Thousands of animals threatened with extinction were shot by trophy hunters last year. Attempts to protect dwindling lion and elephant populations have been thwarted by hunters. They are now allowed to shoot twice as many critically endangered black rhinos as before. How has this happened?

'TROPHY HUNTERS EXPOSED – Inside the Big Game Industry' is an explosive investigation which reveals for the first time how a top fundraiser for Donald Trump, Vladimir Putin's right-hand man, the head of a paramilitary death-squad and a former WWF Director have shot record-breaking lions, elephants, rhinos and leopards.

It exposes the identities of over 500 hunters who have won industry awards for shooting all the 'African Big Five'; the leading figures in the UK industry including a salesman who helps hunters shoot juvenile lions in enclosures; and the extraordinary kill tallies and trophy collections of hunters around the world.

It also lifts the lid on how household brands – and taxes – are funding lobbyists, how the Boy Scouts and Salvation Army in the US are helping the industry recruit a new generation of child hunters, how lobbyists are posing as 'conservation' groups while working to strip wildlife of protections… and how they boast they are able to plough more money into US elections than some of the world's biggest corporations.

'TROPHY HUNTERS EXPOSED – Inside the Big Game Industry' reveals the fears of psychologists and criminologists about how trophy hunting could be fuelling violent crime, and warns that the industry could spark diseases in local communities …

What people are saying about 'Trophy Hunters Exposed – Inside the Big Game Industry'

"It is beyond me that people can get satisfaction from such an unnecessary, senseless and brutal activity. The cruelty endured by these poor animals, who suffer a slow and agonising death, is completely irrational. 'Trophy Hunters Exposed' is a powerful call for action." – Jeremy Cooper, ex-CEO, RSPCA

"This extensively researched book provides a hard hitting and uncompromising expose of Trophy Hunting which is no more, no less, that the ultimate manifesto for its abolition. In this post Covid World into which we are tentatively emerging, Mr Goncalves has deployed his outstanding expertise to provide us with a timely reminder as to the respect and compassion which we must show to all life that we share this planet with." - John Cooper QC, former President and Chair of the League Against Cruel Sports, animal welfare lawyer

"If this book doesn't get trophy hunting banned I don't know what will. An incredible investigation that reveals everything the industry would rather you didn't know." - Judi Dench

"'Trophy Hunters Exposed' lays bare the sordid world of trophy hunting for all to see. A society which allows sentient creatures to be killed for entertainment has serious questions to answer. 'Trophy Hunters Exposed' asks those questions and then answers them in devastating fashion." - Peter Egan

"The trophy hunting industry's 'conservation' façade is comprehensively dismantled in this fast-paced, forensic investigation. The reader is left in no doubt as to the powerful interests behind this cruel bloodsport, and the damage

inflicted on the survival of some of the world's most vulnerable and endangered species. The case for abolition of this archaic pastime has never been made in such a compelling manner." – Nada Farhoud, Environment Editor, Daily Mirror

"The new handbook for campaigners against trophy hunting has arrived. 'Trophy Hunters Exposed' is essential reading for every individual ready to take action against the brutal and unethical killing of wildlife for entertainment. Not an advocate for change yet? You will be after reading this comprehensive exposé of an industry built on cruelty and narcissism that treats innocent lives as mere commodities."- Carrie LeBlanc, Executive Director, CompassionWorks International/Worldwide Rally Against Trophy Hunting

"If there's one book to buy about animals this year, this is it. Trophy hunting is legalised animal abuse on an industrial scale. We cannot call ourselves civilised while we allow trophy hunting. 'Trophy Hunters Exposed' tells us why we must abolish it. Now." – Joanna Lumley

"Slams into trophy hunting with the force of a meterorite. Those of us that love wildlife should be grateful there are campaigners like Eduardo Goncalves prepared to stand so visibly on the front line." - Charlie Moores, The War on Wildlife Project

"An excellently researched and thought provoking book. As a society we should be decrying the trophy hunting industry on both moral and ethical grounds. It is indeed shocking that so few very wealthy people have held the rest of the world to ransom in their quest for gratification. It is indeed shameful that we have allowed this to happen." Linda Park, Co-Founder & Director, Voice4Lions

Trophy Hunters Exposed:

Inside the Big Game Industry

Eduardo Gonçalves

Published by Green Future Books Ltd.
71-75 Shelton Street, Covent Garden, London, England,
WC2H 9JQ

Sales of this book will go to support the Campaign to Ban
Trophy Hunting. To find out more visit
www.bantrophyhunting.org

About the author

Eduardo Gonçalves is an award-winning campaigner, journalist and conservationist who has spent almost 30 years working on virtually all the big issues of our time - climate change, wildlife conservation, forestry protection, the nuclear arms race, homelessness, open government and animal cruelty, including stints as a WWF consultant and CEO of a major animal welfare charity.

In 2018, he founded the Campaign to Ban Trophy Hunting, which is today supported by some of the biggest names in music, sport, film and TV. In 2019, the Campaign to Ban Trophy Hunting persuaded the UK government to support a ban on imports of hunting trophies.

"Trophy Hunters Exposed: Inside the Big Game Industry" is the culmination of a 2-year investigation in which he draws on his experience working inside government; his time as an investigative journalist; and his endless knowledge of animal welfare issues and the bloodsports industry to produce a master-class exposing the inner world of one of the cruellest industries in existence.

The Daily Mail has described Eduardo as "Britain's most prominent anti-hunting activist". He has been presented with the prestigious 'Animal Heroes Award' for services to wildlife by the Daily Mirror.

He is married to Siobhan Mitchell, and has two children. His website is www.eduardogoncalves.com.

CONTENTS

Preface

Pope Francis, in his Encyclical Letter "Laudato Si – On Care for Our Common Home", refers frequently to the dignity and value of every creature. He says: "This is the basis of our conviction that, as part of the universe, called into being by one Father, all of us are linked by unseen bonds and together form a kind of universal family, a sublime communion which fills us with a sacred, affectionate and humble respect."

This interconnectedness also includes the animal kingdom and our need to preserve all species. It would be clear from this document alone that Catholic teaching would be in defence of animals hunted for trophies.

We seem, perhaps all too slowly, to be recognising that we have a common responsibility with all peoples – our brothers and sisters throughout the world - to care for our planet, "our common home". This means accepting the challenge to be responsible and knowledgeable stewards of the world in which we live.

That stewarding needs to embrace the physical world, with its climate, minerals and resources, and the creatures that inhabit this world. Nature is a complexity which exists with fine and exacting balances and where we intrude on Nature's cycle we endanger species. We are learning about the diversity of creatures just at the time that we are beginning to understand how destructive we are being and that in this generation we are now seeing the extinction of 200 species every single day, in what is being called the "Sixth Global Mass Extinction".

We need to urgently reverse this destruction. But there remains one notable exception to concerns expressed about the protection of the diversity of our wildlife – our persistent cruelty towards some animals in the pursuit of trophies. We continue to slaughter animals, often in the cruellest fashion, for sport and fun. How can we claim any dignity in that? What pride can there be in arming ourselves with guns to kill defenceless creatures which are no threat to us?

We seem to have become very confused about the gift of life, be it human or animal. There are arguments that can be understood, whether a person might agree with them or not, about the killing of an animal for its meat – but for a trophy to hang on the wall? There can be no justification in that, particularly when a whole species is facing extinction.

A radical change in thinking is needed, now.

John Arnold
Bishop of Salford
Environment spokesperson, Catholic Church of England & Wales

Foreword

In 2015, there was international uproar following the killing of a Zimbabwean lion called Cecil.

The animal was shot with a bow and arrow by Walter Palmer, an American dentist and trophy hunter. For many people it came as a shock to discover that 'safari hunting' – something many associate with colonialism – was still taking place. Others were horrified at the act of killing an innocent animal simply for 'sport and 'show'. Others still were concerned at the conservation implications. Lion numbers have seen an extraordinary collapse over the past half-century. For many wildlife experts, trophy hunting is an unnecessary additional threat to a species that is already at risk of extinction.

Yet, just a few years on from 'Cecil-gate', lions remain one of the most sought-after animals by trophy hunters around the world. Shooting the biggest lions can grant you entry into the highly-coveted Safari Club International (SCI) Records Book, the industry's 'Guinness Book'. Should you join this elite group, you will be in the company of public figures such as Donald Trump donor/fundraiser Steve Chancellor and former Revlon president and WWF Director Michel Bergerac.[1]

John J Jackson III, ex-President of SCI, is on this list too.[2] Jackson leads an organisation which lobbies for

---

[1] SCI Record Book of Trophy Animals – edition IX, Volume 1, Africa Field Edition, 1997. Safari Club International

[2] SCI Record Book of Trophy Animals – edition IX, Volume 1, Africa Field Edition, 1997. Safari Club International

restrictions on the hunting of threatened species to be taken away. With no satire intended, it calls itself 'Conservation Force'. It is one of a number of hunting groups which are now branding themselves 'conservation' organisations. Worryingly, some international conservation bodies appear to have fallen for it. Jackson has been admitted as a member of the lion experts committee of IUCN, the world's biggest conservation organisation which – among other things - determines the extinction risk of wildlife such as lions.[3]

'Conservation Force' has been granted official observer status within CITES, the Convention on International Trade in Endangered Species, the body created to stop trade in threatened species. Its responsibilities include deciding what restrictions there should be on the trophy hunting of lions. Jackson is not a big cat biologist.[4] He has no relevant scientific qualifications. He does, though, have multiple entries in SCI's Records Book - including for some of the many lions he has shot. In a book which features his trophy room – said to be one of the greatest in the world, and which includes the bodies of lions, polar bears, elephants and leopards - he says the following: "I can plainly see the African lion that has leaped into the air the moment its head snaps backward and explodes with smoke from my bullet."[5] Calls for him to be expelled from IUCN have been ignored.[6]

---

[3] www.conservationforce.org

[4] www.conservationforce.org

[5] "Great hunters – their trophy rooms and collections", Safari Press Inc, 1997

Over the past 20 years, over 500 trophy hunters have won the 'Africa Big Five' award from SCI, one of its most prestigious prizes.[7] It is handed to hunters who shoot lions, leopards, elephants, rhinos and buffaloes. A hunter has to kill at least one of each in order to be eligible. Winners include Russian President Vladimir Putin's former right-hand man Sergey Yastrzhemskiy and Japto Soerjosoemarno, leader of an Indonesian paramilitary death squad.[8] Some achieved this using only a bow and arrow.[9]

Safari Club International is one of a number of hunting organisations that gives prizes to hunters who kill the most animals for 'sport'. It, alone, has approximately 80 different awards.[10] One requires hunters to kill hundreds of animals on each and every continent of the planet. There are some hunters who apparently do not need prizes to motivate them, though. Zimbabwe's Ron Thomson has shot over 5000 elephants, as well as at least 50 lions.[11] Tony Sanchez Arino, a friend of former Spanish King Juan Carlos (himself a keen elephant hunter), has notched up fewer elephants but more lions.[12] Neither have put their names

---

https://secure.avaaz.org/en/community_petitions/Grethel_Aguilar_Expel_Trophy_Hunters_from_the_IUCN/

[7] Safari magazine – Awards 2015, Safari Club International

[8] Safari magazine – Awards 2015, Safari Club International

[9] Safari magazine – Awards 2015, Safari Club International

[10] Safari magazine – Awards 2015, Safari Club International

[11] "Who would want to kill a lion? Inside the minds of trophy hunters", Elle Hunt, Guardian/Observer, 4 November 2018

[12] "Talking African Dangerous Game Hunting with Tony Sanchez-Arino", David E. Petzal, Field & Stream, February 17, 2012

forward for SCI awards. For some, the sheer thrill is reward enough. As John J Jackson III puts it: "Nothing else in life is more satisfying than an elephant hunt."[13]

Far from protecting endangered species, the law today is failing wildlife. As many as 1.7 million animals have been killed by trophy hunters over the past decade.[14] Hundreds of thousands of these animals were from species that are protected by law because scientists believe they are at risk of extinction.[15] We are told that we face a biodiversity crisis every bit as serious as the climate crisis. Yet the slaughter, inexplicably, continues unabated. The law prohibits a person from shooting an elephant or rhino for its tusks or horns. But it is legal for the same person to shoot the same elephant or rhino for its trophies – including the tusks and horns.[16] International trafficking syndicates are known to be using this loophole[17], yet no concerted action has been taken to close it.

Chickens farmed for fast food arguably receive greater welfare protections than wild animals pursued by trophy hunters. Special prizes are handed out by SCI and other groups to hunters who kill animals – including

---

[13] "Controversy swirls around the recent US suspension of sport-hunted elephant trophies", Christina Russo, blog.nationalgeograophic.org, May 6, 2014

[14] "Killing For Trophies: An Analysis of Global Trophy Hunting Trade", IFAW June 14, 2016

[15] CITES Trade Database (UNEP-WCMC)

[16] Convention on International Trade in Endangered Species of Fauna and Flora (CITES) https://www.cites.org/eng/disc/text.php

[17] "Killing for Profit: Exposing the Illegal Rhino Horn Trade", Julian Rademeyer, Zebra Press 2012

large ones such as elephants - using only bows and arrows, crossbows or old-fashioned 'muzzle-loader' rifles.[18] Hunting magazines and forums are replete with tales of animals left with terrible, painful wounds. Cecil the lion took 11 hours to die after being shot with an arrow (he was still choking on his own blood the day after he'd been shot).[19] There are cases of badly wounded big cats being pursued for several days.[20] Official reports suggest many animals suffer serious injuries after being hit but are lost by hunters.[21] They will die slow deaths from infection and sepsis.

Opinion polls suggest the majority of voters in countries around the world abhor trophy hunting.[22] But this is an industry far from being on the retreat. On the contrary: it is actively lobbying to open up new areas of wilderness to hunters, and to reduce the age at which children are permitted to go hunting for 'leisure'.[23] Thanks to their efforts, attempts by governments and conservation groups to classify the lion as endangered failed,[24] despite the clear evidence showing the species' calamitous population decline. Hunting groups openly boast about their successful campaign against efforts to

[18] Safari magazine – Awards 2015, Safari Club International

[19] "Lion Hearted , The Life and Death of Cecil & the Future of Africa's Iconic Cats", Andrew Loveridge, Regan Arts 2018

[20] See for instance "The Cave Leopard", Richard Vallecorsa in "African Hunter magazine – Campfire tales, volume one", Mag-Set publications, 2009

[21] See reports by natural resources and wildlife departments of the states of Ohio, Montana, Texas, Michigan and Vermont

[22] See chapter 12

[23] See chapter 2

[24] www.conservationforce.org

stop the trade in lion trophies. In 2019, they persuaded the CITES conference to double the number of black rhinos that trophy hunters are allowed to shoot every year. Black rhinos are classed in the IUCN Red List of Threatened Species as 'Critically Endangered'.[25]

Hunting organisations are now campaigning to further 'liberalise' wildlife laws. They are spending millions of dollars and pounds each year on lobbying, and have poured large amounts of money into the campaigns of candidates at election time, including that of President Trump's Interior Secretary when he ran for Congress.[26] Taxpayers' money has found its way to fund pro-hunting lobbying and to house hunters' trophy collections. The industry has received sponsorship from household brands. It has raised funds through auctioning off hunts of polar bears and wallabies. It has received donations from some unexpected sources such as the Boy Scouts Association. In a bid to recruit a new generation of hunters, the industry has partnered with the Salvation Army to provide 'shooting programmes' for hundreds of thousands of children.[27]

'TROPHY HUNTERS EXPOSED – Inside the Big Game Industry' provides a hitherto-unseen insight into trophy hunting, the industry's key players, the lobbyists and the donors. It shows how the industry is undermining conservation laws at precisely the time when wildlife needs protection more than ever. It reveals

---

[25] https://www.iucnredlist.org/species/6557/152728945

[26] www.opensecrets.org – see also "How Trump's wildlife Board is rebranding trophy hunting as good for animals", Jake Bullinger, The Guardian 17 July 2018

[27] See chapter 2

the incredible tallies of some of the world's 'top' trophy hunters, the extraordinary contents of their trophy rooms, and the records and industry awards which encourage hunters to shoot thousands of the planet's most vulnerable animals. It also provides a unique insight into the minds of trophy hunters and what drives them to travel around the world to kill animals for pleasure. It reveals that some of the world's most notorious serial killers were trophy hunters and that some psychologists fear the industry's bid to entice a new generation of young hunters could increase violent crime.[28]

It reveals, too, what people around the world really think about trophy hunting, what they want from our politicians, and argues that the time has come to adopt a new 'contract' with nature if wildlife is to survive. The time has come to decide whether or not to close this chapter in our history. This book provides the public and policy-makers with the facts so that we can make an informed decision. The choice is now in our hands.

Ranulph Fiennes

---

[28] See chapter 11

Introduction

The coronavirus pandemic has thrown a spotlight on the wildlife trade as never before.

China's 'wet markets' have provided a fertile environment for diseases of animal origin to make their way into the human population. The tragic consequences have been on a scale until now unseen in modern history. Yet these markets represent only one side of the modern-day wildlife industry.

In 1973, government representatives from around the world gathered in Washington, DC to sign an historic treaty which established CITES, the Convention on International Trade in Endangered Species of Fauna and Flora. The atmosphere was one of optimism and enthusiasm. Strict rules were drawn up to address the perilous collapses of wildlife populations driven by insatiable demand for animal products. Threatened species were named in a list of three appendices ordered by their vulnerability. Trade in Appendix I species, it said, "must only be authorized in exceptional circumstances."[29]

The reality is that while the treaty has regulated some trade, it is far from being the conservation mechanism some had hoped. Trade has continued, even in the most endangered animals. For instance, in 2017 (the most

---

[29] Article II, Fundamental Principles, Convention on the International Trade in Endangered Species of Fauna and Flora, 3 March 1973

recent year for which reliable data is currently available) "exceptional circumstances" were granted for more than 75,000 animals and body parts of species which CITES classes as the most endangered in the world.[30] Permits were signed off for commercial trade as well as acquisition for 'personal use' and 'medicines' of live and dead animals from no fewer than 150 threatened species.

They include 52 kinds of monkey and other primates, 20 cetaceans (e.g. whales and dolphins), 17 'big cats', as well as 7 types of bear, 5 rhino species, and 5 different kinds of pangolin.[31]

The total includes many seizures. However it excludes many items. For example, not included are batches of baleen – the filtering system inside the mouths of whales – for which 'personal use' exceptions were granted. Asian elephants and dozens of captive-bred scimitar-horned oryxes were legally procured for 'personal use' too. The scimitar-horned oryx is extinct in the wild.

The total also does not include over 200 tonnes of minke whale meat sent from Norway to Japan, or 3,000 tonnes of fin whale meat imported by Japan from Iceland.[32]

Also considered "exceptional circumstances" were cosmetic products extracted from the Irrawaddy dolphin, fur and bones from leopards, tusks from Mediterranean monk seals, and leather products from giant pangolins – the latter were given the green light to enter the US. Tiger rugs and skins were traded as were live tigers,

---

[30] CITES Trade Database (UNEP-WCMC)

[31] CITES Trade Database (UNEP-WCMC)

[32] CITES Trade Database (UNEP-WCMC)

some of which were sent from the US to Libya. Trade in Bornean orangutans, clouded leopards, black-headed spider monkeys, golden lion tamarins, and a further six species of the primate family were all given the go-ahead too.[33] British traders sold Bush dogs to Panama, North Korea was allowed to purchase jaguars from Cuba, and permission was given to sell chimpanzees, red pandas and orangutans to circuses.

Asian countries such as China were the destination of many of the animals and body parts of big cats, cetaceans and primates which made their way around the world in 2017. But they were not alone: chimpanzees were also exported to Belarus and Vietnam; Sumatran orangutans were given permits to enter Kazakhstan; gibbons were traded with Ukraine.[34]

The list of 75,000 animals and their body parts also does not include endangered birds or reptiles. Nor does it include species listed in Appendix II or III of CITES which are also legally protected – at least in theory.

Nor, perhaps most importantly, does it include the many thousands of CITES-listed animals that were shot for hunting trophies. In 2017, as many as 35,000 bodies and parts of animals that are at risk of extinction made their way into the trophy rooms of hunters around the world, all with the implicit blessing of CITES.[35] In fact the multi-million dollar trophy hunting industry is to all intents and purposes largely exempted from CITES' rules. This is on the extraordinary grounds that trophy hunting holidays – which can sometimes cost $100,000

---

[33] CITES Trade Database (UNEP-WCMC)
[34] CITES Trade Database (UNEP-WCMC)
[35] CITES Trade Database (UNEP-WCMC)

or more – are considered to be a 'non-commercial' activity.[36]

Among the many CITES Appendix I species that can be hunted with few if any meaningful restrictions are leopards: their numbers are falling, according to IUCN.[37] Also permitted is sport hunting of cheetahs, about which the IUCN Red List tells us there are just 6,674 mature individuals left in the wild[38]. Lions and elephants, including their most fragile populations, can be hunted for 'sport' too.[39]

Pumas, vervet monkeys and zebras have joined the growing list of animals that are being quietly bred in captivity to become cut-price trophies adorning the walls of hunters' homes.[40] Some 75,000 bodies and parts of animals raised for quick, easy and untarnished trophies were taken home by hunters during this past decade.[41] In South Africa alone, over 50 different species have been bred for the bullet.[42]

---

[36] The CITES Appendices

[37] Stein, A.B., Athreya, V., Gerngross, P., Balme, G., Henschel, P., Karanth, U., Miquelle, D., Rostro-Garcia, S., Kamler, J.F., Laguardia, A., Khorozyan, I. & Ghoddousi, A. 2020. Panthera pardus (amended version of 2019 assessment). The IUCN Red List of Threatened Species 2020: e.T15954A163991139.

[38] Durant, S., Mitchell, N., Ipavec, A. & Groom, R. 2015. Acinonyx jubatus. The IUCN Red List of Threatened Species 2015: e.T219A50649567.

[39] Lion and elephant populations in a number of countries are listed in Appendix I of CITES

[40] CITES Trade Database (UNEP-WCMC)

[41] CITES Trade Database (UNEP-WCMC)

[42] CITES Trade Database (UNEP-WCMC)

Some scientists now believe that the trade in hunting trophies may – just like the 'wet' wildlife trade – pose a serious threat to human health. Professor Irvin Modlin of the Yale University Medical School and the South African Veterinary Association (SAVA) are among those to have expressed concerns about the risk of disease transmission resulting from the booming trade in bones of lions shot in 'canned hunting' operations.[43] The animals in these facilities are bred in often in appalling and unsanitary conditions before being killed by trophy hunters within fenced-in enclosures. The hunter takes home the skull and skin for their taxidermist to transform into a trophy. The skeletons often end up in China where they are turned into 'lion wine'.

SAVA believes there is a risk of TB being transferred by the production of this wine, and that there is also a risk to local communities who are sometimes given meat from the dead lions after they have been deboned. Tuberculosis is a major issue in Africa, killing around 500,000 people a year, and is a leading cause of mortality in countries such as South Africa. Dr David Cooper, a leading African wildlife veterinarian who has been studying TB and animal-human transmission for 20 years, describes the threat as "a ticking time-bomb".[44]

The links between trophy hunting and high-risk wildlife trade are becoming ever closer. In its response to Covid-19, China is promoting the use of bear bile as a

[43] "China's ban on wildlife consumption is an overdue death knell for lion bone industry", Don Pinnock, Daily Maverick, 24 February 2020

[44] https://www.facebook.com/pg/Wild-Vet-1647229828897122/posts/

potential treatment.[45] 'Moon bears' (Asian black bears) have long been bred in captivity to be 'milked' - often in conditions of considerable cruelty - for the bile in their gall bladders which is used in several traditional Chinese medicines. Less well-known is the fact that there has been a huge rise in the number of bear bodies and body parts going to China in recent years - an 80-fold increase between 2007-2017 alone.[46] The rate of growth in bear body parts acquired as 'hunting trophies' has risen even faster, by a factor of 300.[47] US customs officials report that they are seizing fast-growing numbers of Chinese 'medicines' acquired from bears.[48]

Polar bears can be legally shot in Canada by trophy hunters. Some have been shot for their penises as well as for their bile. The baculum — or penis bone — from bears is highly sought after for its alleged medicinal benefits. A recent surge in sightings of three-legged black bears in North America is thought to be linked to growing demand for bear paw soup by wealthy Chinese consumers.[49]

Ironically, CITES rules – or the relative lack of them when it comes to killing threatened species for 'sport' - has helped create a buoyant market in animal trafficking. Crime syndicates have gleefully taken advantage of the

---

[45] "China promotes bear bile as coronavirus treatment, alarming wildlife advocates", Rachel Fobar, National Geographic, March 25, 2020

[46] CITES Trade Database (UNEP-WCMC)

[47] CITES Trade Database (UNEP-WCMC)

[48] CITES Trade Database (UNEP-WCMC)

[49] https://www.animals24-7.org/2020/05/29/three-legged-bears-in-the-great-smokies-may-be-no-accident/

flimsy regulations, killing large numbers of rhinos for their horns by posing as trophy hunters. In some cases they have flown in bewildered peasants and prostitutes, plucked from remote Asian villages, to act as their proxies.[50]

Over 17,000 tigers and tiger body parts have been traded or seized in the past 5 years: more than 80% were destined for the traditional Chinese medicine market. Many were labelled as 'trophies'.[51]

China has no historical or cultural tradition of trophy hunting. Yet Chinese 'hunters' now constitute the single largest nationality in pursuit of white rhino 'hunting trophies', beating America into second place.[52] Ten years ago Chinese hunters sought only 18 hunting trophy import permits from CITES officials. By 2017 that figure had soared to 2,142, a rise of nearly 1200%.[53] Today, China is second only to the US for the total number of 'hunting trophy' imports of wild animals, having leapfrogged long-established markets such as Germany and Spain.[54]

In the face of mounting public abhorrence, hunting lobbyists have sought to counter negative publicity by portraying the industry as a benign sport. They point, for instance, to examples where foreign hunters have generously donated elephant meat to 'poor African villagers'. Conservationists believe this may only serve

[50] "Killing for Profit: Exposing the Illegal Rhino Horn Trade", Julian Rademeyer, Zebra Press 2012

[51] CITES Trade Database (UNEP-WCMC)

[52] CITES Trade Database (UNEP-WCMC)

[53] CITES Trade Database (UNEP-WCMC)

[54] CITES Trade Database (UNEP-WCMC)

to fuel the bushmeat trade, however.[55] The industry also claims that trophy hunting is helping endangered animals in their fight for survival. At times, the PR carries echoes of Orwellian 'doublethink'. Just as Winston Smith was taught that war is peace, freedom is slavery, and ignorance is strength, we are now expected to believe that killing animals for pleasure is 'conservation'.

The NRA, the notorious pro-gun group, is among the many organisations which now make this claim – it even goes so far as to call itself a 'conservation' organisation.[56] In fact, a number of hunting lobby groups have emerged in recent years which label themselves 'conservation' organisations. Some of these new 'conservationists' have acquired positions of considerable influence within the world's main wildlife protection institutions. In the US, they are helping to re-write public policy altogether - from within the government.[57]

The strategy is nothing if not audacious. It appears to be working, however. Some of the world's most endangered species have – following campaigns by industry lobbyists – seen protections taken away from them. Studies indicate their populations are in decline.[58]

The lobbyists have succeeded in transforming the various regulations and institutions into a morass of contradictions. The trafficking of trophies such as rhino

---

[55] "Elephant trophy auction covers for opening bushmeat trade", Animals 24-7, Merritt Clifton, February 22, 2020 https://www.animals24-7.org/2020/02/22/elephant-trophy-auction-covers-for-opening-bushmeat-trade/

[56] See chapters 2 and 3

[57] See chapter 3

[58] See chapter 3

horns is banned; but not the shooting of rhinos for trophies … such as their horns. Locals cannot kill endangered wildlife for food, however hungry or desperate they may be; however rich foreigners can saunter in and kill the same animal solely for sport. Kill a domestic cat for thrills and you can expect to be punished; kill a wild cat for thrills and you could win a prize with Safari Club International.[59] Apes are off-limits, but 40 other species of primates - with whom we share more than 90% of our DNA - are popular. And cheap.[60] Killing snow leopards is prohibited in case it pushes them further towards extinction; killing African leopards, on the other hand, apparently makes them less likely to go extinct. Go figure.

The trophy hunting industry is today one of the world's most powerful political lobbies. It has been handed enormous individual donations by some of America's most influential men and women. It is being funded by oil companies and their executives, major banking institutions, gun makers, and the owners of some of the world's most popular drinks brands. It openly boasts of pouring more money into US elections than some of the country's biggest corporations. Among the beneficiaries has been a congressman who went on to become Donald Trump's Interior Secretary - and thus the man with overall responsibility for America's hunting laws and trophy trade.

The success of the lobbyists explains why, against the odds – and indeed the mores of modern society – trophy

---

[59] Safari magazine – Awards 2015, Safari Club International
[60] CITES Trade Database (UNEP-WCMC)

hunting has survived where related activities of the same genre have long ago died out or been banished. Bloodsports such as bearbaiting, dogfighting and fox-hunting are now outlawed in many western nations. However wealthy hunters from those nations can still travel to Africa or Asia to engage in bloodsports.

Imagine for a moment if the tables were turned. What would be the reaction were large numbers of Africans or Asians to descend upon Hampshire (UK) or New Hampshire (US) to kill local wildlife for amusement?

This is a book which seeks – perhaps for the first time - to shine a light on the industry, how it works, and how it is subverting real conservation. It explores the many troubling ethical questions raised by killing living, sentient creatures for 'trophies', some of which may have potentially serious ramifications for the safety of our communities.

Much has been said about American hunters, yet relatively little is known about those from the rest of the world. However one of the industry's all-time biggest prize-winners is British.[61] Indeed UK brokers are selling hunts where you can shoot juvenile lions that have been bred in captivity, and horrific big cat hunts using packs of hounds.[62] A British businessman is among those within the industry promoting father-and-son hunting holidays where they can 'bond' over killing a bagful of animals.[63]

Some of the world's other leading trophy hunters come from Germany and Spain, France and Russia, and

---

[61] Safari magazine – Awards 2015, Safari Club International

[62] See chapter 5

[63] See chapter 5

even Belgium and Switzerland.[64] Among the industry's most colourful and controversial figures are hunters hailing from the Middle East and southern Africa.[65] The reader will be introduced to trophy hunters from different parts of the world who have some of the biggest kill tallies ever recorded in history. Some of these record-holders are alive – and still hunting – today.

In 2019, the South American nation of Colombia became the most recent country to ban all trophy hunting within its borders. Explaining the judicial ruling which declared trophy hunting to be unlawful, magistrate Antonio Jose Lizarazo said that it was "not constitutionally allowable to kill or mistreat animals for the sole purpose of recreation. Animals are not things, they are beings with feelings."[66] There are many issues where moral ambiguity exists and debate on the finer points of detail is legitimate. As Colombia's judicial system has ruled, and as the evidence provided by the ethics experts cited in this book, trophy hunting is not one of them.

So where now? The British prime minister, Boris Johnson, has made clear on a number of occasions his intention to move ahead with a ban on hunting trophy imports and exports. He has made the pledge in parliament and on social media. It was in his government's 2019 Queen's Speech (twice) and was included in the Conservative Party's election manifesto, which – as 'first father' Stanley Johnson reminded a group of MPs and Peers at a Parliamentary event in

---

[64] See chapter 6
[65] See chapter 7
[66] "Colombia to ban sport hunting", phys.org, February 7, 2019

January 2020 - was endorsed by the general public at the ballot box.

Motions and statements of support for a trophy ban have been made and signed by politicians spanning 9 political parties in the UK's parliament, which is almost certainly a record. A series of opinion polls by different survey companies show the strength and consistency of support for tough action amongst every demographic, geographic and voting group in the country. 'Brexiters' and 'Remainers' support a ban with equal vigour. As far as tests of political legitimacy go, this has clearly been met. And amply so.

We have nearly been here before – at least in part. In 2016, UK Environment Minister Rory Stewart – in response to a question from fellow Conservative MP Henry Smith – repeated a commitment first announced in Parliament on 24 November 2015 that "the Government will ban lion trophy imports by the end of 2017 unless there are improvements in the way hunting takes place in certain countries, judged against strict criteria."[67] His successor as Minister, Liz Truss MP, confirmed the government's position, saying: "Unless we see improvements in the way hunting takes place, judged against strict criteria, we will ban lion trophy imports within the next two years."[68] In February 2019,

[67] http://www.parliament.uk/business/publications/written-questions-answers-statements/written-question/Commons/2016-06-14/40644/

[68] "Conservatives break pledge to ban lion hunt trophies from being imported into UK", Jane Dalton, The Independent, 10 February 2019 https://www.independent.co.uk/environment/lion-hunting-trophy-imports-ban-uk-us-africa-pledge-wildlife-zac-

however, The Independent newspaper reported that the government had "broken a pledge to ban imports of lion hunting trophies."[69] Had the government stuck to their guns (as it were), the lives of some 50 lions could have been spared.[70]

We must not make the same mistake again. We cannot let this opportunity to reclaim the right to call ourselves a civilised society slip from our grasp a second time.

But there is arguably another imperative now too. The Covid-19 pandemic that is rampaging throughout the globe provides yet further justification, if any were needed, for swift and decisive action – not just nationally but internationally. Trophy hunting is part of a wildlife industry that has inflicted careless acts of barbarity on the world's fauna, the consequences of which have come back to haunt us in almost apocalyptic fashion. Surely if there were a time and place for a moratorium on wildlife trade - including in hunting trophies, commercial trade or for so-called 'personal use' – that moment is here and now. But such a moratorium must be swiftly followed by a comprehensive ban, a resolution for which should be

goldsmith-mps-a8772386.html

[69] "Conservatives break pledge to ban lion hunt trophies from being imported into UK", Jane Dalton, The Independent, 10 February 2019 https://www.independent.co.uk/environment/lion-hunting-trophy-imports-ban-uk-us-africa-pledge-wildlife-zac-goldsmith-mps-a8772386.html

[70] This is an estimate based on the number of lion trophies recorded as having been imported into the UK since 2016 (source: CITES Trade Database (UNEP-WCMC))

brought to the next CITES Conference of the Parties that is scheduled to take place in 2022.

CITES has many friends and as many detractors. There is no question that there is a need for strong international institutions which ensure that human economic activities do not cost the earth. However it is clearly counter to its fundamental purpose, and its legitimacy as an international institution, that CITES should allow such huge volumes of trade in wildlife to continue - and grow. It is even more absurd that it should apply what can best be described as a 'laissez-faire' approach with regards to trade in wildlife. CITES-listed species are animals which the international community has determined are threatened with extinction. Yet CITES currently allows them to be killed for no other reason than to provide sordid entertainment for a privileged few.

It is equally counter to its purpose and legitimacy that IUCN, the world's quasi-governmental conservation entity, should grant access and positions of influence to some of the world's leading hunters and hunting lobbyists, in particular to those who possess no scientific experience or relevant qualifications.

So to Boris Johnson, and indeed to Ivonne Higuero (the Secretary General of CITES) and the incoming IUCN Director General, the message from this book – and from voters and communities everywhere - is clear: the time to ban trophy hunting has come. Like the abolition of bear-baiting, dog-fighting and other great moral evils that have thankfully been consigned to history, future generations will likely look back in astonishment and ask: how on earth did we let it go on for so long?

My sincere and grateful thanks go to the Olsen Animal Trust, the Anthony V Martin Charitable Foundation, Peter Egan, Penny Morgan, Ros Coward, Julian Richer, Damian Aspinall and many many others for their support and advice, both on this book and the wider campaign to abolish trophy hunting. Thanks are also due to Beth Jennings of Claws Out for permission to reproduce the cover photograph, and to Richard Peirce for permission to reproduce a section from his own excellent book "Cuddle Me Kill Me".

Particular thanks are due to Luis Filipe for his skilful research and thoughtful critiques, Jose Cristiano for helping make it possible for the book to be written at all, and above all to the incredible rock that is Siobhan Mitchell without whom this – and much else besides – would surely never come to fruition.

This book is written in an entirely personal capacity and reflects my own views on the various issues touched upon. Any mistakes are mine and mine alone.

Profits from the sale of this book will be donated to the Campaign to Ban Trophy Hunting.

Eduardo Goncalves – May 2020

Part 1: The Industry

Chapter 1: How The Industry Works[71]

Trophy hunting is a business. A big business. And as with any successful business, alluring marketing and slick sales strategies matter.

Advertisements in industry magazines paint an enticing image of the excitement and fulfilment that awaits the prospective hunter. "The spirit of adventure" can be yours, as can an "amazing experience and trophies." Puns and wordplay are deployed. If you're after a trophy leopard, one company invites the client to go with them - "for prime spots".

A narrative of nostalgia for the empire and for when times were 'simpler' is woven. One company promises hunting on foot "like the good old days." Its hunting concession "is as wild as South Africa gets", a place "where rhino roam and lions roar under a cloudless sky". Another charms the reader: "When we are not trekking across her face, she calls out to us to return. This is what we do. This is Africa."

Africa is depicted as a place "where nature feels unexplored, unvisited, like walking the tracks of the explorers before us. It is the fusion of man and nature that is an unforgettable experience." To get you in the mood you can, if you wish, "have lunch in a cave with

---

[71] The case studies, quotes and prices in this chapter are taken from the websites, brochures and advertisements in industry publications of multiple trophy hunting companies (or 'outfitters', as they are often referred to) from around the world. For a selection, visit www.africahunting.com or www.bookyourhunt.com

native bushman drawings scattered on the overhanging walls."

If you yearn to find your tribe, hunting holiday operators are there to help. "It may be the people. The land. The camaraderie around a crackling campfire. The PH (professional hunter) and tracker who started out as strangers but leave you as friends."

Whatever your tastes, you are number one - the hunting companies will cater to your every whim. "Natural picturesque surroundings, an array of wildlife, diverse culture and mouth-watering cuisine are the perfect blend for a true African adventure. The focus is on the adventure, providing a personalised experience. Allow us to take your dream, expand it and turn it into a lifelong memory by exploring the abundance of options that can be personalized for hunters."

One trophy hunting forum carries the following description of a well-known African hunting centre: "The romantic black and white movie world of the Victorian-era safari, when sporting gentlemen clad in pressed trousers and starched shirts ventured out to bag the big one, is replicated down to the last detail. Native workers… slather hunting guests in luxury, pressing their clothes daily, providing hot water for showers, and fixing morning and evening feasts, all painstakingly prepared." Another proudly proclaims that it provides "a colonial atmosphere and grandeur from a forgotten era."

When not hunting, other activities can be laid on such as scenic helicopter tours, deep sea fishing, even elephant-back riding. Health spas and massages are available in the comfort of your room. Hot air ballooning, champagne breakfasts and sunset cruises can all be arranged. A trip to Robben Island – once home to incarcerated ANC leaders such as Nelson Mandela – can be thrown in for a modest fee.

The brochures and websites cruelly highlight the differences between local have-nots and global jet-setting have-yachts. One tempts prospective clients with the promise that their lodge "is a place where opulence and service are of the utmost importance; where every day is tailored to be a world-class experience for our valued guests. From sun up to sun down, we happily cater to your every whim.

"The lodge has its own private sparkling plunge pool with a beautiful sundeck and our guests are welcome to enjoy our fully stocked lodge bar and private cinema." It adds: "You will want for nothing." A private landing strip is available "for your convenience".

Getting ready

Having been wooed by the advertising, you now need to purchase the proper equipment. First on the shopping list is the rifle. Next to a picture of a trophy hunter in the wilderness lovingly cradling his chosen weapon, one advertisement in a hunting magazine reads: "Getting there is half the fun… especially when your sub MOA rifle weighs 4 lbs 13 oz".

"Behind every revolution is a patriot" proclaims another, a large US flag emblazoned across it. The ad is for a new rifle model called 'Patriot'. "Few things are more American than a great rifle. And the new Patriot is the sum of all those that came before it, from its fluted barrel, fluted bolt and adjustable trigger to its flush-fit magazine and classic stripped stock."

Bullets aren't just bullets. "There's more to ammunition than just making noise and blowing smoke", according to one manufacturer. Another promises to give you "terminal performance without equal and excellent accuracy" and "the best performance for hunting any game species anywhere in the world." For one manufacturer, the message is all in the strapline: "Accurate. Deadly. Dependable."

Quality ammunition is "the least expensive hunt insurance you can buy", another company suggests. To ensure quality, the company is "constantly testing them in the laboratory and in the field." There is no such thing as one-size-fits-all. "Several styles are offered, tailored to the game and conditions the hunter expects to encounter." Trading on their reputation for efficiency and quality engineering, a maker of bullets and scopes proclaims: "Made in Germany. Deadly anywhere." It adds: "We don't speak German (but..) when ultimate accuracy and performance is your goal… we all speak that language. "

Technology and new gadgets are helping to make trophy hunting an even more exciting experience. One manufacturer of sights says that its latest product features "true ballistic range. With blink of an eye speed, precise readings, and rugged dependability" it is "the ultimate rangefinder for any serious hunter. It features 6x magnification, ranging out to 1200 yards, Scan Mode, and vivid OLED display technology for unsurpassed light transmission. For hunters who demand the absolute best, this is it."

You can also purchase audio aids to help you locate your target animal. "Hear the outdoors come alive" reads one advertisement, which promises "in-ear hearing enhancement with superior digital sound up to 6x normal hearing." Members of Safari Club International, the world's largest trophy hunting group, can expect a special discount.

For Americans hunting at home, they can now purchase an all-terrain vehicle with a special weapons storage compartment: "Introducing the 2nd Amendment Package – box concealed under the rear seats!"[72]

If you're a trophy hunter, it is surprisingly easy to take your firearms abroad with you. Often it is a case of simply checking in your rifle at the airport. Ammunition is permitted too. You may be required to request a permit for temporary export of your preferred weapon and to fill in customs paperwork at your destination. However, as befits high-class clientele, the industry has special 'fixers' who can meet and greet you at the airport and arrange this on your behalf.

What's on the Menu?

Consumers expect variety and choice when they visit the supermarket, so why not when they go trophy hunting? Many safari firms, commonly known as 'outfitters', pride themselves on being able to provide a large number of different animals for hunters to choose

---

[72] "The Journal of the Texas Trophy Hunters", Nov/Dec 2017 (ttha.com) vol 42, no.6

from. It is not uncommon to find 50 or more different species on offer.

You will want to find the 'best' outfitters to hunt with. Size matters, particularly if you want your animal to make it into Safari Club International's prestigious 'Records Book' of the world's biggest trophies. One company in British Columbia brags that it's the company to go with if you want "HUGE grizzly and black bear".

Safari Club International offers prizes for hunters who shoot the most animals. Clients thus want to be assured of getting as much bang for their buck as possible. One company quotes a satisfied customer who says: "You will use more rifle in a week in Africa than you might in five or even ten years of hunting in the United States."

Some outfitters specialise in different types of hunting. Several, for instance, cater for those who prefer to shoot big game using only bows and arrows or handguns. One company, which exclaims that South Africa "is truly a bowhunter's paradise", adds: "We have exclusive access to some of the most sought after big five/dangerous seven hunting areas in all of Africa. Lion, elephant, buffalo, leopard, rhino, crocodile and hippo make up Africa's dangerous seven and we offer hunting opportunities for all seven species to both bow and rifle hunters!" A happy client gives the firm's professional hunting guide the thumbs-up: "I took all of the Big Five with Hannes (the professional hunter) and I'm still coming back!"

If you enjoy the spectacle of hunting with hounds, the leopard is among the animals on offer. Shooting an African caracal – a medium-sized cat - will usually cost as little as $250. If you choose to hunt it with hounds you can expect to add another $1000 to the price tag.

Companies put on special promotions to make their product stand out from the crowd. One ad features a picture of a large dead leopard and entices readers with the offer of a giveaway if they can find a better deal elsewhere. "I own 3 magnificent private hunting ranches which have a hunting surface area of over 200,000 acres and is home to 50,000 animals. If you can find another hunting outfitter who can beat me on the above points I will give you a free hunt."

It includes a quote from a hunter who was able to brag about his great deal to his peers. "There were 27 guys on the airplane ride home from the States, and when we compared pictures, I had the best time overall. Most had shot 2 or 3 good trophies. I had pictures of 9 – 9 true 'trophy' animals." Another chimes: "The hunting was beyond our wildest dreams!"

You can find 'shoot one get one free' deals too: pay to kill a male lion and the company will throw in a lioness at no extra cost. A 'price comparison' website helps you find the best offers available – simply enter your desired trophy species and/or the country you want to hunt in.[73]

There are providers of last-minute 'discount deals' for late cancellations. One even offers Black Friday sales. Its circular breathlessly exclaims: "I have 2 discounted Cape buffalo bull hunts available for 2020 in South Africa. You can expect a bull from 38" - 42". To further

---

[73] www.bookyourhunt.com

sweeten the deal "you can take a dark bull giraffe for a trophy fee of only $2,000! ONLY $6,900 All-in!"

Hardened trophy hunters looking to complete collections, win prizes or gain new entries in record books may look specifically at who the firm has hired as their professional hunter or guide. Some "PHs", as they're known, run their own operations. One boasts he has helped his clients acquire the most 'Top 10' trophies of all time and that he has also won the SCI International Professional Hunter of the Year award.

As well as mammals, many hunters seek out bird or "wing shooting" holidays. One company warns prospective customers that they will shoot so many birds with them that they should "expect hot barrels and sore shoulders". "If the rush of flushing quail gets your blood pumping then you have found the right place," it pledges.

Many businesses encourage hunters to bring their family along. Some even allow young children to take part in hunts. In the words of one firm: "Why not bring the kids along? We're passionate about the next generation of hunters." Another has photographs on its website of children with monkeys that they have just killed. Yet another has images of two young children with warthog and antelope trophies on their social media page. The accompanying message reads: "Hunting buddies for life! These 5 yr and 4yr old boys had a blast."

"Few things are as precious to us as accommodating parents who bring their kids along for their first hunting trips" reads the promise on a company's website. "Change the world one child at a time by taking your child on the ultimate hunting safari in the heart of Africa… Ultimately your heart will swell to bursting when your child puts down his or her first buck," it concludes. The company offers some rare animals for trophy hunters to shoot, including white lions.

A number of firms sell 'starter' or first-time hunter deals. One company's marketing materials pitch their product to those "who wish to get their feet wet on some of the most sought after animals that Africa has to offer". Another has a 5-day package deal which it says is "perfect for the hunter on a first trip to Africa as well as those with limited time or a strict budget."

The same firm has a "Family Plains Game Hunting Package", a bulk offer in which the whole family can kill as many as 6 animals. A version of the deal is available as a father and son 'bonding' hunt - "but it's also the perfect opportunity for any 2 friends or family members to enjoy a classic African plains game hunt together at an affordable price.

"Regardless of whether you want a hunt for two friends or a husband and wife, a father and daughter or a father and son hunting package, each guest will get the hunting adventure of a lifetime," it enthuses. There is a 'Hunters Dream Package', a 'Serious Hunter Package', and a 'Golden Package' to choose from.

Some companies market 'honeymoon hunts' and corporate packages where management teams can go to strategize and 'connect' whilst shooting animals. "The bigger your group or package, the better the price break," promises one. It's not alone. Another says its aim is to "provide an unforgettable experience where you and your team can witness the beauty of the outdoors while building camaraderie, trust and enthusiasm among employees. We believe in the importance of teamwork and will do everything necessary for you to enhance the energy and connectivity among your team."

One of the companies offering corporate packages also specialises in breeding African wildlife within the United States. This means hunters can now shoot African Big Game without ever having to leave America. There are dozens if not hundreds of such ranches in the US, mainly in Texas. They maintain herds of zebras, giraffes and a host of rare animals. "They want a trophy so it looks as though they have been on an African safari, but without having to pay the price of going to Africa," says Priscilla Feral of Friends of Animals. There are now more blackbuck antelope, a species native to Africa, in the state of Texas than on the entire African continent. "Zebra mares forage here near African impala antelopes, and it is easy to forget that downtown San Antonio is only two hours to the east", muses a reporter who visited one of these ranches.[74]

A report by Texas A&M University said that America's exotic wildlife industry is today a billion-dollar industry. The industry's rate of growth has been breath-taking. The Texas Parks and Wildlife Department estimated the state's exotic wildlife population to be approximately 195,000 animals in 1994. John T. Baccus, a retired Texas State University biologist, thinks the current figure is closer to 1.3 million.

---

[74] "Blood and beauty on a Texas Exotic-Game ranch", Manny Fernandez, New York Times October 19, 2017

One well-known exotics ranch has a runway for private planes to land on, and World War II tanks that you can drive around and shoot. If you prefer to hunt after dark, night-vision goggles are available. Children are welcomed.

America's new 'Jurassic Parks' are growing in popularity. One visitor explained: "It offers a hunting experience the whole family can enjoy." Another enthusiast agreed: "Over the years, I have had the good fortune to enjoy some of the finest sporting facilities our State has to offer for both corporate and personal trips", adding that it worked as "a week-long trip hosting corporate guests, or just enjoying a weekend getaway with family and friends." Another proclaimed his joy at being given the hunting trip as a gift. "What a lucky guy! This was a Christmas present I received from my wife. I couldn't have asked her for a better surprise!"

'Canned hunting' – where animals are bred in captivity for trophy hunting and shot in enclosures - is becoming increasingly popular throughout the world, particularly in the US and South Africa. Since the 1990s, over 30,000 hunting trophies from 58 captive-bred species have been exported from South Africa alone.[75] Animals particularly popular with hunters here include rhinos, zebras and sheep.

The industry has been widely condemned, even by some in the trophy hunting world such as Safari Club International (SCI). However SCI's annual convention continues to allow canned hunt operators to exhibit.[76]

---

[75] CITES Trade Database (UNEP-WCMC)
[76] "Undercover video finds trophy-hunting convention vendors selling captive-bred lion hunts", Justine Coleman, The Hill, 12

It is a profitable business, not least as lion breeders can sell their animals simultaneously for trophies and for Asia's bone trade once the hunter has taken the skull and skin to the taxidermist. The number of trophies entering Britain from "canned" hunting operations has trebled in recent years.[77] In addition to lions, "canned" animals shot by British hunters include leopards and zebras.[78] In recent years, UK hunters have brought home over 200 trophies of lions and other captive-bred animals including monkeys and baboons that had been bred on hunting ranches in Zambia.[79] British hunters have shot 'canned' wildcats too. A bear and a white rhinoceros, both of them bred in captivity, also feature on official records of hunting trophies coming into the UK.[80]

Current estimates of the numbers of captive 'big game' animals in South Africa are around 10,000.[81] As many as 6,000 or more lion cubs alone are bred in captivity here each year for hunting and trade.[82]

An investigation by South Africa's EMS Foundation has uncovered links between the industry and crime syndicates implicated in international wildlife trafficking: "Organised elephant and rhino trafficking groups, because they have the existing killing and

---

February 2020
[77] CITES Trade Database (UNEP-WCMC)
[78] CITES Trade Database (UNEP-WCMC)
[79] CITES Trade Database (UNEP-WCMC)
[80] CITES Trade Database (UNEP-WCMC)
[81] LionAlert https://lionalert.org/canned-hunting/
[82] "Cuddle me, Kill me – a true account of South Africa's captive lion breeding and canned hunting industry", Richard Peirce, Struik Nature, 2018

smuggling infrastructure in place, can, and have, extended their activities to wild lions. These same syndicates are producing processed lion 'cake' and tiger 'jelly/cake' in South Africa from tigers and lions in the South Africa big cat captive industry."

They add: "There are reports that these body parts are shipped out to SE Asia in cargo ships and through military/diplomatic channels. They are also leaving the country in parcels and luggage to other African transit countries (and then presumably from there on to Southeast Asia)."[83]

WWF says that it has evidence that the industry is fuelling renewed poaching of wild lions: "An increase in reports of lion poisonings and killings in Mozambique, Zimbabwe, South Africa, Uganda and Tanzania show there is an escalating trend in the trade of lion body parts, the result of which is an impending threat to some national populations".[84]

While lions make up the majority of animals bred for trophy hunting, many other big cats are now available too. Records from CITES show hunters are being granted permits for trophies of captive-bred leopards, cheetahs, jaguars, and even tigers.[85] In fact, in South Africa there are now some 60 businesses breeding tigers.[86]

---

[83] "The Extinction Business – SA's Lion Bone Trade', EMS Foundation www.emsfoundation.org.za & Ban Animal Trading www.bananimaltrading.org , July 2018

[84] "The Extinction Business – SA's Lion Bone Trade', EMS Foundation www.emsfoundation.org.za & Ban Animal Trading www.bananimaltrading.org , July 2018

[85] CITES Trade Database (UNEP-WCMC)

[86] "Tiger Breeding in South Africa", Stephen Wiggins, IWB 24

If you know where to look, you can shoot one for a trophy. Records show that American and Danish hunters are among the customers to have bagged a captive-bred tiger trophy here.[87]

Outside of South Africa, captive-bred bobcats, Canadian Lynxes and Eurasian lynxes can all be shot in North America[88]. A growing number of cougars bred in captivity in Argentina are being shot by foreign hunters.[89]

The industry doesn't stop at big cats. Sheep, crocodiles, hippopotamuses and honey badgers are among the animals bred to satisfy demand from trophy hunters.[90] A number of trophies of captive-bred birds are recorded by CITES too, including falcons from Qatar and Brazilian vultures.[91] Hunters can shoot captive-reared buzzards and bustards for sport in Pakistan.[92]

American and South African ranches may be breeding some of the world's most iconic and threatened animals for sport hunting, but they are not alone. In recent years, hunters have travelled from all over the world to the UK to shoot Indian hog deer, Barasinghas, and the Pere David's Deer.[93] The latter, a Chinese species, is classed by IUCN as Extinct in the Wild.[94]

April 2018 https://iwbond.org/2018/04/24/tiger-breeding-in-south-africa/

[87] CITES Trade Database (UNEP-WCMC)

[88] CITES Trade Database (UNEP-WCMC)

[89] CITES Trade Database (UNEP-WCMC)

[90] CITES Trade Database (UNEP-WCMC)

[91] CITES Trade Database (UNEP-WCMC)

[92] CITES Trade Database (UNEP-WCMC)

[93] CITES Trade Database (UNEP-WCMC)

[94] Jiang, Z. & Harris, R.B. 2016. Elaphurus davidianus. The IUCN Red List of Threatened Species 2016: e.T7121A22159785

UK hunting trophy imports of captive-bred wildlife: 1994-2018[95]

Addax; African wild cat; Arabian oryx; Barbary sheep; Black bear; Blackbuck; Caracal; Dama gazelle; Egyptian goose; Hamadryas baboon; Lechwe; Leopard; Lion; Markhor; Nile crocodile; Nilgai; Scimitar horned-oryx; Serval; Southern White Rhinoceros; Spur-winged goose; Tsessebe; Vervet monkey; Yellow baboon; Zebra

Captive-bred hunting trophies exported by South Africa, 1991-2018[96]

Aardwolf; Addax; African elephant; Arabian oryx; Barbary sheep; Bay duiker; Blackbuck; Blue duiker; Bontebok; Bontebok hybrid; Brown hyena; Caracal; Chacma Baboon; Cheetah; Civet cat; Cougar; Egyptian goose; Equus hybrid; Eurasian lynx; Grivet monkey; Hamadryas baboon; Hartman zebra; Hippopotamus; Honey badger; Indian hog deer; Knob billed duck; Kori bustard; Lechwe; Leopard; Leopard tortoise; Lion; Little egret; Namaqua dove; Nile crocodile; Orange-winged amazon; Oryx hybrid; Pale chanting goshawk; Pygmy falcon; Rainbow lorikeet; Red lory; Rock monitor; Scimitar horned oryx; Serval; Sheep; Sitatunga; Southern Black Korhaan; Speckled guinea; Speckled pigeon; Spur winged goose; Tiger; Tsessebe; Urial; Vervet monkey; Western crowned pigeon; White

---

[95] CITES Trade Database (UNEP-WCMC)
[96] CITES Trade Database (UNEP-WCMC)

rhinoceros; White tailed whistling duck; Wood bison; Yellow-naped amazon

Top 10 'canned hunting' trophy exports from South Africa, 1991-2017 (species & no. of trophies)[97]

Lion: 11,813 + 1829kg bones
Nile crocodile: 9,443 + 3 litres oil
Lechwe: 4,064
Scimitar-horned oryx: 1,067
Bontebok: 839
Barbary Sheep: 621
Hartmann Zebra 440
Caracal: 319
Blue duiker: 218
White rhinoceros: 109

Going on safari

Hunting concessions in Africa range from state-owned land such as parks, to communal areas and private ranches and farms. Some are colossal. Chewore, Zimbabwe's largest hunting concession[98], is over 1 million acres in size.[99] That is larger than the US state of Rhode Island or the UK county of Hampshire.

The hunting rights on these estates are typically acquired by safari companies via tender. In Namibia and

---

[97] CITES Trade Database (UNEP-WCMC)
[98] http://zimfieldguide.com/mashonaland-west/sapi-chewore-dande-and-doma-safari-areas
[99] https://www.chipitanisafaris.net/camps-zim.htm

Zimbabwe they are allocated by the government. The length of the lease usually ranges from 5 to 10 years. The safari company hires a professional hunter ('PH') who undergoes an accreditation process. They are required to accompany the trophy hunter and maintain an official record of the hunt. In the main, Professional Hunters are white Africans from South Africa and Zimbabwe, although there are also some American and European ones.

Some big companies have numerous hunting concessions which they own or lease in several countries; others are smaller operations. You can book direct online, through agents, or attend industry auctions, conventions and exhibitions where hunting holiday operators make a brisk trade.

In North America, alligators, cougars, lynxes, wolves and wild sheep are among the many species which trophy hunters can shoot. Alaska is popular for those wanting reindeer or mountain goats. One firm here has acquired hunting concessions in the Arctic. In its marketing materials, it proclaims: "We respect the wildlife, the land, and each other. As a result we hunt hard, have fun, and enjoy a high hunting success rate."

Its spring grizzly bear hunt comes highly recommended: "The hides of these beautiful bears are the thickest and most luxurious in the world." Wolves are an optional extra. "We highly recommend the heavier-belted magnum calibers in a bolt action with a minimum bullet weight of 250 grains", the publicity material adds. "If you wish to consume liquor it is recommended you bring your favorite adult beverage."

Hunters from around the world flock to Canada every year for its black bears. They are among the most hunted animals on the planet.[100] Despite being threatened with extinction by climate change, Canada lets foreign trophy hunters come and shoot its polar bears too.[101]

Further south, Mexico and Argentina are becoming increasingly popular destinations. Cougars can be hunted from February to September in South America. Wild pampa sheep and imported European wild boar are available here too.

Animals can be hunted on their own or as package deals. In North America, a 5-day black bear/wolf 'combo' for instance will cost around $4500, while a 10-day cougar/lynx package is approximately $8500. Many other combinations are available, such as an 8-day wolf/coyote hunt priced at $4800, or a 10 day deal which includes black bear, migratory birds and deer at a cost of $12,000. Cougar on its own can cost around $7500, lynx $4500 and grizzly bear $8000.

In Africa, the cost of hunting elephants typically starts at around $45,000 and can go up to $70,000. A wild lion is around $35,000, while a leopard is approximately $25,000. White rhinos can cost as much as $150,000. [102] [103]

---

[100] CITES Trade Database (UNEP-WCMC)

[101] CITES Trade Database (UNEP-WCMC)

[102] Average price taken from nine hunting companies: Cape to Cairo, CMS Safari, Mukulu African Hunting Safari, Allen Schenk Safari, Worldwide Trophy Adventures, Hunt-Nation, African Hunting Lodge, Book My Hunt, and phirimasafaris.com

[103] "Trophy hunting by the numbers – the United States' role in global trophy hunting", HSI-HSUS, February 2016

The rights to kill two critically endangered black rhinos recently sold for $350,000[104] and $400,000 apiece[105].

The cost of a 'dream' African safari can quickly reach six figures. There is the cost of taxidermy and of shipping one's prized trophy to take into consideration. A growing number of operators provide professional photographers and videographers to record every detail of your adventure. The luxury trimmings – the serenity spa, wine tasting, cigar bar and so on – may have to be paid for separately.

While the cost of trophy hunting can seem like a fortune, though, the price of life for many species is cheap. You can pay $100,000 for a hunting holiday, yet the trophy fee for some animals is $100 or less.

South Africa is the hub of the African safari hunting industry, followed by Namibia which is particularly popular with Europeans wanting cheetah trophies (US hunters are currently not allowed to import cheetah body parts). A cheetah can cost less than $4000.

Some African nations are popular for their more unusual trophy species. Uganda, for instance – which was described as the 'Pearl of Africa' by Winston Churchill – is popular for those wanting to bag a spotted hyena, black-backed and side-striped jackals, Burchell's zebras or Rothschild's giraffes. Central and western Africa has populations of forest elephant and dwarf

---

104
https://www.theguardian.com/environment/2015/may/21/texan-paid-350000-kills-endangered-black-rhino-africa
[105] https://www.nytimes.com/2019/09/08/us/trump-black-rhino-trophy-hunter.html

buffalo. In Cameroon, "rainforest hunting is exciting and the local Pygmy people are excellent trackers."

For those seeking adventure down under, there is an Australian safari firm that will help you acquire trophies of "all the available species of Australia including the 14 South Pacific big game animals". Feral goats and rams and the "world's biggest rusa" can be shot on a 2 million acre hunting estate which also claims to have thousands of buffalo and salt water crocodiles. Australia is recommended for hunters wanting to add dingo trophies to their collections.

In neighbouring New Zealand, privately-owned estates and mountain properties offer "monster" red stag and Himalayan tahr. "We can help you tailor your hunting experience to include fun activities for family and non-hunters that will be truly memorable." Wallabies are available elsewhere in the country.[106]

Not far away are New Caledonia and Mauritius where you can shoot Javan rusa stags. New markets in Eastern Europe and Asia are opening up all the time. Azerbaijan, like Kazakhstan, is said by fellow hunters to be 'excellent' for Siberian brown bear.

Whilst it may no longer have much in the way of large predators (most were hunted to extinction long ago) Europe still has a number of countries which welcome trophy hunters. One firm provides no fewer than 62 species to choose from. The menu includes lynxes, wildcats, reindeer and golden jackals. Driven hunts, where a line of beaters force game towards

---

[106] What to Hunt - Wallabies Hunting; New Zealand Department of Conservation https://www.doc.govt.nz/parks-and-recreation/things-to-do/hunting/what-to-hunt/wallabies/

waiting guns, can be arranged in Poland, Hungary, Romania and Spain as well as in the UK.

Virtually every country in western Europe has something to offer. Turkey is an increasingly popular destination. Romania has brown bears and wolves. Shooting these animals can count toward one of Safari Club International's many prizes for globe-trotting hunters. Beavers and arctic foxes are among other animals which can legally be shot by trophy hunters. Specialist bookings agents can help by "selecting the trip that is right for you and your companions".

The Conventions

Every year, thousands of trophy hunters descend on the conventions of major industry groups such as Safari Club International and the Dallas Safari Club. These conventions serve as a market-place for the sale of a range of hunts. Animal trinkets can be found here too, some of them made from the bodies of endangered species. An undercover investigation by Humane Society International of SCI's 2019 convention in Nevada found canvasses made from elephant ears, belts made of hippo skin, and elephant skin furniture. A table made out of a hippo's skull was among the many other items for sale.[107]

It is at these conventions that many trophy hunts are auctioned off, the proceeds of which help support SCI's lobbying work in Congress and elsewhere. Lots offered for auction at the 2019 convention included a 10-day

---

[107] "A Humane World: Kitty Block's Blog" – "At Safari Club Convention, vendors peddle canned lion hunts, elephant and hippo body parts: January 18, 2019

polar bear hunt which raised $60,000. Elephant and leopard hunts in Namibia raised over $40,000. Bidders parted with thousands of dollars for the chance to hunt wild sheep in Tajikistan and Mexico, brown bears in Alaska, sable and hippos in Zambia, and to snap up a 21-day 'Dangerous Game' hunt in Tanzania.[108]

In 2020, 2 hunters paid $340,000 for a "hunt of a lifetime" personally guided by Donald Trump Jr.[109]

There are a number of other major industry conventions and exhibitions around the world. The Jagd and Hund fair held in Dortmund each year is possibly the largest hunting event in Europe. At the 2020 fair, undercover reporters from Bild magazine recorded trophy hunt operators offering to shoot leopards in the legs first so that the paying client could then kill the animal at close range.[110]

Spain's Cinegetica exhibition is not far behind and claims to have received 40,000 visitors in 2019.[111] Before being postponed due to Covid-19, hundreds of hunting companies had booked stall space for its 2020 fair. They included firms offering hunts of polar bears, cheetahs, monkeys, and all of the 'African Big Five'. There were also companies selling hunts of 'canned lions', and hunts where children under 11 could join in.

---

[108] From Auction.safariclub.org

[109] "Paid: $340,000 to hunt deer with Don Trump Jr. in fundraising record", Paul Bedard, Washington Examiner 14 February 2020

[110] https://www.thesun.co.uk/news/10862611/evil-trophy-hunters-pay-thousands-kneecapped/

[111] https://www.cazavision.com/cinegetica-2019-record-40000-visitantes

Some businesses due to take part sell honey badger and reindeer hunting trips on their websites.[112]

Abu Dhabi's International Hunting & Equestrian Exhibition is also bidding to be among the biggest, and trophy hunting companies are now eyeing markets in Asia with increasing interest. In 2019, the first ever China Hunting Show was held in Shanghai. Among the companies exhibiting was a South African company selling hunts of captive-bred tigers.[113]

Shipping

After the hunter has shot the animal, it is taken back to the lodge or camp for skinning. The skull has the flesh removed and is boiled. The trophy will then usually be subjected to a treatment process called dipping. Sometimes called dip and pack, or dipping and disinfection, it is a process which seeks to kill any bacteria or pathogens before the trophy is transported. Concerns have recently been raised about lion bones being a possible transmission vector for tuberculosis, however.[114] The process usually requires skins, skulls and other body parts to be submerged in an acid solution for up to 48 hours, and then salted before being dried.

---

[112] See Exhibitors List at https://cinegetica.es/soy-visitante/

[113] "South Africa selling tiger and lion hunts to Chinese nouveau riche", Louise de Waal, Conservation Action Trust, 25 June 2019

[114] "China's ban on wildlife consumption is an overdue death knell for lion bone industry", Don Pinnock, Daily Maverick, 24 February 2020

Once you have your desired trophy, you will wish to take it home with you. In the UK an import permit fee of £67 is payable to import a "specimen or any number of specimens as long as they are of the same species of genus." However, the government agency responsible "may waive the fee payable for import and re-export applications which are non-commercial and if the import, export or re-export will benefit the conservation of the species."[115] Many trophy hunters claim that it does.

There are a number of brokers and freight companies which specialise in transporting trophies by sea and air. After the international furore that followed the killing of Cecil the lion, over 40 of the world's leading airlines – including British Airways, Virgin and Emirates - stopped hunters from sending their trophies home on their planes. A number still allow them, though. Among them is Turkish Airlines. The company was recently implicated in an investigation by World Animal Protection which found that poachers were using their freight arm, Turkish Cargo, to illegally transport wild-caught parrots out of the Democratic Republic of the Congo, Nigeria and Mali. The birds were destined for countries in the Middle East and Asia.[116] Other commercial companies that still allow hunting trophies to be carried include South African Airways and Ethiopian Airlines.[117]

---

[115] "Fees for CITES applications for animals", AHVLA (Animal Health & Veterinary Laboratories Agency, June 2013)

[116] From www.Ladyfreethinker.org

[117] "Airlines put hunting trophies on infrequent-flyer list", Animal Welfare Institute, Spring 2018 www.awionline.org

Cargo airlines are much more important to the industry than commercial carriers, however. FedEx is technically the world's biggest airline by virtue of the huge volumes it transports every year. Its fleet is three times the size of British Airways' and has almost 700 planes flying to 375 destinations. Its closest competitor flies to just over 300. Page 161 section 13 of the Fedex Service Guide January 6, 2020 (updated April 20, 2020) states: "Taxidermy-finished hunting trophies or completely processed (dried) specimens of whole animals or parts of animals are acceptable for shipment into the U.S."[118] Page 184 adds: "FedEx SameDay City may accept certain shipments of animal heads and other parts for taxidermy if properly packaged."

The list of 'Standard DHL Prohibited Commodities' which forms part of DHL Express Shipping Guidelines, on the other hand, states: "The following commodities are not acceptable for transport by DHL under any circumstances... Hunting (Animal) trophies, animal parts such as ivory and sharks fin, animal remains, or Animal-by-Products and derived products not intended for human consumption, prohibited for movement by the CITES Convention and/or local law."[119]

Some hunters have sought to circumvent bans by airlines by switching to sea freight. While shipping times are longer – up to 12 weeks from southern African to the US - costs can be 25% lower.[120]

---

[118] https://www.fedex.com/content/dam/fedex/us-united-states/services/Service_Guide_2020.pdf

[119] https://www.dhl.com/en/express/customs_support/express_import_guidelines.html

Taxidermy – which usually consists of turning the trophy into a 'shoulder mount' or 'full (body) mount' – can either be done in the country where it was hunted or back in the hunter's home nation. They will usually be bubble-wrapped and placed in custom-built wooden crates.

On ships, the entire container will often be filled with crates of hunting trophies. Shipping companies sometimes remove horns and antlers to reduce the charges payable. As many hunters kill a number of different animals on their expeditions, they can be packed in bulk. A typical crate of 6 'plains game' animals including zebras and baboons will cost about $1700 up to a weight of 100kg, and around $4000 for consignments weighing up to 300kg. Insurance, customs paperwork and packaging costs are added on top, as is the cost of road transfer from the destination port to the hunter's home.

Some freight forwarding companies do little more than ship hunting trophies. One such company, Trophy Shippers, markets itself to clients as a pro-hunting firm. "First and foremost, we're hunters, too." Hence, says the company, it "understands what goes into planning the hunt of a lifetime because we've taken that trip." Theirs, moreover, is a business "for the hunter by the hunter. We recognise that your blood, sweat, tears and hard-earned money go to the hunt and a memory that lasts a lifetime. Your hunting trophy represents the hunt, the people, the process, the adventure, the adrenaline rush, the memory,

---

[120] "Killing for Trophies – an analysis of global trophy hunting trade", IFAW, 14 June 2016

and the story that will last for not only your life but generations to come.

"The only concern that you have is making the shot." After all, "when the memory fades, the trophy lasts forever."[121]

Taxidermy

Taxidermists regard their profession as akin to an art form. "The respect for animals and nature conveyed in the art of taxidermy is myriad and it is in this spirit that you must undertake the hobby," according to 'The Essential Guide to Taxidermy – from Trap to trophy', an industry 'bible'. "Essentially you must reflect the awe in which mankind must hold nature if it is to continue to thrive and reside within it. Such a respectful, spiritual approach to this often methodical undertaking is wise as it will see you connect more with creatures you work upon. In turn, you will produce work with a vividness seldom seen in those less sensitive," it adds.[122]

Virtually any animal can be turned into a shoulder or full mount. The cost will be around $500 (shoulder mount) and $1250 (full mount) for a baboon, $750/$3000 for a cheetah, $2500/$10,000 for a giraffe, $1000/$4000 for a leopard, and $1000/$5000 for a lion.

Should you so desire, taxidermists can also arrange to prepare your ostrich trophy ($1000/$2500), porcupine ($500/$2000), vervet monkey ($500/1000) or warthog ($600/$2000). A rhino will set you back $4000/$8000.

---

[121] https://www.trophyshippers.com/
[122] "The Essential Guide to Taxidermy – From Trap to Trophy", Dalton Harriott, Triangle Circle Square Press, 2015

Special effects can be added. You can arrange for the bear to have its mouth open, as if it were growling. Or you can mount your full-size bear trophy on a 'habitat base' to replicate how it looked in the wild. Without irony, one industry leader promises that its added foliage "help bring the subject to life".

Your trophy can be turned into a variety of ornaments, trinkets and home furnishings. One firm, for instance, promises to transform your elk teeth into "fine elk ivory jewellery". There are businesses that will make a rug out of grizzly bear, cougar, wolf or baboon skin. Fly whisks can be made from the tails of elephants, rhinos or giraffes for as little as $350. Or they can turn the hoof of your zebra into ashtrays ($400) or bookends (starting at $500 per pair). Hippo feet are also available.

For $270, zebra hooves can be turned into a gun rack. A wide range of warthog novelties can be purchased: letter openers and bottle openers ($185), corkscrews ($225), and beer mugs ($495) among them. You can have your elephant feet turned into a serving tray ($750), barstool ($1100), footstool ($950), wastepaper basket ($950), or an umbrella stand ($1050). Your elephant's ears can be turned into a map of Africa (prices start at $1500) or a painting of the African Big Five (from $2600). Other options include a pack of 6 coasters ($295), a belt ($395), or a pillow ($275 – 375).

You can even have your own scrotum pouch made. The cost: $295.

Trophy hunting is exempted from many of CITES' restrictions on wild animal trade because it is – somewhat bizarrely - not considered to be a 'commercial' activity. Nevertheless, hunting trophies – some of them of animals that appear to have been shot very recently – regularly make their way into the brochures of auction houses. Some are sold in shops too.

British auctioneers Tennants are a company which specialises in the sale of hunting trophies. At a June auction in 2019, items on offer included a black bear full body (guide price £1,500), a leopard skin (£350), a turtle's head (£380), a zebra head (£1,600), a giraffe neck and head (£4,500), a full body cougar (£1,500), and an elephant's foot (£300). The auction withdrew the lot of an African lioness - which it claimed had been "ethically-sourced" - after questions were raised about the legality of its provenance.[123]

Other items to have made it into their catalogues include a waste-paper bin made from a pair of rhino feet[124] and an elephant foot tea caddy.[125]. Tennants has previously sold black rhino horns for upwards of

---

[123] "Critics slate auction of stuffed animals for using dead creatures as souvenirs", Tom Parry, Daily Mirror 13 June 2019

[124] Tennants auction catalogue
https://bid.tennants.co.uk/m/view-auctions/catalog/id/728?page=5&view=grid

[125] https://bid.tennants.co.uk/m/lot-details/index/catalog/728/lot/488396?url=%2Fm%2Fview-auctions%2Fcatalog%2Fid%2F728%3Fpage%3D6%26view%3Dgrid

£20,000.[126] Other items to go under the hammer include a baboon skull[127] and the heads, paws and tails of otters.[128]

'Get Stuffed', in Islington, London, is a shop crammed with hunting trophies of animals from around the world. Some date back several decades, whereas others have been hunted more recently. Its foreign mammals section includes trophies of lions, a tiger, leopard, polar bear, various primates, a full-body giraffe, and a young zebra. There are also some rare and endangered animal trophies including a red panda and a snow leopard.[129]

The Great British Shooting Show

A number of companies hoping to sell trophy hunting holidays at the "Great British Shooting Show" at the Birmingham NEC in February, 2020, published their schedule of trophy fees. They included Anlem Trust Safaris which had ostriches available for £349 and porcupines for £194. Zebras were only £852 each.

---

[126] Tennants auction catalogue https://bid.tennants.co.uk/m/view-auctions/catalog/id/79?page=2&cat=247

[127] Tennants auction catalogue https://bid.tennants.co.uk/m/lot-details/index/catalog/289/lot/241804?url=%2Fm%2Fview-auctions%2Fcatalog%2Fid%2F289%3Fpage%3D3

[128] Tennants auction catalogue https://bid.tennants.co.uk/m/view-auctions/catalog/id/728?page=7

[129] Get Stuffed https://www.thegetstuffed.co.uk/

Namib Hunting Safaris had baboons available for just £50. Jackals were on offer for the same price. The cost of a monkey with Thorndale Safaris was £43. They also had a number of birds going cheap – Egyptian goose for £28, and guinea fowl at £14.

The trophy fees for animals available from Legelela Safaris included Bat Eared Fox for $600, Civet Cat at $1750, and Genets for $300. Wild cats and White Tailed Mongoose were both available for $350. Nduna Hunting safaris had a special offer for hunting caracals with packs of hounds for £800. Some trophy hunting firms offered tantalising deals, including free baboons, jackals and monkeys.

The show's website proudly announced: "If one of the items on your bucket list is an international hunting trip, Europe offers the finest wild boar, mouflon, ibex and chamois hunting in some spectacular and beautiful locations. Argentina offers amazing dove shooting and then there's the Dark Continent of Africa. Africa offers the international hunter the ultimate hunting safari experience. With more international hunting and safari outfitters attending the British Shooting Show than any other event, your dreams can become a reality." Children under the age of 15 would be allowed in free.

After local protests and widespread media coverage[130], the NEC announced it would no longer allow companies involved in trophy hunting to take part[131]. Organisers of

---

[130] See for instance "Fury as NEC hosts 'barbaric' expo plugging the chance to SHOOT lions, giraffes and elephants", Alison Stacey, Birmingham Mail 7 July 2019
https://www.birminghammail.co.uk/news/midlands-news/fury-nec-hosts-barbaric-expo-16543244

the show announced they would take their trade to Liverpool instead. The local authorities there moved swiftly to shut down the exhibition altogether.[132]

[131] "NEC statement over 'barbaric' expo plugging chance to SHOOT lions, giraffes and elephants", James Rodger, Birmingham Mail, 12 July 2019
https://www.birminghammail.co.uk/news/midlands-news/nec-statement-over-barbaric-expo-16560344
[132] "Controversial shooting show due to be held in Liverpool is cancelled", Liam Thorp, Liverpool Echo 8 October 2019

Chapter 2: The Key Players - Safari Club International, the NRA et al

Safari Club International (SCI)

"Since 2000, SCI has spent $140 million on protecting the freedom to hunt through policy advocacy, litigation and education for federal and state legislators to ensure hunting is protected for future generations." – Safari Club International[133]

Safari Club International, the world's largest trophy hunting organisation, celebrates its 50th anniversary in 2021.

The organisation was the brainchild of Casper Johnny 'CJ' McElroy, or 'Mac' as he was known to many, a hunter from California. When McElroy started hunting, the sector consisted of only a handful of small associations. He first brought together the Southern California Safari Club and the Safari Club of Los Angeles. They were joined by sister organisations in Chicago and elsewhere shortly after. New chapters quickly emerged throughout the US.[134]

Advocacy campaigns were launched to promote the image of trophy hunting. An 'American Wilderness Leadership School' was created to recruit young people.

---

[133] https://www.safariclub.org/about-us

[134] More background on CJ McElroy and the founding of SCI can be found at https://www.africahunting.com/threads/c-j-mcelroy-founder-of-safari-club-international.3317/

Representatives were sent to lobby the conferences of the newly-established Convention on the International Trade in Endangered Species (CITES).

The first foreign branch was established in Spain in 1977 followed soon after by dozens of others. The first meeting with a US President took place in the White House that same year, to protest against the Endangered Species Act.[135] Under McElroy, the new group quickly became one of America's – and the world's – most powerful industry lobby groups.

In 1977, the first SCI Records Book was published. Not only was it to become the industry's most important standard: it was to influence the way trophy hunting was practised. It actively encouraged hunters to shoot the biggest animals – the 'fittest' of the species – in order to give them a chance to enter this hallowed publication. Awards schemes were created, giving prizes to hunters who shot the most animals in the most continents.

Safari Club International today has some 200 chapters in different parts of the world as well as right across the US. SCI members are calculated to have killed at least 2000 lions, 1800 leopards, 800 elephants and as many as 500 black rhinos, according to various estimates.[136][137]

Its focus is protecting hunters' 'rights'. The SCI-affiliated 'Hunt Forever' website describes the

---

[135] https://www.safariclub.org/blog/scis-50th-anniversary-horizon

[136] "Killing for trophies – an analysis of global trophy hunting trade", IFAW

[137] "At Safari Club Convention, vendors peddle canned lion hunts, elephant and hippo body parts", Kitty Block, HSUS 18 January 2019

organisation as being "the foremost advocate in the world devoted to protecting the freedom to hunt. SCI will not falter or waiver in its devotion to this mission".[138] It works to protect "your freedom to hunt covered from Alabama to Zimbabwe."[139] Its strapline is: "First For Hunters".

The group lobbies to strip back legal protections which restrict sport-hunting of wildlife. It has powerful supporters, including former US President George Bush and a number of leading American politicians and generals.[140]

Its annual convention is legendary, or notorious, depending on one's perspective. Around 1,000 companies from across all sectors of the industry come to exhibit and sell their wares within the 500,000 square foot convention centre in Reno. Firearms manufacturers and taxidermists are numerous. SCI says that over 20,000 people visit its main convention each year. In a recent post-event report to members, the organisation said that "there were outfitters from everywhere with hunts on every huntable species so choices are still good to fill a bucket list."[141]

Andrew Loveridge is the scientist who radio-collared 'Cecil' the lion before he was shot by American dentist Walter Palmer, a SCI member who won a Safari Club

---

[138] https://huntforever.org/about/

[139] For more information about SCI's advocacy work visit https://www.safariclub.org/protect-freedom-hunt

[140] "Big names backing big-game hunter", Paul Salopek, Chicago Tribune 13 May 2001 https://www.chicagotribune.com/news/ct-xpm-2001-05-13-0105130268-story.html

[141] SCI Convention report, www.africahunting.com

International prize for shooting animals in North America. Loveridge describes his visit to one of SCI's conventions in his recent book '*Lion Hearted*': "The 4-day convention is a huge marketplace, and the 3 halls, each the size of a vast aircraft hangar, were filled to capacity with stalls selling hunting safaris. For sale were expeditions to hunt polar bears, buffalo, lions, elephants, exotic sheep – pretty much any species it is possible to hunt. Intermingled were stalls selling expensive, bespoke hunting rifles, expedition and hunting gear, wildlife art, trinkets and taxidermy services."[142]

The lives of approximately 1000 animals are 'sold' to prospective hunters during the event.[143] Despite criticising canned hunting in public, companies that sell canned lion hunts come to exhibit at SCI's event.[144]

In 2019, undercover investigators from Humane Society International discovered that one of the exhibitors at the convention was CZ-USA - a firearms manufacturer whose weapons have been found in African game reserves implicated in rhino poaching. The US Commerce Department and the Department of Homeland Security launched an investigation into CZ

[142] "Lion Hearted , The Life and Death of Cecil & the Future of Africa's Iconic Cats", Andrew Loveridge, Regan Arts, 2018

[143] "Trophy Hunters Gather At Safari Club International Convention To Bid On Big Game Kills", Kathryn Snowdon, Huffington Post 01/02/2017

[144] "Undercover investigation exposes illegal wildlife items, including elephant skin furniture, hippo skull table and stingray belts, for sale at Safari Club International's 2019 convention", HSI/HSUS 18 January 2019 https://www.hsi.org/news-media/undercover-investigation-safari-club-international-011819/

and its subsidiary company in the US to see if laws had been broken. The company had already been warned previously that its weapons were being used by poachers to shoot protected wildlife in South Africa.[145]

The 2019 convention also hosted businesses selling items such as elephant skin sofas, bracelets made from elephant hair, and belts made from the skin of sharks. Buckets containing hippo teeth were on display. One stand was selling a knife with a handle made from the tusk of narwhal.

The convention hosts a number of special fundraising events each year. In 2020, Donald Trump Jr – the President's son – was the guest speaker at SCI's Convention. The 'rump' Beach Boys led by Mike Love were the highlight act, to the disgust of Beach Boys co-founders Brian Wilson and Al Jardine. They publicly disowned their former bandmates and signed a petition in protest.[146]

Other recent offerings include a 'Conservation Leadership Award Gala' co-hosted by gun-makers Berretta. The event features an 'Oscar-style' award ceremony, gourmet dinner, entertainment, and a series of auctions. There was a 'SCI Protect Your Freedom to Hunt Lunch'. The featured speaker was Jack Carr, described as "a devoted supporter of the 2nd Amendment

---

[145] "Potentially illegal wildlife products, unethical captive-bred lion hunts exposed at SCI Convention", HSUS/HSI

[146] "Beach Boys founder denounces band's Reno gig, calls for boycott to protest trophy hunting", Benjamin Spillman, Reno Gazette Journal, 4 February 2020
https://eu.rgj.com/story/news/2020/02/04/brian-wilson-beach-boys-boycott-sci-reno-2020-trump-jr/4650001002/

and hunting and wildlife organizations" and "author of a new political/military thriller titled 'The Terminal List'." Proceeds from the lunch went towards SCI's "Hunter Action Fund (HAF) SuperPac", a mechanism for raising money for campaigns at election time.[147]

The auction of a World Heritage Rifle Series raised $260,000. SCI's Foundation raised over $1.5 million.[148] Rick Parsons, SCI's CEO, exclaimed: "On Saturday evening, the party atmosphere was palpable. Bidding on auction items was competitive and folks were whooping and hollering in support because everyone knew that the money was going for the cause."[149]

In a press release, SCI President Paul Babaz added: "This Convention exhibited the embodiment of the concept of HUNTER PRIDE."[150] Babaz made a direct appeal to attendees to donate to its election campaign SuperPac fund which, according to SCI, "resulted in thousands of dollars being raised on the spot."

Babaz is an investment manager and trophy hunter from Louisiana. He describes himself on social media as a "hunter, conservationist, #2 advocate, sustainable use advocate!"[151] He sits on the Board of the National Rifle

---

[147] "Enhance your SCI convention experience by attending special events", Ammoland.com, November 29, 2018

[148] SCI Convention report, www.africahunting.com

[149] "Safari Club International's 47th Annual Convention A Rousing Success", Ammoland, 16 January 2019 https://www.ammoland.com/2019/01/safari-club-internationals-47th-annual-convention-a-rousing-success/#axzz6KXXOCspu

[150] SCI Press Release 14 January 2019 https://www.safariclub.org/press/scis-47th-annual-convention-rousing-success

[151] https://www.facebook.com/PaulBabazSCI/

Association (NRA). An article endorsing him in AmmoLand magazine sets out his platform: "The need to align SCI with like-minded groups such as the NRA helps strengthen the fight against both the radical anti-hunting groups and those who would rob us of our Second Amendment rights. Hunting and firearms are tightly woven in the fabric of America and what affects one will surely affect the other."[152]

In 2019, Babaz was "terminated" by Morgan Stanley and quietly stepped down from his SCI role. According to the Guilliano Law Group's 'Stockbroker Fraud' website, Babaz was removed by the securities broker dealer on October 4, 2019 after allegations were made that he had carried out trades without the authorisation of clients, and that official documents relating to a number of transactions had been "improperly used by Babaz".

It added that documents from the Financial Industry Regulatory Authority (FINRA) appear to show that Babaz had been identified in a number of further complaints including "accusations of his misconduct". One complaint alleges "misrepresentations had been made concerning an annuity" sold by Babaz. Two complaints have been settled with combined damages exceeding $100,000.[153]

Babaz was succeeded as SCI President by businessman Steve Skold. However Babaz remains a member of the NRA's Board. In his recent bid for re-election, he gave an interview to Guns America Digest in which he states: "I have owned and shot AR's and what

---

[152] From www.Ammoland.com, January 28, 2019
[153] "Morgan Stanley stockbroker terminated for unauthorized trading", https://stockbrokerfraud.com/paul-babaz/

some classify as 'Assault Weapons' long before it they were called 'Assault' weapons! I can say unequivocally that I oppose and will always oppose any sort of ban on firearms or gun accessory."[154]

On Valentine's Day, Babaz posted the following reminder to his supporters on Facebook: "Valentine's Day is a great day to cast your vote to protect your rights and show your love of Freedom!"[155]

In April 2019, SCI appointed a new CEO to replace the outgoing Rick Parsons. W Laird Hamberlin holds a number of SCI hunting records and awards. Laird, from the US state of Georgia, has hunted in Africa, Asia, the South Pacific, South America, Europe and throughout the US, Canada and Mexico. He has killed the African Big 5 (lion, elephant, rhino, leopard, buffalo), has hunted hippos and crocodiles, and has numerous SCI 'Inner Circles' and 'Grand Slam' hunting awards to his name.

SCI is officially opposed to canned hunting. However, Hamberlin has hunted pumas with an Argentinian company called Telleria, which is registered as a 'criadero' or registered breeding facility for puma. According to a hunting industry report on Telleria, "cats are specifically captive-bred there, individually marked (presumably with a passive ID tag) and released into an enclosure. They may then be hunted and, because they were privately raised animals rather than wild puma, an

[154] https://www.gunsamerica.com/digest/nra-board-candidate-paul-babaz/

[155] https://www.facebook.com/PaulBabazSCI/posts/2262806170680580

export permit is available." Hamberlin is named as having hunted with Telleria in 2013.[156]

Upon his appointment, he issued a statement: "We are in an unprecedented period of attacks on hunting, particularly international hunting that has been SCI's brand for many years. Hunting here in the US is also under attack and is a right that we will help to preserve. SCI has always been the leading organisation defending the rights of all hunters around the world."[157]

As well as lobbying politicians, SCI has an in-house team of lawyers. It is active in the courts challenging laws and regulations that protect wildlife. It has brought more than 50 cases before the courts and filed a number of briefs with the US Supreme Court on cases involving the Second Amendment (the right to bear arms) and the right to hunt imported exotic wild animals on private ranches in the US.[158]

SCI has been involved in cases relating to imports of elephant and lion trophies from endangered populations, removing protections from black bears and grizzly bears, and hunting in America's wildlife refuges.[159]

Safari Club International's 'PAC' – Political Action Committee – is one of the largest in the US. PACs are

[156] "Who can export Argentina puma hunting trophies", The Hunting Report, 1 July 2014 http://huntingreport.com/who-can-export-argentina-puma-hunting-trophies/

[157] "W Laird Hamberlin named SCI CEO", www.huntfover.org

[158] https://www.safariclub.org/litigation

[159] "Safari Club International sues to protect hunting in Alaska", Jake VanDeLaare, Wide Open Spaces, 29 January 2017 https://www.wideopenspaces.com/safari-club-international-sues-to-protect-hunting-in-alaska/

used to funnel financial contributions to the campaigns of election candidates. Contributions from SCI's fund totalling hundreds of thousands of dollars are made every year to political campaigns.[160] SCI boasts that its PAC is bigger than that of some of America's largest corporations including General Motors and Delta airlines.[161]

In 2018, Safari Club International and Dallas Safari Club together made major donations to candidates in the US' mid-term elections, over 90% of which went to Republicans.[162] Ryan Zinke, who later became the US Interior Secretary – and thus responsible for America's hunting laws and trophy import regulations - received thousands of dollars from Safari Club International for his 2014 and 2016 election campaigns to the US Congress.[163] Other leading politicians to have received donations from SCI include the US Senate leader Mitch McDonnell.[164] McDonnell received $8,000 towards his

160
https://www.opensecrets.org/pacs/lookup2.php?strID=C00122101
[161] https://www.safariclub.org/donate
162
https://www.opensecrets.org/orgs/recipients?id=D000000757 ;
https://www.opensecrets.org/orgs/summary?topnumcycle=2018&toprecipcycle=All%20cycles&contribcycle=All%20cycles&lobcycle=All%20cycles&outspendcycle=All%20cycles&id=D000025229
[163] "High-ranking Trump official attends hunting convention", Miranda Green and Timothy Cama, The Hill 3 February 2018 https://thehill.com/policy/energy-environment/372166-high-ranking-trump-official-attends-trophy-hunting-convention
[164] "Hunting club that suspended U.S. hunter donates to top lawmakers", Susan Cornwell, Reuters 31 July 2015
https://www.reuters.com/article/us-zimbabawe-wildlife-lion-

campaign in 2014.[165] Mike Pompeo, the US Secretary of State, received $2,000 when he was running for the House of Representatives in 2016. Former House speaker John Boehner received $5,000 in 2014 and a further $2000 in 2016.

Between 2016-2018, Safari Club International handed over almost $1.2 million in campaign contributions to Congressional candidates. In 2016, for instance, contributions were made to 151 candidates running for the House of Representatives – there are 435 members of the House, hence the equivalent of over one third of the House. That same year, 47 candidates to the Senate received contributions from Safari Club International. There are 100 Senators.

SCI has long had close relations to leading figures inside the US Administration. A leaked memo from the 1990s shows that SCI leaders were being briefed by senior members of the US government about NGO campaigns and Congress members' concerns around trophy hunting.[166] The internal memorandum, stamped confidential, describes how Don Barry, Acting Assistant Secretary of the Interior, met with SCI CEO Rick Parsons. Barry had warned Parsons that an animal welfare group's criticisms of 'Campfire', a controversial African trophy hunting programme supported by US

---

club-idUSKCN0Q506C20150731
165

https://www.opensecrets.org/pacs/pacgot.php?cmte=C00122101&cycle=2014

166 Memorandum from head of SCI CITES Delegation Rick Parsons to SCI President Skip Donau & Bill Brewster dated June 9, 1997

Government money, had led to several members of Congress asking questions about the government's position on elephant and cheetah trophy hunting. "He (Don Barry) showed Rick (Parsons) two letters from influential Congressman… the other was from several (at least 8) members of the Congressional Black Caucus. There were several other letters as well, one from some liberal Congressmen and one from some Conservative Republican Congressmen, both very negative about CAMPFIRE."

"Barry told Rick that the HSUS attack was a serious matter, that it was now clearly focusing on elephant sport hunting, and that he suggested that the Congressional Sportsmen's Caucus needed to deal with the issue. He also said, that this kind of language in letters was going to make it harder for the Department to find a policy compromise on an issue like cheetah. He pointed out that the elephant was 'only' a threatened species which (sic) the cheetah was an endangered species. Thus if Congress could get this upset over elephant sport hunting, Barry assumed that Congress would be extremely upset over sport hunting for the cheetah, an endangered species… Please respond as soon as possible".

SCI has set up a sister 'charitable' wing called SCI-Foundation (SCIF). The Foundation's logo features a lion, a shield and spears. "The shield expresses defense of our rights as hunters. The crossed spears represent our willingness to fight to protect those rights. The lion, of course, depicts our courage in that endeavour."[167]

---

[167] https://safariclubfoundation.org/society-of-the-lion-shield/

SCIF works to 'educate' young people and others about hunting.[168] Its latest annual report shows children being taught to shoot and taking part in a trophy hunt.[169]

While technically a separate organisation, in practice it often works hand-in-hand with SCI on campaigns. SCIF's 'Fighting For Lions' campaign was, according to its Executive Director Bob Benson, "a collaborative effort between SCI and SCIF to keep the African lion off of the USFWS (US Fish & Wildlife Service) Endangered Species List. Our team has stood strong and taken the fight to the anti-hunting establishment."[170] The Foundation raised $1.3 million for its successful campaign to stop lions from being listed as endangered by the US government and from being included in Appendix I of CITES.[171] Had the lion received either of these protections, it would have been virtually impossible for American hunters to bring home their trophies. According to some estimates, lion numbers have fallen from around half a million after World War II to approximately 20,000 today.

---

[168] "Outdoor education – developing the next generation of hunter conservationists",
https://safariclubfoundation.org/education/

[169] Safari Club International Foundation 2018 Annual Report
http://safariclubfoundation.org/wp-content/uploads/2018/11/2018-AR-2sm.pdf

[170] Safari Club International Foundation 2013 Annual Report
http://safariclubfoundation.org/wp-content/uploads/2018/10/AnnualReport2013.pdf

[171] Safari Club International Foundation 2013 Annual Report
http://safariclubfoundation.org/wp-content/uploads/2018/10/AnnualReport2013.pdf

SCI and SCIF seek to influence decisions within international conservation bodies such as CITES. In 2019, SCIF issued a voting guide for CITES conference delegates calling on them to downgrade protections on a number of species, and also to oppose proposals brought by African nations and conservationists to bring in tougher regulation and monitoring of hunting of endangered species including giraffes.[172]

SCI Foundation has been allowed to participate in a number of meetings of CITES committees including its Animals Committee[173] and Standing Committee[174]. One of its key initiatives is called the 'African Wildlife Consultative Forum' (AWCF). This is an initiative which brings together officials from most of the countries in sub-Saharan Africa and often meets ahead of CITES conferences to discuss upcoming votes.

At the end of the 2019 CITES conference in Geneva, Safari Club International wrote a report for members celebrating the success its lobbying efforts. It said that the conference had "ended well for hunters" although it complained that a vote to allow the sale of rhino horn had been rejected by delegates. It also criticised "the unnecessary listing of the giraffe on Appendix II" of CITES. However, it joyfully reported the fact that it had

---

[172] Safari Club International & Safari Club International Foundation 'Sustainable Use Voting Guide'
https://www.safariclub.org/sites/default/files/inline-files/CoP18%20English%20Voting%20Guide%20-%20Final_0.pdf
[173] https://firstforwildlife.wordpress.com/2015/09/17/cites-animals-committee-a-success-for-science-based-conservation/
[174] https://www.safariclub.org/international-affairs

succeeded in ensuring that "leopard quotas are secure for years to come."

The report also boasted that lions "will remain on CITES Appendix II, where they belong, and without additional trade restrictions. For years now the team from SCI and SCIF have worked to keep trade restrictions on lions minimal." Further good news was the fact that the proposal to double the quota for black rhino trophy hunting had passed.

The newsletter concludes that SCI and SCI Foundation 'experts' at the conference had "made sure that good sense prevailed."[175]

As part of its efforts to recruit children to the sport, the Safari Club museum in Tucson has 400 different trophy species on display. Within the 40,000 square foot space is 'McElroy Hall', named after SCI founder CJ McElroy, where "hundreds of disembodied heads ... are lined up in long rows on knotty pine walls", including many of the 425 trophies McElroy is said to have acquired over his hunting career.[176] SCI Foundation has an 'America's Hunting Heritage' programme which provides videos and lesson plans about hunting for teachers to use in schools.[177] SCI also has a school in

[175] https://safariclubfoundation.org/wrap-up-report-on-cites-cop18/

[176] "What's Behind Tucson's International Wildlife Museum?", Jim Nintzel, Tucson Weekly 6 April 2015 https://www.tucsonweekly.com/TheRange/archives/2015/04/06/whats-behind-tucsons-international-wildlife-museum

[177] https://www.safariclub.org/blog/americas-hunting-heritage-program-earns-emmy-nomination

Wyoming which trains teachers in how to present a positive image of trophy hunting to young people.[178]

SCIF also has a partnership with the Salvation Army to deliver "outdoor learning experiences to youth related to wildlife conservation education, shooting sports and hunting".[179] Since 2009, more than 200,000 children have taken part.[180]

SCI's Foundation has a joint programme with the Boy Scouts of America too. It encourages children to receive "hunter education" lessons. In 2018, almost 3,000 boy scouts took part.[181] The Boy Scouts Association of America is listed as being a major financial donor to the SCI Foundation.[182]

SCI's Records Book

In 1977, Safari Club International launched its Records Book. It was to become one of the organisation's most foremost – and, from a conservation perspective, devastating - initiatives.

---

[178] https://safariclubfoundation.org/american-wilderness-leadership-school/

[179] https://www.safariclub.org/blog/partnering-salvation-army-outdoors

[180] Safari Club International Foundation 2018 Annual Report http://safariclubfoundation.org/wp-content/uploads/2018/11/2018-AR-2sm.pdf

[181] Safari Club International Foundation 2018 Annual Report http://safariclubfoundation.org/wp-content/uploads/2018/11/2018-AR-2sm.pdf

[182] Safari Club International 2017 Annual Report http://safariclubfoundation.org/wp-content/uploads/2018/10/AR2017-Finalsm.pdf

The Records Book encourages hunters to shoot the biggest animals of each species listed by stipulating a minimum 'score' or size/weight for a trophy to be eligible. In so doing, it has driven a process of artificial selection within species which has left many - including lions and African elephants – fighting for their survival, according to scientists.[183]

In his opening message in the 1997 edition of the Records Book, SCI President Lance Norris writes: "The SCI Record Book has become the standard that international hunters use to record their hunting accomplishments and to compare their trophies with others. No other record book is so widely used and quoted, and no other measuring system is as well-known and utilized by the world's hunters, professional hunters, guides and outfitters and wildlife managers as ours is."[184]

The measurement system used for lions is called 'method 15'. It specifies that a trophy must have a minimum score of 23 to be eligible for entry. The score is calculated by adding the width and length, in inches, of the animal's skull. Lion trophies that have made it into the record books include one shot by top Donald Trump fundraiser Steven Chancellor in April 1995 in Botswana. The animal's skull was 16 8/16 inches long and 10 14/16 inches wide, giving it a total score of 27 6/16. For many years, Chancellor held the world record for the biggest lion ever shot by a trophy hunter.[185]

183
https://www.nationalgeographic.com/news/2017/11/wildlife-watch-trophy-hunting-extinctions-evolution/
[184] SCI Record Book of Trophy Animals – edition IX, Volume 1, Africa Field Edition, 1997. Safari Club International

Leopard trophies use the same measurement system. The minimum score for leopards is 14. The Records Book is dismissive of concerns about the leopard's declining numbers: "Experienced observers of African fauna cannot help but wonder why the status of the leopard is regarded so negatively, for it is obvious that populations are healthy in many parts of the continent."

Record-breaking leopard hunters include former New Mexico Governor Tom Bolack, and leading German trophy hunter Egon Lechner (see Chapter 5).[186] Other prominent names on the list include SCI founder CJ McElroy, Trump fundraiser Steve Chancellor, ex-Revlon President and WWF Director Michel Bergerac, 'Conservation Force' founder John J Jackson III, and the leader of an Indonesian paramilitary death squad called Japto Soerjosoemarno.[187]

The measurement system for African Elephants is the combined weight of each tusk in pounds. As recently as the late 1990s the minimum score was 100 – in other words, a combined weight of 100 pounds for the two tusks.[188] However the diminishing size in elephant tusks resulting from hunting and artificial selection has forced SCI to now lower the entry bar to 90 lb.[189]

---

[185] SCI Record Book of Trophy Animals – edition IX, Volume 1, Africa Field Edition, 1997. Safari Club International

[186] SCI Record Book of Trophy Animals – edition IX, Volume 1, Africa Field Edition, 1997. Safari Club International

[187] SCI Record Book of Trophy Animals – edition IX, Volume 1, Africa Field Edition, 1997. Safari Club International

[188] SCI Record Book of Trophy Animals – edition IX, Volume 1, Africa Field Edition, 1997. Safari Club International

[189] SCI Online Record Book 2020

Among those to have multiple record-breaking entries in the elephants section are Bolack, McElroy, Bergerac, and John J Jackson. Handgun hunter Larry Kelly has two entries.[190] Many of these names also appear in the Records Book for the biggest-ever black and white rhinos ever to have been shot.

SCI Fundraising

While membership fees generate around $4 million every year[191], one of SCI's main money-makers is its annual convention in January each year which raises approximately $15 million[192]. Award-winners are handed their prizes at glittering galas during the convention. However they must pay for the actual award itself as well as for their dinner, both of which come at a cost.

Safari Club International offers dozens of different prizes to hunters who shoot the most animals, who kill them in the greatest number of places, and who use 'novel' ways to kill them. If, for instance, a hunter has succeeded in achieving the 'African 29' – where you

---

https://www.scirecordbook.org/

[190] SCI Record Book of Trophy Animals – edition IX, Volume 1, Africa Field Edition, 1997. Safari Club International

[191] SCI Financial Statements years ended June 30 2017 and 2018 https://www.safariclub.org/sites/default/files/2019-01/FinStatement_SCI_FY18.pdf

[192] "SCI Moves Its 2018 Annual Hunters' Convention From Mandalay Bay", AfricaHunting.com, 12 October 2017 https://www.africahunting.com/threads/sci-moves-its-2018-annual-hunters-convention-from-mandalay-bay.40560/

have to shoot 29 different species of African wildlife - or killed all the species needed to receive the 'Animals of Africa' prize, the hunter has to pay out $2,850 to receive the award. Shipping is extra.

The same goes for the African Big Five. Similarly, if you've completed the Grand Slam of Turkeys or have shot everything you need to receive the Goats of the World prize, the cost is $2850. There are some prizes that are a little less expensive, though. The Global Hunting award and the 'Top Ten' prize come in at $2500. So does the prize for achieving the 'Sheep of the World' goal.[193]

For each level of the 'Inner Circles' awards there is both an entry fee and a listing fee which together come to several hundred dollars. As you go up the scale of Inner Circles – from copper to bronze, and all the way up to Diamond – you can expect to pay again. And again. Simply to put forward your name for entry into the 'Pinnacle of Achievement' category, the 'Zenith Award' or 'Crowning Achievement' you have to pay $800 - each.

If you get as far as SCI's World Hunting Award, you can design your own statue. But you will need to pay for it in advance.[194]

Many of the world's leading trophy hunters are wealthy businessmen, so it is perhaps unsurprising to learn that a significant proportion of the hunting industry's income comes from 'high net worth individuals' and major corporations. However some of

---

[193] Safari magazine – Awards 2015, Safari Club International
[194] Safari magazine – Awards 2015, Safari Club International

the money entering SCI's coffers has arrived from unexpected quarters.

Safari Club International's corporate sponsors include household names such as Yamaha[195], Zeiss[196], and Swarovski Optik.[197] The SCI Foundation has received donations of more than $100,000 from Beretta, the gun manufacturers[198], and gifts of over $50,000 from companies involved in hunting and shooting such as Game Frontiers of Tanzania Ltd, Midway USA Inc and Trijicon Inc.[199]

Some of America's biggest corporations have made major donations too. They include the Atlanta Beverage Company – owners of Budweiser - and controversial multinational oil conglomerate Halliburton.[200] A string of vineyards, insurance companies and private family trusts are on the list of major givers.

---

[195] "Yamaha Renews SCI Corporate Sponsorship" https://www.safariclub.org/blog/yamaha-renews-sci-corporate-sponsorship

[196] "Carl Zeiss Sports Optics and SCI Renew Partnership" https://www.safariclub.org/blog/carl-zeiss-sports-optics-and-safari-club-international-renew-partnership

[197] SCI Corporate Sponsors https://www.safariclub.org/sci-corporate-sponsors

[198] Safari Club International Foundation 2017 Annual Report http://safariclubfoundation.org/wp-content/uploads/2018/10/AR2017-Finalsm.pdf

[199] Safari Club International Foundation 2017 Annual Report http://safariclubfoundation.org/wp-content/uploads/2018/10/AR2017-Finalsm.pdf

[200] Safari Club International Foundation 2017 Annual Report http://safariclubfoundation.org/wp-content/uploads/2018/10/AR2017-Finalsm.pdf

So are the Boy Scouts of America Foundation and the US State of Michigan, both of whom have handed over cheques for more than $10,000, as has Morgan Stanley (the company for which SCI President Paul Babaz worked before having his employment there terminated).[201] There are four-figure donations from several charitable foundations, a fine art gallery, wildlife artists, and a German firm specialising in fine crystal.

Among the most unusual are cheques received from Kirkwood School District R-7 and Napoleon Community Schools. The Kirkwood School District R-7, of St Louis, Missouri, covers 10 schools ranging from pre-school through to high school, and donated up to $2,490. The Napoleon Community Schools, a public school district authority in the state of Michigan representing 6 schools from pre-school to high-school, donated up to $4,900.[202] Less surprisingly, the NRA has made significant donations.

Fundraising platforms including JustGive (not to be confused with JustGiving), Wonderful Giving, YourCause, Combined Federal Campaign and the Benevity Community Impact Fund have been used to pass on some of the largest donations made to SCI. So has the matching fund of Chevron employees. Other SCI corporate sponsors include oilboomUSA, Global Rescue, Boyt Harness Company, Norma, SportEAR, Tracking

[201] Safari Club International Foundation 2017 Annual Report http://safariclubfoundation.org/wp-content/uploads/2018/10/AR2017-Finalsm.pdf

[202] Safari Club International Foundation 2017 Annual Report http://safariclubfoundation.org/wp-content/uploads/2018/10/AR2017-Finalsm.pdf

Point, Havalon Knives, Gaston, Kenetrek Boogts, Doubletap, Mossy Oak, and Outdoor Channel.[203]

A 2016 investigation by Ethical Consumer magazine found that a number of household brands have been directly or indirectly involved in trophy hunting. Nikon, it said, was selling hunting equipment and promoted safaris and "dangerous game adventure(s) on the dark continent." Nikon was also a partner of the 'Raised Hunting' TV hunting show. Swarovski Optik, meanwhile, has sponsored the NRA's Youth Hunter Education Challenge.

Of the 30 companies it reviewed, 83% "had some involvement in selling sport hunting accessories or marketing products at hunters."[204] In addition to Swarovski Optik, a number of other hunting optics manufacturers were found to be sponsoring hunting organisations and related initiatives. Vista Outdoors sponsored the annual 'Daughters at the Range' event which encourages families and their daughters to take part in sport shooting. Vortex Optics' website contained a Trophy Room on its website with images of animals killed using its products.[205]

In all, 76% of companies that sold hunting accessories had sponsored hunting organisations. Over half were

---

[203] Safari Club International Foundation 2017 Annual Report http://safariclubfoundation.org/wp-content/uploads/2018/10/AR2017-Finalsm.pdf

[204] "Shooting Wildlife", Ethical Consumer, Anna Clayton, February 15, 2016

[205] "Shooting Wildlife", Ethical Consumer, Anna Clayton, February 15, 2016

members of hunting groups including the Boone & Crockett Club and Safari Club International.

Brands/Companies that sponsor or are members of hunting organisations[206]

Alpen/Alpen Outdoor Corporation (USA), Bresser/Jinghua Optical & Electronics Co Ltd (China); Burris/Beretta Holding SpA (Italy); Bushnell/Vista Outdoor USA; Hawke/Deben Group Industries (UK)Leica/LeicaCamera AG (Germany); Leupold/Leupold & Stevens Inc (USA); Meoptica/Meoptica sro (Czech); Minox/Minox GmbH (Germany); Nikon/Nikon Corporation (Japan); Steiner/Beretta Holding SpA (Italy); Swarovski/Swarokski Group (Austria); Vanguard/Vanguard (China); Vortex/Sheltered Wings Inc (USA); Zeiss/Carl Zeiss Stiftung (Germany)

Brands/companies that sell hunting accessories and/or market optics to hunters[207]

Acuter/Synta Technology (Taiwan); Barska/Micro World Corp (USA); Bosma /Guangzhou Bosma Corp (China); Carson/Carson Optical (USA); Celestron/Synta Technology (Taiwan); Eschenbach/Escehenbach Holding GmbH/Equistone Partners Europe (Germany/UK); Kowa/Kowa Group (Japan);

---

[206] "Shooting Wildlife", Ethical Consumer, Anna Clayton, February 15, 2016

[207] "Shooting Wildlife", Ethical Consumer, Anna Clayton, February 15, 2016

Opticron/Opticron (UK); Pentax/Ricoh Imaging Co ltd (Japan); Visionary/Optical Hardware (UK); Vision King/Vision King Optical Technology (China)

Individuals who give more than $100,000 to SCIF are classed as 'African Lion level' donors; those who give more than $50,000 are 'African Elephant' donors, givers of $25,000 or more are 'Rhino level' and so on. SCIF also has a 'Hunter Legacy 100 Fund', an exclusive club for those who make regular large donations.

There is a 'Society of the Lion and Shield' for SCIF's biggest supporters. 'Pacesetter' donors are those who give more than USD $50,000, while 'Partner' donors hand over USD $10,000 or more. You can also make major donations to SCIF via a 'Planned Giving & Estate Planning' scheme, where in effect rich hunters can include SCIF in their wills and/or make donations to the organisation through stocks and the sale of other assets such as land.

Paul Babaz, along with Beretta, has donated more than $100,000 to SCI Foundation, earning him the status of 'African Lion level' donor.[208] Steve Chancellor, a major donor to Donald Trump's Presidential campaign and to the Republican Party, is among other to have made some of the largest donations to Safari Club International with a cheque of between $25,000 - $49,000 to SCI Foundation. He is recognised as a 'Rhino Level' donor by SCI Foundation.[209]

[208] Safari Club International Foundation 2017 Annual Report http://safariclubfoundation.org/wp-content/uploads/2018/10/AR2017-Finalsm.pdf

[209] Safari Club International Foundation 2017 Annual Report

Leopard Level donors are those who have given between $10-24,000. They include the Boy Scouts of America Foundation, Independent Charities of America, Justgive, Morgan Stanley c/o Cybergrants Inc., the NRA, and the US State of Michigan's taxpayers.[210]

Next comes the 'Cape Buffalo' level for those who make donations of between $5-9,000. This group includes the Banovich Fine Art Gallery, the Bellevue Foundation, the Cadillac/Yellowstone Club, Halliburton, and Justin Vineyards & Winery.[211]

Further down the scale is the Elk Level ($2,500-4,900). It includes Chevron Matching Employee Funds, YourCause LLC trustee, Napoleon Community Schools, and Wonderful Giving.[212]

There is also a 'Caribou Level' ($1,000-$2.490). Among those listed are Budweiser's owners the Atlanta Beverage Company, the JP Morgan Chase Foundation, Kirkwood School District R-7, and SCI's London Chapter.[213]

---

http://safariclubfoundation.org/wp-content/uploads/2018/10/AR2017-Finalsm.pdf

[210] Safari Club International Foundation 2017 Annual Report http://safariclubfoundation.org/wp-content/uploads/2018/10/AR2017-Finalsm.pdf

[211] Safari Club International Foundation 2017 Annual Report http://safariclubfoundation.org/wp-content/uploads/2018/10/AR2017-Finalsm.pdf

[212] Safari Club International Foundation 2017 Annual Report http://safariclubfoundation.org/wp-content/uploads/2018/10/AR2017-Finalsm.pdf

[213] Safari Club International Foundation 2017 Annual Report http://safariclubfoundation.org/wp-content/uploads/2018/10/AR2017-Finalsm.pdf

'Hunter Legacy 100 Fund' donors include Trump donor Steve Chancellor together with his wife Terri (who is also an award-winning trophy-hunter); NASCAR[214] race-team owner Richard Childress and his wife Judy; and Danial & Charlotte Peyerk,[215] trophy hunters and parents of Chris Peyerk who in 2018 paid $400,000 to shoot a critically endangered black rhino.[216]

Auctions of trophy hunting trips at its annual convention remain one of the main ways SCI raises funds. The trips are usually donated by safari companies. Trophies, fur coats and furniture made from wildlife body parts were among the other items sold at its convention in January 2020. Among items on offer was a wallaby hunt in New Zealand[217], a deer hunt in Scotland[218], and a hunting trip in pursuit of tuskless elephants[219].

[214] The National Association for Stock Car Auto Racing

[215] Safari Club International Foundation 2017 Annual Report http://safariclubfoundation.org/wp-content/uploads/2018/10/AR2017-Finalsm.pdf

[216] "Trophy hunter can bring home rhino killed for $400,000", Ben Hoyle, The Times 10 September 2019

[217] https://www.onlinehuntingauctions.com/5-day-New-Zealand-Arapawa-Sheep-and-Wallaby-Hunt-for-One-Hunter-and-One-Observer_i35311445

[218] https://www.onlinehuntingauctions.com/5-day-Scotland-Scottish-Red-Deer-Hunt-for-One-Hunter-and-One-Observer_i35311455

[219] https://www.onlinehuntingauctions.com/10-day-Zambia-Tuskless-Elephant-Hunt-for-One-Hunter-and-One-Observer_i35311791

The NRA (National Rifle Association)

"How do you spell conservationist? H-U-N-T-E-R!"
– NRA website

The NRA, America's and the world's most powerful gun rights group, is increasingly turning its attention to trophy hunting.

Around 3.5 million of the NRA's 5 million members are thought to be hunters.[220] With trophy hunting in the spotlight, it has now launched a major campaign to fight back against campaigns to ban trophy imports which it sees as a potential threat to gun ownership.

Wayne LaPierre, CEO of the National Rifle Association, describes the NRA as "the strongest voice of freedom on the planet".[221] The NRA views trophy hunting as primarily one about hunters' 'rights' and protecting the 'freedom' to hunt: "As the nation's oldest civil rights organisation, the NRA fights nonstop for American freedom and its 5.5 million members, gun owners, hunters and shooters."[222]

In response to what it calls a 'culture war' being waged against hunters, it has launched an initiative called the 'NRA Hunters' Leadership Forum' to win the battle for public opinion. The NRA's Ross Seyfriend explains why its campaign to defend trophy hunting is now a priority. "The NRA's dedication to the

---

[220] https://www.nrahlf.org/about-us/
[221] "The Journal of the Texas Trophy Hunters", Nov/Dec 2017 (ttha.com) vol. 42, no.6
[222] https://www.nrahlf.org/about-us/

preservation of the Second Amendment and the protection of our right to keep and bear arms is very simply what we do. However, that is not all we do, or have done. The privilege to hunt with those arms has also been a dedicated cause for NRA for a very long time; but in a relatively quiet way. With the launch of the NRA Hunters' Leadership Forum the NRA's support of the hunting sports and all that related to hunting is no longer in the background."[223]

Keith Wood, also of the NRA, adds: "Hunting has always been part of NRA's cause, but often not its focus. The organisation is stepping into the void now to fight another battle."[224]

The NRA posts content on its social platforms for members and other hunters to share. One such item – entitled "The fight to save hunting" – urges members to get behind the campaign: "In hunting's darkest hour, only the NRA has the muscle and the backbone to reject the animal rights extremists. To save hunting, you must understand the terms of the battle. Because the animal rights extremists fighting to destroy hunting have an even more destructive goal: the systematic diminishment of humanity itself."[225]

In capitals the message "HELP US EXPOSE THE EVILS OF THE ANIMAL RIGHTS MOVEMENT" is displayed. Underneath it says: "The truth behind the animal rights movement is nothing less than evil. We are

---

[223] "We are Hunters", Ross Seyfriend
https://www.nrahunting.com/we-are-hunters/
[224] "Only the hunter knows", Keith Wood
https://www.nrahunting.com/only-the-hunter-knows/
[225] https://www.nrahunting.com/

going to expose them – but we need your help to do it. Can we count on you to fight?" A button which takes you to a donations page is provided.[226]

In an article entitled 'The Animal Rights Dream - Their dream is our nightmare', contributor Rick Rafferty makes the following extraordinary claim: "Radical extremist groups with deep ties to organised violence are working around the clock to sully the image of the American and international hunter. They have destroyed multi-million dollar businesses and whitewashed their anarchist intentions through a sympathetic mainstream media."[227]

No evidence is provided to support these serious allegations. However, another headline in capitals reinforces the message: "FIGHT BACK AGAINST THE DICTATORS – Refuse to have your way of life stolen from you by the ignorant dictators of the animal rights movement. Help NRA Hunting bring the fight to these hypocritical elites."[228]

Leading hunter and NRA supporter Phil Phillips has written an article for the campaign entitled: "How do you spell conservationist? H-U-N-T-E-R!"[229] Hunters are working to create their own "freedom-loving platforms" to spread the message.[230] A number of video-

---

[226] https://www.nrahunting.com/

[227] https://www.nrahunting.com/the-animal-rights-dream/

[228] https://www.nrahunting.com/a-million-little-dictators/

[229] "How Do You Spell Conservationist? H-U-N-T-E-R!" NRA Hunters Leadership Forum, Phil Phillips 15 August 2018 https://www.nrahlf.org/articles/2018/8/15/how-do-you-spell-conservationist-h-u-n-t-e-r/

[230] "How Hunters are Adjusting to Social Media Bans", Frank

sharing platforms including www.ugetube.com and www.letsgoshooting.org have already been set up.

The NRA, like SCI, has instituted initiatives to encourage women and children to take up hunting. They include a 'Youth Hunter Education Challenge'[231] and a 'Women's Wilderness Escape'.[232] Youth Hunting camps promote "fun and adventure", according to the NRA's Tom Claycomb III. On their arrival at one of these camps, children are given a 'goodies bag', the Pledge of Allegiance is recited, and then a local pastor leads the group in prayer. "Group one starts at the shotgun station, group two at the .22 range, group 3 at the black powder range, group 4 at the archery range, group 5 at the knife sharpening/gun cleaning station and group 6 at the survival station."

At the end of the day there is a raffle. Every child gets something to take home. "This year there were 25 guns, 10 bows, backpacks, knives and more given away. Some kids are super lucky and win an actual elk, deer or duck hunt."[233]

The NRA's 'Women on Target' is another initiative which encourages women to take up hunting.[234]

Miniter, NRA 7 March 2019
https://www.americanhunter.org/articles/2019/3/7/how-hunters-are-adjusting-to-social-media-bans/

[231] https://yhec.nra.org/

[232] https://wwe.nra.org/

[233] "Youth Hunting Camp Promotes Fun and Adventure", Tom Claycomb III, NRA Hunters Leadership Forum, 28 November 2018 https://www.nrahlf.org/articles/2018/11/28/youth-hunting-camp-promotes-fun-and-adventure/

[234] "The Thrill of the Chase – Women and their North American Big Game Trophies", Kathy Etling & Susan Campbell Reneau, Safari

The NRA has recently been hit by a series of internal disputes between longstanding CEO Wayne LaPierre and the group's controversial president Oliver North, who became internationally famous for his role in the Iran-Contra scandal. Questions have been asked about the CEO's spending habits after The Wall Street Journal reported that a top NRA executive "signed a document agreeing that the gun-rights organization would be 99% owner of a company formed to buy a $6 million Dallas mansion for NRA CEO Wayne Lapierre".[235]

A court case is currently underway in the US involving LaPierre who is allegedly seeking to prevent a TV channel from airing film footage showing him shooting an African elephant. Court documents say that the film shows LaPierre firing multiple gunshots at the animal and also show his wife, Susan LaPierre, cutting off the elephant's tail. The couple then "posed for photos while sitting on the deceased elephant," according to legal papers.[236]

Press

[235] "NRA Promised $6.5 Million to Buy Mansion for CEO Wayne LaPierre, Document Shows", Mark Maremont, Wall Street Journal, 13 August, 2019 https://www.wsj.com/articles/nra-promised-6-5-million-to-buy-mansion-for-ceo-wayne-lapierre-document-shows-11565714149?shareToken=stca02bb3318b24d81b6db9a2920a1ce65

[236] https://www.thetrace.org/2020/01/nra-wayne-lapierre-elephant-hunt/

Dallas Safari Club (DSC) & Houston Safari Club (HSC)

"Protecting Hunters' Rights: Advocacy is a part of DSC's mission. DSC and DSC-PAC have been very successful in defeating legislation that would have severely curtailed hunting rights and negatively impacted vast tracts of hunting habitat. Your contributions to the DSC-PAC go directly to efforts that support and help elect pro-hunting, pro-Second Amendment candidates at the federal and state levels". – Dallas Safari Club[237]

There are a number of other influential groups within the hunting industry. One of them is Dallas Safari Club (DSC). Launched in 1972, DSC describes its mission as being to "promote and protect the rights and interests of hunters worldwide".[238]

DSC has a major annual hunting convention similar to that of SCI. Around 1000 exhibitors and 30,000 attendees took part in the 2019 event.[239] Its convention was thrown into the media spotlight in 2014 when DSC controversially auctioned a trophy hunt of a critically endangered black rhino.[240]

---

[237] https://www.biggame.org/who-we-are/our-mission/#

[238] About DSCF https://www.biggame.org/2020/03/20/dsc-message-covid-19/

[239] https://www.biggame.org/convention/

[240] "Rhino Hunt Auction Stirs More Controversy", Brian Clark Howard, National Geographic, 14 January 2014 https://www.nationalgeographic.com/news/2014/1/140113-

Dallas Safari Club and Safari Club International often work together. DSC supported SCI President Paul Babaz's campaign for election to the board of the National Rifle Association: "Paul Babaz is an NRA Benefactor member, veteran, hunter, and firearms collector nominated by the NRA Nomination Committee. A lifelong hunter and sportsman, Paul is a passionate Second Amendment advocate and political activist, even serving as co-chair of President Trump's Second Amendment Coalition. For decades, Paul has shown his commitment to the NRA beyond donations. He's an active supporter of the NRA Foundation, member of the Hunters' Leadership Forum's President's Club and is past Chairman of Friends of the NRA Piedmont Committee. He also serves on the NRA's Hunting & Wildlife Conservation and Legislative Policy Committees."

The endorsement statement added: "He enjoys hunting with his daughters in his spare time."[241]

Like SCI, Dallas Safari Club has its own Foundation and a Political Action Committee to which donations "will be directed to campaigns and candidates in order to preserve the hunting heritage".[242] DSC boasts that it has been "very successful in defeating legislation that would have severely curtailed hunting rights" and that donations to its PAC are helping "elect pro-hunting, pro-

dallas-safari-club-rhino-permit-auction/

[241] "Dallas Safari Club Endorses Kevin Hogan and Paul Babaz for NRA Board of Directors", Dallas Safari Club https://mailchi.mp/biggame.org/dsc-endorses-babaz-and-hogan-for-nra-board?e=17301be748

[242] https://www.biggame.org/who-we-are/pac/

Second Amendment candidates" at every level of government within the United States.[243] The Foundation's website pledges that DSC will "seek to influence public opinion" and "support litigation where necessary to protect the rights of sportsmen and sportswomen."[244]

Dallas Safari Club gives grants to the prominent hunting lobby group 'Conservation Force'[245] and to the NRA's Youth Hunting Education Challenge.[246]

Another benefactor of DSC funding is 'Conservation Visions',[247] an organisation which - like Conservation Force - promotes the message that hunting animals for sport supports conservation. Its President and CEO is Shane Mahoney, who is also a Director of Conservation Force.[248] Mahoney sits on an IUCN Committee which has drawn criticism from conservationists for promoting the "sustainable use" (i.e. trophy hunting) of wildlife[249]. According to DSC documents, its grant to Conservation Visions funds "Shane Mahoney's role as a Conservation and Hunting Advocate, Advisor, and Communicator for the organization" and includes money to make

---

[243] Our Mission – Protection Hunters Rights https://www.biggame.org/who-we-are/our-mission/

[244] Hunter Advocacy https://dscf.org/advocacy/

[245] https://dscf.org/advocacy/

[246] https://dscf.org/grants/

[247] https://dscf.org/grants/

[248] https://www.conservationforce.org/shane-mahoney

[249] https://www.iucn.org/commissions/commission-environmental-economic-and-social-policy/our-work/specialist-group-sustainable-use-and-livelihoods-suli/suli-north-america

promotional videos, social media outreach and public speaking.[250]

In 2015, DSC applied to become a member of IUCN, the global conservation body. Its application was accepted.

Kids Outdoor Zone is another organisation which benefits from DSC's grants. It is described as "an organization that trains men in local churches to use the outdoor sports to train and mentor kids in their community. To date KOZ has trained over 500 men to use activities such as shooting and hunting, to mentor local at-risk youth one Saturday morning each month. KOZ has a presence in 18 states and Canada."[251]

The work and mission of Houston Safari Club (HSC) is similar to that of both Safari Club International and Dallas Safari Club. It works to "protect the rights of hunters and the hunting heritage through advocacy, policy and legislation"[252] and "supports initiatives that protect the tradition of hunting and hunters rights."[253]

Although less well-known than SCI and HSC, it is influential and supported by the rich and powerful. Until recently, the city of Houston, Texas was the primary destination for lions shot by American trophy hunters. HSC Executive Director Joe Betar recently attended a White House event with President Donald Trump to celebrate the government's environmental achievements. According to a marketing brochure published by Houston Safari Club, HSC Foundation members have an

---

[250] https://www.dscf.org/grants/

[251] https://dscf.org/grants/

[252] https://houstonsafariclub.org/

[253] https://houstonsafariclub.org/

average net worth between $2.2 million and $2.5 million.[254] Its supporters include Philip Glass, a west Texas rancher who spent $100,000 on a lion hunt in Zimbabwe which was the subject of the 2017 documentary 'Trophy'.[255]

The outrage prompted by the killing of Cecil the lion led HSC to announce that it was launching a Political Action Committee (PAC) fund and that it would be "ramping up" its lobbying operations.[256] HSC has launched a ferocious attack on a bill introduced by US Congressman Raul Grijalva to restrict trophy imports into the US: "To try to do away with it (trophy hunting) because of emotionally uninformed and highly publicized portrayals is not only short-sighted, but would bring about the end of conservation as we know it and, ultimately the demise of the wildlife and wildlife habitat in Africa."[257] Grijalva is Chair of the US House of Representatives Natural Resources committee.

---

[254] Houston Safari Club Foundation 2020-2021 Media Kit https://hscfdn.org/wp-content/uploads/2020/02/2020-2021-HSCF-Media-KitWEB-1.pdf

[255] "Houston Safari Club forms PAC to fight trophy hunting restrictions", Jeremy Wallace, Houston Chronicle 4 September 2019 https://www.houstonchronicle.com/politics/texas/article/Houston-Safari-Club-forms-PAC-to-fight-trophy-14414395.php

[256] "Houston Safari Club forms PAC to fight trophy hunting restrictions", Jeremy Wallace, Houston Chronicle 4 September 2019 https://www.houstonchronicle.com/politics/texas/article/Houston-Safari-Club-forms-PAC-to-fight-trophy-14414395.php

[257] "Houston Safari Club forms PAC to fight trophy hunting restrictions", Jeremy Wallace, Houston Chronicle 4 September 2019 https://www.houstonchronicle.com/politics/texas/article/Houston-Safari-Club-forms-PAC-to-fight-trophy-14414395.php

Other Trophy Hunting organisations

Many of the older trophy hunting groups that preceded SCI and DSC were initially created to establish measurement systems for animal trophies. The world's oldest group is the Boone & Crockett Club, launched by former US President Teddy Roosevelt. When he stepped down, Roosevelt went on a year-long hunting spree in Africa with his son Kermit where they shot hundreds of animals. Kermit and Roosevelt's other son, Theodore Jr, are among the few trophy hunters ever to have shot panda bears. One panda trophy can still be viewed at Chicago's Field Museum. The Roosevelts called their trophy "the Golden Fleece of our trip."[258]

Boone & Crockett's 'Trophy Scoring System for North American Wildlife Trophies' was established in 1930. However, it wasn't the first such system to be invented. That honour goes to Rowland Ward, a British natural history enthusiast, who devised the 'Horn Measurements and Weights of the Great Game of the World' in 1892.

The International Council for Game and Wildlife Conservation, commonly known as CIC, established a trophy formula of its own in 1930. In 2019, a video emerged of CIC's President, George Amman, launching an extraordinary personal attack on British prime minister Boris Johnson and his fiancé, Carrie Symonds.

---

[258] Mongtomery, et. al. "Characteristics that make trophy hunting of giant pandas inconceivable." Conservation Biology, 2020

The remarks were made at the opening of the German hunting fair 'Jagd und Hund', Europe's largest such event. The footage shows Amman - a leading international banker who has had a string of top roles in London, New York and Paris – referring to "Prime Minister Boris Johnson, who shares his table (and something else) with his table-lady, with his animal rights lady".[259]

The Weatherby Foundation promotes what is arguably the most prestigious – and demanding – prize available to trophy hunters, the Weatherby Award. The Foundation also works to "educate youth and the non-hunting public on the beneficial role of ethical sport hunting and its contribution to wildlife conservation."[260] The organisation is named after Roy Weatherby, a hunter and maker of rifles used by the rich and famous, including Roy Rogers, John Wayne and the Shah of Iran.[261]

Weatherby died in 1988 "nearly 45 years after he began his simple quest to find a more effective way to take an animal." The company slogan still reads: "Nothing shoots flatter, hits harder or is more accurate than a Weatherby."[262]

'Hunter Nation', meanwhile, is a new campaigning coalition which seeks to 'reform' the US Endangered

---

259 https://www.facebook.com/cicwildlife/videos/541541003117548/?v=541541003117548

260 https://www.weatherbyfoundation.com/about-us/

261 https://www.weatherbyfoundation.com/about-us/roy-e-weatherby/

262 https://www.weatherbyfoundation.com/about-us/roy-e-weatherby/

Species Act which it claims "has become the favoured tool of anti-hunting groups to take wildlife and habitat restoration efforts away from the State Fish and Game Agencies, to the significant detriment of hunters and sportsmen".[263] Hunter Nation complains that "hunting, which was once an honoured and respected tradition in America, is under attack by the Left who wants to destroy our way of life. These are the same people that want to take our guns, that mock our faith in God, that want open borders and want to destroy the very moral fabric of America. Well, we as proud American hunters will not let that happen! That is exactly why we have joined together to form Hunter Nation! Just like our Nation's earliest patriots, we ask you to unite and join Hunter Nation to help defend our Traditional American Values."[264] A section of Hunter Nation's website invites readers to apply for a series of "dream hunts", including on an exotics farm in Texas.[265]

The group is led by what it calls "America's greatest Hunters and Patriots." They include American rock musician Ted Nugent and country music star Craig Morgan. On the group's website Morgan says: "'Hunter Nation (is) a great group of American Hunters that love and cherish God, family, country, hunting, and conservation." Michael Waddell, a member of Hunter Nation's Advisory Board, adds: "Hunters all have the right and should promote hunting. God's renewable resource is for everyone to enjoy."

---

[263] https://hunternation.org/about/
[264] www.hunternation.org
[265] https://hunternation.org/2020-dream-hunts/

Another leading light within the group is Jason Chaffetz, a Fox News Contributor and former Member of Congress (where he served as Chairman of the Oversight Committee) and author of "The Deep State".[266]

The Sportsmen's Alliance calls on supporters to sign a 'Pledge to Protect Hunting' which reads: "I am proud to be a hunter. It is who I am, to my core, and for this I will not apologise. I am honoured and humbled to represent a long lineage of hunters that have existed as long as mankind itself. For thousands of years we have hunted to sustain our existence, to provide for others. This privilege has created a primal connection to the natural world that few people can relate to."

It continues: "It is an honor to be a hunter. I embrace this and accept my responsibility to convey the myriad of positive attributes hunting provides for wildlife, wild places, conservation and society as a whole. I will articulate hunting's ability to nurture the mind, body and soul. I will convey these attributes to respect the quarry, the traditions and the spirituality hunting provides...

"I pledge to advocate for hunting, to spread my enthusiasm among my fellow hunters and rid our community of complacency. I pledge to fight for what's right so hunters are rightfully viewed as the pillars of the wildlife conservation community."[267]

Together with Safari Club International they are suing the state of New Jersey so they can hunt bears on public land.[268] It has a Government Affairs Department which

---

[266] https://hunternation.org/team/

[267] https://www.sportsmensalliance.org/get-involved/pledge-to-protect-hunting/

[268] "Hunting Leaders File Lawsuit Challenging New Jersey Black

consists of "a team of experienced lobbyists, lawyers, and campaign specialists who are on the front lines protecting and advancing our outdoor heritage in all 50 state legislatures, in Washington DC, in the courts, and at the ballot box."[269]

Another group, the Congressional Sportsmen's Foundation[270] claims to be "the most respected and trusted sportsmen's organisation in the political arena".[271] Set up in 1989, it lobbies members of Congress, US state Governors and members of state assemblies across the country alongside the Governors Sportsmen's Caucus and the National Assembly of Sportsmen's Caucuses. It claims to have succeeded in creating "an unprecedented network of pro-sportsmen elected officials that advance the interests of America's hunters and anglers" thus ensuring that it is able "to protect and advance hunting."[272] The network, it says, includes 300 members of Congress, 27 US Governors and 2000 law-makers at state level.[273]

Its board includes ex-SCI President Paul Babaz; the US President of FN, one of the world's largest firearms manufacturers; a representative from gunmakers Smith & Wesson; the President of Shell Oil; and the chairman and the vice-president of the Boone & Crockett Club.

Bear Hunt Ban", 4 October 2018
https://www.sportsmensalliance.org/news/hunting-leaders-file-lawsuit-challenging-new-jersey-black-bear-hunt-ban/
[269] https://www.sportsmensalliance.org/government-affairs/
[270] www.congressionalsportsmen.org
[271] http://congressionalsportsmen.org/about
[272] http://congressionalsportsmen.org/about
[273] http://congressionalsportsmen.org/about

Francisco Bergaz, from the Bacardi family, and Brad Franklin, a senior executive from Yamaha – which has been a corporate donor to SCI - are also on CSF's Board.

The group is working to persuade US states to allow hunting on Sunday, and is one of a group of hunting groups which supports 'Families Afield' - a campaign against "barriers to hunting"[274] by children and which urges states to open their doors "to greater opportunities for young hunters and their families to enjoy hunting traditions together."[275]

The National Shooting Sports Foundation is the trade association of the USA's firearms industry. It represents over 12,000 manufacturers, distributors, retailers, shooting ranges and hunting organisations. "As the firearms industry's trade association, NSSF is working day in and day out to promote, protect and preserve our industry and our sports."[276] Its government relations department is there to "determine threats or benefits to the industry, develop strategies to address those activities and act through lobbying, grassroots advocacy and public affairs efforts."[277]

Other active trophy hunting organisations include the Christian Bowhunters of Texas and the Christian Outdoor Alliance. The latter's mission is "to guide youth and outdoorsmen to a relationship with Jesus Christ through experience in God's great outdoors."[278]

---

[274] http://www.familiesafield.org/pdf/FamiliesAfield_Report.pdf

[275] http://www.familiesafield.org/Supporters.cfm

[276] https://www.nssf.org/about/

[277] https://www.nssf.org/government-relations/

[278] "The Journal of the Texas Trophy Hunter", November/December 2017, volume 42 no.6

Chapter 3: How the industry is weakening wildlife laws

"Nothing has been so consistently fulfilling to me as my hunting. It has stirred an insatiable appetite for more."[279] - John J Jackson III, former President of Safari Club International; Founder and Chairman of 'Conservation Force'; IUCN committee member

Politicians, the press and public opinion are almost uniformly – and vehemently - opposed to trophy hunting. In response to this, the industry's strategy has been to claim that trophy hunting is helping tackle poverty in Africa and that shooting animals for sport supports wildlife conservation.

Trophy hunters say that it is only by serving a human function – as a souvenir for the hunter – that a wild animal has value. It has no intrinsic right to exist as such. Without trophy hunting, it is nothing: there is no need for it, nor any imperative to conserve it. Furthermore, animals – and nature – are incapable of surviving without human intervention. The environment cannot manage itself; 'man' must do it. Hence the need for 'management culls', for instance (which can be sold at a healthy profit to trophy hunters).

The industry has reframed killing animals for sport as what it calls 'sustainable' or 'wise use' of a natural

---

[279] "Great hunters – their trophy rooms and collections", Safari Press Inc, 1997

resource no different to inert matter which meets an essential human need.

At the forefront of this campaign is an organisation founded by a former President of Safari Club International. It calls itself 'Conservation Force'. It is one of a host of hunting organisations old and new which now use 'conservation' and other wildlife-friendly words in their names and mission statements. Some hunting prizes now include the word 'conservation' in their title too. Safari Club International (SCI) has described itself in public as a conservation organisation. For instance, a newspaper article by a SCI President commences: "Safari Club International, a wildlife conservation organisation…".[280]

Conservation Force is registered as a charitable foundation. According to its website, its objectives are "wildlife conservation, education, research and serving the greater public good. It serves the public through support and development of conservation infrastructure locally, nationally and internationally".[281] Its work, though, is primarily as a lobbying and litigation group. It campaigns on behalf of the hunting industry to reduce restrictions on the hunting of protected species, and lobbies and sues to have trophies of endangered wildlife allowed back into the US.

The group was set up by John J Jackson III, a Louisiana lawyer and "lifetime sportsman"[282]. While at the helm of Safari Club International, he set about reshaping its lobbying strategy. He used his law firm to

---

[280] Alfred 'Skip' Donau, Tucson Citizen, 31 July 1998

[281] https://www.conservationforce.org/corporate-description-

[282] https://www.conservationforce.org/about

provide *pro bono* legal support to hunting groups to challenge and overturn bans on trophy imports and hunting. His operation became "an around-the-clock international communication headquarters and advocacy 'war room'."[283]

His client list reads like a Who's Who of the world's leading hunting organisations. They include the International Professional Hunters Association (IPHA), Dallas Safari Club, Houston Safari Club, the African Safari Club of Florida, the Professional Hunters Association of South Africa, as well as the organisation of which he was President, Safari Club International.[284] Together they have been challenging the legal protections given to threatened wildlife under the US Endangered Species Act which meant that hunters couldn't bring home trophies of their favourite animals.

Conservation Force won a lawsuit that re-opened elephant trophy imports from South Africa, Namibia, Tanzania, Ethiopia and Cameroon.[285] The 'Polar Bear Initiative Committee' campaigned to amend the Marine Mammal Protection Act to make it possible to allow in polar bear hunting trophies.[286] Polar bears can now once again be shot by American hunters and their trophies brought into America.[287]

In 1997, the year after he stepped down as SCI President, Jackson dissolved his law firm and launched 'Conservation Force' as a full-time endeavour.[288] The

283 https://www.conservationforce.org/about
284 https://www.conservationforce.org/what-they-say-about-us
285 https://www.conservationforce.org/john-jackson
286 https://www.conservationforce.org/john-jackson
287 CITES Trade Database (UNEP-WCMC)

group started filing legal petitions demanding that the protection status of animals under the US Endangered Species Act (ESA) be downgraded. It filed and intervened in over a dozen ESA and CITES law suits. It succeeded in re-establishing import permits for trophies of endangered Zambian elephants[289], 'downlisted' the conservation status of the endangered Canadian Wood Bison[290], and successfully petitioned for the markhor, a central Asian goat, to be downgraded from endangered to threatened[291] - all of which made it easier for hunters to bring home their trophies.

Conservation Force secured permission for leopard trophies to be imported from Mozambique[292], where the animal is vulnerable; overturned a ban on trophy hunting in Costa Rica[293]; and defeated several efforts to stop white rhino hunting[294].

It developed an 'Enhancement Initiative' which argued that trophy hunting of endangered-listed species in the wild actually improved their conservation prospects[295]. The campaign led to 'enhancement' permits being issued to trophy hunters to shoot critically-endangered Black Rhinos.[296]

[288] https://www.conservationforce.org/about
[289] https://www.conservationforce.org/john-jackson
[290] https://www.conservationforce.org/john-jackson
[291] https://www.conservationforce.org/john-jackson
[292] https://www.conservationforce.org/john-jackson
[293] https://www.conservationforce.org/john-jackson
[294] https://www.conservationforce.org/john-jackson
[295] https://www.conservationforce.org/john-jackson
[296] https://www.conservationforce.org/john-jackson

When Conservation Force stopped official moves to list a rare desert sheep as endangered - which would have meant hunters could no longer bring their trophies into the US[297] - Dennis Campbell, a multi award-winning and record-holding hunter, wrote that Jackson "almost single-handedly prevented the desert sheep of Baja, Mexico, from being uplisted as endangered by the US Fish & Wildlife Service."[298]

Don Causey, writing in The Hunting Report, adds: "Without Jackson's efforts, most observers agree, elephant hunting by Americans would be a thing of the past".[299] In fact, John Jackson and Conservation Force have drawn near-adulation from the many pro-hunting groups they have worked with around the world, a list which runs into hundreds.[300] According to Ron Gabriel of Boone & Crockett, for instance, Conservation Force "has become perhaps the most powerful legal force in the US and the world on behalf of hunters."[301] Ray Lee of the Foundation for North American Wild Sheep - a group that promotes trophy hunting of mountain sheep - agrees: "Conservation Force is perhaps the most effective organisation at promoting sport hunting and advocating for hunters' rights worldwide".[302]

Eduardo de Aaroz, president of the International Professional Hunters Association, adds that "the work done by John Jackson III is unparalleled, being focused

[297] https://www.conservationforce.org/john-jackson
[298] https://www.conservationforce.org/what-they-say-about-us
[299] Don Causey, Editor - The Hunting Report (12/96)
[300] https://www.conservationforce.org/about
[301] https://www.conservationforce.org/what-they-say-about-us
[302] https://www.conservationforce.org/what-they-say-about-us

on world-wide legal actions to re-open or maintain the sustainable use of renewable natural resources", adding that "this is how hunting is called today".[303] James Swan of Outdoorhub.com is equally effusive: "Superheros (sic) are big these days. If we were to hold an election for hunting's version of Spiderman, I would nominate Louisiana attorney John Jackson III, because Jackson has spun an international network of connections with a tireless motivation to make things happen".[304]

Conservation Force is currently campaigning to allow American hunters to bring home cheetah trophies[305] and to remove the threatened cape mountain zebra from the US Endangered Species Act.[306] It is also running campaigns promoting the "benefits to elephant from regulated hunting"[307] as well as the "benefits of regulated leopard hunting"[308].

Conservation Force has been trying to improve the image of trophy hunting too. Jackson has given a number of talks around the world including on "Hunting for an acceptable image: building public acceptance for sustainable use of wildlife", "Preaching beyond the choir: promoting hunting in the 21st century through effective communications", and "Image-building for acceptance and recruitment".[309]

---

[303] https://www.conservationforce.org/what-they-say-about-us
[304] https://www.conservationforce.org/what-they-say-about-us
[305] https://www.conservationforce.org/about
[306] https://www.conservationforce.org/news-updates-alerts
[307] https://www.conservationforce.org/news-updates-alerts
[308] https://www.conservationforce.org/news-updates-alerts
[309] https://www.conservationforce.org/john-jackson

Conservation Force has sought to directly influence negotiations over wildlife protections within CITES. It claims victory for defeating a proposal by the Kenyan government to list all African Lions on Appendix I of CITES, which would have curtailed the hunting of lions.[310] It says that it was Conservation Force which drafted a CITES resolution which defines hunting quotas, thus enshrining trophy hunting as allowable for threatened species.[311]

John Jackson and Conservation Force are also working to 'reform' CITES[312]. It has been able to work from within in furthering this aim. Conservation Force has been granted official International Observer status at CITES. Jackson himself has been allowed to participate in its conferences, working groups and committees[313]. At the CITES conference in Geneva in 2019, Conservation Force – along with Safari Club International and Dallas Safari Club – were often called by the conference chair to give their views on items under discussion.

Conservation Force has promoted the interests of controversial groups such as the Professional Hunters Association of South Africa (PHASA), a body that was kicked out of some international hunting bodies over its support for canned lion hunting. On its website, Conservation Force carries the following endorsement from PHASA: "Conservation Force, in the person of John Jackson, represents PHASA's interests at CITES and other forums of importance to our industry. (T)here

---

[310] https://www.conservationforce.org/john-jackson
[311] https://www.conservationforce.org/john-jackson
[312] https://www.conservationforce.org/about
[313] https://www.conservationforce.org/conferences

is no doubt that his continued efforts play a large role in protecting our rights and interests and hence the financial support given to Conservation Force".[314] The African Professional Hunters Association has also expressed its gratitude to Conservation Force for representing its interests within CITES: "We thank you for being our voice with the US Fish & Wildlife Service and CITES."[315]

Conservation Force has been particularly active within IUCN, the global conservation body. Jackson has been a member of IUCN's African Lion Working Group for more than 15 years. In fact he is a member of a number of IUCN Commissions and 'specialist groups' going back as far as 25 years.[316] IUCN has accepted funds from Conservation Force to develop a 'conservation hunting' project.[317] An IUCN symposium in London on the theme of 'Recreational Hunting, Conservation and Rural Livelihoods' was co-sponsored by Conservation Force.[318]

In addition to setting up Conservation Force, Jackson has helped found a number of other influential hunting lobby groups including the Congressional Sportsmen's Caucus and Foundation, and the Governors Hunting Heritage Conference.[319]

Away from his legal and lobbying work, Jackson is one of the world's top trophy hunters. His name appears regularly throughout SCI's Records Book. He has been

[314] https://www.conservationforce.org/what-they-say-about-us
[315] https://www.conservationforce.org/what-they-say-about-us
[316] https://www.conservationforce.org/john-jackson
[317] https://www.conservationforce.org/corporate-description-
[318] https://www.conservationforce.org/corporate-description-
[319] https://www.conservationforce.org/john-jackson

on at least 38 elephant hunts and killed 14 elephants.[320] In a recent magazine interview, he confessed that elephant hunting was to him "the most intimate, real relationship one can have with elephant. Nothing else in life is more satisfying than an elephant hunt."[321]

His home includes a large room filled with his hunting trophies from around the world. It features giraffes, zebras and bears.[322] He describes it as being "like a mirror. It reflects the wild places I have been and long to return to. It reflects the places, species, and cultures that have possessed and forever hold me captive".[323]

If CITES or IUCN officials are unaware of Jackson's interests, it is difficult to understand how - as he openly talks about them on Conservation Force's website. He is a life member of the Dallas Safari Club, the Houston Safari Club, the Congressional Sportsmen's Assembly, the Alaskan Professional Hunters Association, the International Professional Hunters Association, and the Professional Hunters Association of South Africa.[324] He has been awarded honorary life membership of the African Professional Hunters Association.[325] He is a

---

[320] "Controversy swirls around the recent US suspension of sport-hunted elephant trophies", blog.nationalgeograophic.org, May 6, 2014, Christina Russo

[321] "Controversy swirls around the recent US suspension of sport-hunted elephant trophies", blog.nationalgeograophic.org, May 6, 2014, Christina Russo

[322] "Great hunters – their trophy rooms and collections", Safari Press Inc, 1997

[323] "Great hunters – their trophy rooms and collections", Safari Press Inc, 1997

[324] https://www.conservationforce.org/john-jackson

member of the African Safari Club of Florida, the Chairman's Club of Congressional Sportsmen's Foundation, the National Shooting Sports Federation, the National Taxidermist Association, the Boone & Crockett Club, the Pope & Young Club, and the North American Professional Hunters Association.[326] Jackson has won multiple awards and honours from hunting groups around the world too.

Hunting industry awards presented to John J Jackson III/Conservation Force[327]

Outstanding member of the Year award, Safari Club International, 1992

Special Recognition Award, Safari Club International 1994

Medal of Distinction, International Game Foundation of HIH Prince Abdorreza, 1994

Wildlife Utilization Award, Professional Hunters Association of South Africa, 1995

Excellence in advocacy of our hunting heritage award, Foundation for North American Wild Sheep, 2003

Conklin Conservation Commendation, Conklin Foundation, 2004

Recognition Award, Grand Slam Club/Ovis, 2005

Ox of Okavango Award, African Professional Hunters Association, 2006 and 2011

---

[325] https://www.conservationforce.org/john-jackson
[326] https://www.conservationforce.org/john-jackson
[327] https://www.conservationforce.org/john-jackson

President's Award, Guide and Outfitters Association of British Columbia, 2008
Board of Directors award, Grand Slam Club/OVIS 2010
Honorary Life membership: Tanzania Professional Hunters Organisation, 2010
International Statesmen Award, Wild Sheep Foundation 2010
Peter Hathaway Capstick Hunting Heritage Award, Dallas Safari Club, 2013
Coenraad Vermaak Distinguished Award, Professional Hunters of South Africa, 2017

Andrew Loveridge, the scientist who radio-collared Cecil the lion, tells of how he took Conservation Force at their word and asked them to help fund lion research. In his book 'Lion Hearted – the life and death of Cecil and the future of Africa's iconic cats', he recounts a meeting with Jackson and other hunters at Safari Club International's annual convention – and the reaction he received when they realised that Loveridge was the man responsible for a ban on lion hunting in Zimbabwe.

"Over an early morning breakfast, we told him about the research and how we'd worked with Zimbabwe National Parks to temporarily suspend trophy hunting in the area around Hwange National Park as a measure to allow the lion population to recover.

"John started to look a bit queasy, and not because of the greasy breakfast. A conversation about suspended trophy hunting was not what he had expected, and this was clearly not welcome news.

"Things went downhill from there.

"We were due to speak to a group of professional hunters and safari operators, mostly from Zimbabwe. They listened politely to the presentation I had prepared.

"When I finished, there was a stony silence, followed eventually by a few sceptical questions.

"At the end of the meeting, one of the hunters summed up the mood with a comment I will always remember. He said, 'Well, maybe hunting does have an effect on lion populations, but we can't let the anti-hunters see any of these results'."[328]

In 2016, New Jersey's senate voted to ban hunting trophies of 'Big Five' animals (lion, leopard, rhino, elephant and Cape Buffalo) and all animals listed under Appendix I or II of CITES or considered critically endangered, endangered, or vulnerable by IUCN from its airports and sea port facilities. Conservation Force – together with the state's taxidermy industry and a group of trophy hunters - took the government of New Jersey to court demanding that the law be struck down. The judge agreed on the basis that the New Jersey law conflicted with the federal Endangered Species Act which permits importation of trophies from those species.[329]

However, Conservation Force had less luck when they tried to sue Delta airlines that same year. Delta had refused to ship the trophy of a critically endangered black rhino. The animal had been shot following an auction hosted by Dallas Safari Club, sparking

[328] "Lion Hearted – the life and death of Cecil and the future of Africa's iconic cats", Andrew Loveridge, Regan Arts, 2018

[329] "Federal judge strikes down NJ ban on trophy importation", August 30, 2016: www.theoutdoorwire.com

international furore. The case was brought with Corey Knowlton, the hunter who had paid $350,000 to kill the rhino. Court documents show that Conservation Force claimed that "Delta's ban on transport of Big Five trophies has a chilling effect on US hunters because the trophy is such an essential and tangible reminder of the hunting experience".

The court disagreed. Delta's ban on transporting hunters' trophies remains in place.

Others who have played a key role in Conservation Force include Bert Klineburger, a trophy hunter who has been inducted into SCI's Hall of Fame[330] and some of whose trophies feature in SCI's Records Book[331]; Philippe Chardonnet, a past Executive Director of pro-hunting group IGF and who – like Jackson – has sat on important IUCN committees[332]; Renee Snider, arguably the most prolific female trophy hunter of all time[333]; Jim Teer, a trophy hunter who has won awards with SCI[334]; Don Lindsay, President of the International Professional Hunters Association, IPHA, for 14 years and who was President of the Professional Hunters Association of South Africa (PHASA) between 1982-1991[335]; and Ricardo Longoria[336], a multi-award winning bowhunter[337],

---

[330] https://www.conservationforce.org/bert-klineburger
[331] SCI Record Book of Trophy Animals – edition IX, Volume 1, Africa Field Edition, 1997. Safari Club International
[332] https://www.conservationforce.org/philippe-chardonnet
[333] https://www.conservationforce.org/renee-snider
[334] https://www.conservationforce.org/teer
[335] https://www.conservationforce.org/don-lindsey
[336] https://www.conservationforce.org/ricardo-longoria
[337] Safari magazine – Awards 2015, Safari Club International

President of the Weatherby Foundation[338] and board member of Safari Club International's Foundation[339].

Another person who has been a leading figure in Conservation Force is Shane Mahoney[340]. On the website of Conservation Visions, the organisation of which he is CEO, is a photo of Mahoney posing with a rifle slung over his shoulder.[341] In 2017, Mahoney spoke at Dallas Safari Club's annual meeting where he said that it was "the real deal" when it came to conservation.[342]

On Conservation Force's website, Mahoney is quoted saying hunting "is the generator of our human condition, the crucible of intellect and the fore of creativity. It is our mirror of the world, the image-maker of wild creation; it has defined how we see, literally and figuratively."[343]

Mahoney is Chair of the IUCN North American 'Sustainable Use and Livelihoods Specialist Group'[344], a group which supports trophy hunting.

Jackson explains his own philosophy on trophy hunting as follows: "Our lives are measured by trophies of all sorts, from the hides and heads of game animals to

---

[338] https://www.weatherbyfoundation.com/about-us/presidents-message/

[339] Safari Club International Foundation 2018 Annual Report http://safariclubfoundation.org/wp-content/uploads/2018/11/2018-AR-Finalsm.pdf

[340] https://www.conservationforce.org/shane-mahoney

[341] https://www.conservationvisions.com/

[342] 'They're Trusted To Protect Animals. But "They" Include Trophy Hunters. Inside The Global Conservation Organization Infiltrated By Trophy Hunters'. Buzzfeed, February 13, 2020

[343] https://www.conservationforce.org/why-we-hunt

[344] https://www.conservationforce.org/shane-mahoney

diplomas, graduation rings and expensive cars, all of which symbolise and advertise an achievement worthy of a certain degree of social esteem. Trophyism - the love of trophies - is fundamental to understanding human nature, and how indeed we gained dominion of the planet.

"It is no mere coincidence that disproportionate numbers of men with high status or great wealth in modern American society, business tycoons, military leaders and holders of high state office, are trophy hunters.

"Because trophies carry so much importance, confirmation of the kill is often required in hunting societies.

"For thousands of years trophies have signified manhood and virility. A man is described as 'randy' if he is especially virile or has a high libido. The term 'randy' actually originates from an old Latin word, 'randall', which means 'wolf shield'."

"Because trophies are associated with virility, rhinos are killed for their horns and tigers for their organs."[345]

He tells the story of the first animal he killed. "There is a positive, spiritual side to the trophy too. At the age of 13 I collected my first trophy, a mallard hen, which I very carefully skinned and preserved. That skin was sacred to me... every hunter remembers his first kill vividly and can accurately recount it, not unlike the first time he made love.

---

[345] "Why we hunt: call of the chase / the meaning of trophy in male initiation ", John Jackson, Conservation Force – in www.africahunting.com October 27 2010

"For me that mallard hen was not merely a symbol of my first big step to manhood... that trophy also honours her life as the spirit of her nation, and above all else it is a public statement of gratitude for the gift of her life that I might become a man worthy of her sacrifice.

"Trophies rank a man socially.

"What cannot be denied is that a young man's trophy signifies his passage from childhood to manhood, and if we intend to initiate young men properly then it is essential that we encourage them to collect a trophy from the animals that make their passage possible."[346]

The tactic of rebranding trophy hunting as 'conservation' is being deployed across the industry. A hunting coalition calling itself the American Wildlife Conservation Partners (AWCP) is made up of dozens of pro-hunting organisations.[347] In April 2020, the AWCP wrote to all US state governors demanding that hunters be allowed to hunt despite the Covid-19 pandemic. In a press release, one of the signatories - the Congressional Sportsmen's Foundation - claimed that hunting "remains an avenue to physically and mentally recharge during the COVID-19 pandemic", adding that "it is critical for the sustainability of our nation's treasured natural resources that they are able to continue hunting".[348]

---

[346] "Why we hunt: call of the chase / the meaning of trophy in male initiation ", John Jackson, Conservation Force – in www.africahunting.com October 27 2010

[347] https://www.boone-crockett.org/conservation/conservation_wcp.asp?area=conservation

[348] Press release, Congressional Sportsmen's Foundation, April 9, 2020

In the letter, the signatories plead: "In particular, please consider maintaining the openness of opportunities for the hunting of spring turkey and bear".[349] Signatories included Conservation Force, Safari Club International, the NRA, Dallas Safari Club, and Houston Safari Club.

A number of other so-called 'wildlife conservation' groups are in reality little more than hunting organisations or businesses. The 'Wildlife Research Center', which owns the wildlife.com domain, is a company that develops scent lures and disguises for hunters.[350] It manufactures what it calls "an irresistible formula that attracted deer like nothing they'd ever seen before."[351] Its website features galleries of hunters and says its products "do a great job, making sure hunters have the best scent products available".[352]

The 'Wildlife Management Institute', which is chaired by a former president and CEO of the National Shooting Sports Foundation[353], "supports the wise use of wildlife, including regulated recreational hunting of designated populations."[354] The mission of the 'Texas Wildlife Society' is protecting "hunting heritage".[355] Its

[349] https://files.constantcontact.com/93ba5414201/159e4a71-d392-43f1-9f52-fe3a2118c8e4.docx

[350] https://www.wildlife.com/index.php

[351] https://www.wildlife.com/Wildlife-Research-Center-About-Us-Details.php?Background-and-History-2

[352] https://www.wildlife.com/Wildlife-Research-Center-About-Us-Details.php?Background-and-History-2

[353] https://wildlifemanagement.institute/about/board

[354] https://wildlifemanagement.institute/about

[355] www.texas-wildlife.org

projects include the Texas Youth Hunting Program which "gives young Texans the opportunity to participate in youth hunting activities safely" thus "preserving tomorrow's hunting heritage today."[356] It runs its own Texas Big Game Awards which it describes as "the official hunting program of Texas."[357]

'Bear Trust International' says that "hunting is a part of the world's natural heritage and should be used as one of many tools for effective wildlife management".[358] This is perhaps not surprising given that its Board of Directors includes representatives of pro-hunting groups.[359] Its Executive Director is a professional hunting guide.[360] The organisation's official partners include Dallas Safari Club and the SCI Foundation.[361]

Similarly, 'Ducks Unlimited' was founded by a group of hunters and admits that 90% of its members are hunters.[362] In March 2019, it appointed a new CEO - Adam Putnam – who, it said, was "a lifelong hunter".[363] Its website has a section on 'hunting tips'[364]and offers a waterfowl "hunting party" for the "hardcore duck

---

[356] https://www.texas-wildlife.org/program-areas/category/texas-youth-hunting-program

[357] https://www.texas-wildlife.org/program-areas/category/texas-big-game-awards

[358] https://beartrust.org/vision-and-mission

[359] https://beartrust.org/staff

[360] https://beartrust.org/new-executive-director-of-bear-trust.html

[361] https://beartrust.org/partners

[362] https://www.ducks.org/hunting

[363] https://www.ducks.org/press-room/news-releases/ducks-unlimited-announces-new-ceo?poe=news-releases

[364] https://www.ducks.org/hunting/waterfowl-hunting-tips

hunter"[365]. Its classifieds section leads with the question: "Looking for a great hunt this season? … Look no further!"[366]

The website of the 'National Wild Turkey Federation' also has resources to help you find the best turkey hunts. It promotes turkey hunting 'Grand Slams' which it says are "considered top feats or goals to diehard turkey hunters. The Grand Slam will take you around the country, chasing each of the four most common wild turkey subspecies in the US… then there is the Mt Everest of slams: the US Super Slam. Finishing the Super Slam involves tagging a wild turkey in each of the 49 states that have turkeys".[367]

The 'Camp Fire Club of America' was founded by hunters "to further the interests of sports afield"[368] – another form of words used to describe the hunting of animals for pleasure.

The 'American Woodcock Society-Ruffed Grouse Society', meanwhile, is "dedicated to preserving our sporting traditions… our members are mainly grouse and woodcock hunters." The organisation sponsors several shooting and hunting events[369]. The 'Rocky Mountain Elk Foundation' was founded by a group of hunters from Montana to promote hunting.[370] Its current President and CEO was previously Executive Director at the NRA[371]

---

[365] https://www.ducks.org/ducks-unlimited-events/waterfowl-hunters-party

[366] https://www.ducks.org/media/classifieds

[367] https://www.nwtf.org/hunt/article/chasing-grand-slam

[368] https://www.campfireclub.com/login

[369] https://ruffedgrousesociety.org/about-us/

[370] https://www.rmef.org/rmef-history/

and was recently touted by industry insiders as a possible successor to Wayne LaPierre as CEO of the gun rights group.[372]

The 'Wild Sheep Foundation' has a series of hunting awards[373] and runs youth programmes to recruit new hunters.[374] It has a lobbying arm which works to preserve the "hunting heritage in North America" – "hunting and sportsmen-led conservation are important American traditions that must be ensured in policy."[375] The group's President and CEO was Executive Director of Dallas Safari Club from 1997 to 2008, and a Director of SCI from 1990-97.[376]

The goals of the 'Mule Deer Foundation' include developing programmes "that focus on recruitment and retention of youth into the shooting sports".[377] Its President and CEO, Miles Moretti, supported the appointment of David Bernhardt as US Secretary of the Interior because "David is an avid hunter and outdoorsman."[378] The 'Quality Deer Management

[371] https://www.ammoland.com/2018/05/rmef-announces-new-president-and-ceo/#axzz6LYkcmRYS

[372] https://www.ammoland.com/2020/05/uncertain-future-lies-ahead-for-national-rifle-association/#axzz6LYkcmRYS

[373] https://www.wildsheepfoundation.org/awards/hunting/north-american-awards

[374] https://www.wildsheepfoundation.org/mission-and-programs/youth-programs

[375] https://www.wildsheepfoundation.org/mission-and-programs/advocacy

[376] https://www.wildsheepfoundation.org/about/staff

[377] https://muledeer.org/about-us/mdf-goals/

[378] "MDF supports David Bernhardt for DOI Secretary as

Association' promotes a 'Rack Pack' youth programme "to create and enrich future hunters".[379] Its website has a "Hunting Heritage" page which features a young woman being 'blooded'.[380]

The 'IWMC (International Wildlife Management Consortium) World Conservation Trust' lobbied CITES delegates at its 2019 conference to downlist a number of threatened species popular with hunters, including Zambia's elephants[381] and the markhor[382]. It also asked them to vote against the inclusion of the giraffe on CITES Appendix II.[383] It has opposed plans for the creation of a whale sanctuary in the south Atlantic.[384] Several of its members have served on CITES' Secretariat, including its President Eugene Lapointe, who was Secretary General of CITES from 1982 to 1990.

LaPointe[385] and the IWMC World Conservation Trust[386] have been publicly supportive of Ron Thomson, a hunter

Confirmation Hearings Begin" – press release, March 28, 2019

[379] https://www.qdma.com/hunt/hunting-heritage/

[380] https://www.qdma.com/hunt/hunting-heritage/

[381] https://www.iwmc.org/cites-cop/cites-cop18/facts/302-facts-prop-10/file.html

[382] https://www.iwmc.org/cites-cop/cites-cop18/facts/308-iwmc-voting-guide-recommendations/file.html

[383] https://www.iwmc.org/cites-cop/cites-cop18/facts/308-iwmc-voting-guide-recommendations/file.html

[384] https://www.iwmc.org/iwc-66/255-defeat-of-so-called-sanctuary-welcomed/file.html

[385] https://twitter.com/IWMCWCT/status/1122989482997878786

[386] https://www.iwmc.org/docman/iwmc-document-catalogue/newsletter-archive/2009/117-2009-october-november-

who has shot over 5000 elephants[387] and who heads an organisation called the 'True Green Alliance'. Thomson recently described NGOs' calls for a ban on wildlife trade with China as "tantamount to treason"[388] and said that animal welfare groups are "the paedophiles of the wildlife industry."[389] Thomson claims to have "by far hunted more than any other man alive."[390] He has received awards from Conservation Force and Safari Club International for his work.

Another organisation which promotes hunting in the name of conservation is 'Conservation Frontlines'. It works "all-out to 'branding' sustainable hunting" and to "equip hunters with knowledge and arguments to campaign as reliable and authentic advocates and communicators of the conservation hunting message."[391]

US President Donald Trump has publicly denounced elephant hunting as a "horror show"[392] and tweeted that "(I) don't approve of killing animals. I strongly disagree with my sons who are hunters".[393] Despite this, there

december-enews/file.html

[387] https://news.sky.com/story/hunter-ron-thomson-totally-unrepentant-about-killing-5-000-elephants-11688494

[388] https://www.mahohboh.org/tga-response-to-call-for-permanent-ban-on-wildlife-trade-in-china/

[389] Telling the Truth Where and When the Truth Matters, April 7, 2020 Ron Thomson https://www.mahohboh.org/telling-the-truth-where-and-when-the-truth-matters/

[390] "Who would want to kill a lion? Inside the minds of trophy hunters", Elle Hunt, Guardian/Observer, 4 November 2018

[391] https://www.conservationfrontlines.org/about-us/

[392] https://twitter.com/realdonaldtrump/status/932397369655808001?lang=en

have been a number of significant changes to wildlife laws since Donald Trump was sworn in as President in January 2017 which have delighted trophy hunters. The US government is currently moving ahead with plans to open up as much as 1.4 million acres of publicly-owned land in 74 national wildlife refuges to hunting. It is also looking to amend laws which protect the grey wolf from hunters in 48 states.[394] According to Newsweek, the Trump administration plans to end protections for species that are currently designated as threatened and make it easier to remove species from the endangered list.[395]

The US has also begun allowing hunters to bring back trophies of lions and elephants from Zambia and Zimbabwe. Imports from these countries had previously been banned because of particularly grave concerns about the conservation status of those animals there.

The manner in which the decision was made public gave a clear clue as to what – or more accurately, who - was behind it. Rather than an announcement in the Federal Register, or on the White House website or by the US Fish & Wildlife Service (FWS) - the government agency which oversees trophy import regulations – the

[393]

https://twitter.com/realdonaldtrump/status/18036685791468339
3

[394] "Trump administration announces plans to expand hunting and fishing access in wildlife refuges", CBS News, Sophies Lewis, June 6, 2019

[395] "Trump administration plans to end some protections for endangered species after UN report warns of 'mass extinction event'", Nicole Goodkind, Newsweek May 10 2019

decision was made during a meeting of the so-called African Wildlife Consultative Forum, a pro-trophy hunting coalition.[396] The announcement itself was made by Safari Club International.

Former US-FWS Director Dan Ashe described this as "unsettling, raises concerns about impartiality, and warrants skepticism".[397] Humane Society International commented that it was "not surprising a hunting outfitter advertised elephant hunts in Zimbabwe as soon as the SCI announcement was made public."[398] It added "that SCI, the largest pro-trophy hunting lobby group, announced this decision suggests an uncomfortably cozy and even improper relationship between trophy hunting interests and the Department of the Interior".

On the same day the lifting of the elephant trophy ban was announced, US Secretary of the Interior Ryan Zinke - himself an avid hunter – announced the creation of a new official advisory body called the International Wildlife Conservation Council (IWCC). Despite its title, its remit would be to "recommend removal of barriers to the importation into the US of legally hunted wildlife" while also "developing a plan for public engagement and education on the benefits of international hunting" including the "economic benefits that result from US

---

[396] "Lions next in line of fire as US rolls back curbs on African hunting trophies," Oliver Milman, The Guardian, 16 November 2017

[397] "From the desk of Dan Ashe - "We can conserve elephants without hunting them", January 4, 2018 www.aza.org

[398] "Interior department to allow imports of elephant and lion trophies from Africa, reversing Obama policies", blog.humanesociety.org November 15, 2017

citizens traveling abroad to hunt." Under the terms of its charter, IWCC's job was set out as "lowering barriers to import legally hunted wildlife into the United States, which includes streamlining the issuance of import permits; reviewing import bans and seeking ways to remove them; and reviewing ESA listed species".[399]

The body was composed almost entirely of trophy hunters and industry supporters.[400] They included some of the world's leading trophy hunters, SCI 'African Big Five' award-winners, and representatives of hunting weapon manufacturers. Safari Club International, the National Rifle Association and Conservation Force were all represented. Paul Babaz was President of SCI at the time of his appointment and a member of NRA's Board. Erica Rhoad, the NRA's director of hunting policy, was appointed as was John J Jackson III of Conservation Force. The Council was chaired by Bill Brewster, a former U.S. Congressman who has served on the boards of both SCI and the NRA. According to the NRA, Brewster and his wife have been involved in trophy hunting for 50 years. Brewster bought a lifetime membership of the NRA for his 3-day old grandson.[401]

---

[399] U.S. Department of the Interior, International Wildlife Conservation Council Charter, U.S. Fish and Wildlife Service, December 21, 2017. Letter from Susan Lieberman, Vice President of International Policy, Wildlife Conservation Society, et al., to Joshua Winchell, U.S. Fish and Wildlife Service, November 24, 2017.

[400] "Trump wildlife protection board stuffed with trophy hunters", AP, March 15 2018

[401] https://www.americanhunter.org/articles/2014/12/30/hlf-member-spotlight-bill-suzie-brewster/

Steven Chancellor, a major donor and fundraiser for Donald Trump who holds some of SCI's top hunting records[402], was another member. Chris Hudson is a past president of Dallas Safari Club. Peter Horn is a former Vice-President of SCI's Foundation wing and also of gun-makers Beretta. He co-owns a property with one of Donald Trump's sons, Eric, who is also a friend of another council member – TV hunting guide Keith Mark, organiser of 'Sportsmen for Trump' during the 2016 Presidential election campaign. Mark has posted pictures on social media with the President's son and Ryan Zinke, the Secretary of the Interior, standing next to a dead bear and wild sheep.[403]

Other prominent hunting advocates on the committee included Olivia Opre, a former Mrs America contestant who has won the Diana Award, the SCI prize for leading female trophy hunters. Opre has killed almost 100 animals across 6 continents, including a lion and black rhinoceros. Another winner of SCI's Diana Award, Denise Walker, was appointed too. Walker once shot an African elephant from 5 paces and has posted photographs of herself with a dead leopard and other animals.

British hunter and tracker Ivan Carter was born in Zimbabwe and lives in the Bahamas, and is reported to have hunted elephants with Denise Walker. He called the killing of Cecil the lion "the 'Twin Towers' of the hunting world – our 9/11". He was appointed too.[404]

[402] SCI Record Book of Trophy Animals – edition IX, Volume 1, Africa Field Edition, 1997. Safari Club International

[403] "Trump wildlife protection board stuffed with trophy hunters", AP, March 15 2018

Critics pointed out the irony in appointing representatives of groups who have sued the US government in order to force it to expand the list of countries from which trophies can be brought into the US. The committee was eventually disbanded in early 2020 amidst claims it had broken federal rules.

When Ryan Zinke was appointed as Donald Trump's first Interior Secretary, the trophy hunting industry was delighted. Zinke is a former congressman from the state of Montana who received contributions to his election campaigns from SCI.[405] Chris W Cox, executive director of the NRA's Institute for Legislative Action, commented that "America's hunters and recreational shooters have a champion in Secretary Ryan Zinke. Zinke is fighting for our sportsmen and women to have greater access to our public lands."[406]

Zinke oversaw the reversal of a number of Obama-era restrictions on imports of lion and elephant hunting trophies into the US. He also reversed a ban on ammunition linked to the poisoning of bald eagles.[407] Zinke was eventually forced to resign after a series of media allegations.[408]

---

[404] "Trump wildlife protection board stuffed with trophy hunters", AP, March 15 2018

[405] "High-ranking Trump official attends hunting convention", Miranda Green and Timothy Cama, The Hill 3 February 2018 https://thehill.com/policy/energy-environment/372166-high-ranking-trump-official-attends-trophy-hunting-convention

[406] www.doi.gov press release 22/05/2018

[407] "Lions next in line of fire as US rolls back curbs on African hunting trophies," Oliver Milman, The Guardian, 16 November 2017

[408] https://time.com/5480865/controversies-interior-secretary-

However Zinke's deputy and eventual successor, David Bernhardt, was welcomed just as warmly by the industry. The Boone & Crockett Club and the NRA were among the hunting organisations to write to the US Senate urging them to confirm Bernhardt's appointment.[409] The Congressional Sportsmen's Foundation issued a press release in which it stated: "Secretary Bernhardt is an avid sportsman and has consistently demonstrated his personal commitment to increasing public access opportunities for sportsmen and women."[410] "As an avid hunter, shooter and fisherman, Secretary Bernhardt is committed to conserving America's outdoor heritage," added the NRA's Chris W Cox. "Under his leadership the Dept of Interior will continue to pursue conservation policies that respect the rights of America's outdoorsmen and women."[411]

The warm words of praise were not unexpected. Bernhardt was a keynote speaker at the 2018 convention of Dallas Safari Club.[412] As acting Secretary following Zinke's resignation, Bernhardt had signed Secretarial Order 3374 which expanded hunting on dozens of wildlife refuges and thousands of acres of public land.

Following confirmation of his appointment, Bernhardt announced: "The Trump Administration will continue to

---

ryan-zinke-resignation/

[409] https://www.govinfo.gov/content/pkg/CHRG-115shrg26073/pdf/CHRG-115shrg26073.pdf

[410] CSF press release dated April 11, 2019

[411] "Outdoorsman David Bernhardt confirmed as Secretary of the Interior", Guns.com, Chris Eger 14 April 2019 www.guns.com

[412] https://www.biggame.org/wp-content/uploads/2019/05/CampTalk-March-2019-Web.pdf

prioritise access so that people can hunt, fish, camp, and recreate on our public lands."[413] He has kept his promise. In April 2020, Bernhardt announced proposals to expand hunting rights on more than 2 million acres of land, including almost 100 wildlife refuges across the US. Hunting groups such as the Boone & Crockett club celebrated. "When finalized, the new rule will continue to add to the Administration's efforts to expand hunting and fishing access on refuges bringing the total expansion to 4 million acres nationwide," it said in a press release. "We thank Fish and Wildlife Service Director Aurelia Skipwith, Secretary Bernhardt and President Trump for this Administration's continued commitment to the sportsmen and women of this country."[414]

The Trump Administration has recently appointed a leading former lawyer for Safari Club International to a key position within the US Fish & Wildlife Service (FWS), the government department responsible for issuing trophy import permits. Anna Seidman, SCI's

---

[413] "Interior orders more access to public lands for American hunters, fishers, outdoorsmen", Penny Starr, Breitbart, 23 Mar 2019

[414] Boone & Crockett press release: 'B&C THANKS DEPARTMENT OF THE INTERIOR FOR EXPANDING HUNTING AND FISHING OPPORTUNITIES ON 97 NATIONAL WILDLIFE REFUGES', April 8, 2020 https://www.boone-crockett.org/news/featured_story.asp?area=news&ID=442&utm_source=Monthly+Newsletter+-+All+Subscribers&utm_campaign=df03209c7c-Jan_2020_Newsletter_01_COPY_01&utm_medium=email&utm_term=0_08394aecbd-df03209c7c-40777141&mc_cid=df03209c7c&mc_eid=bd8e19f230

former Director of Legal and Advocacy and International Affairs, has taken up the role of Assistant Director of International Affairs at US-FWS. Whilst at SCI, Seidman led the group's campaign to overturn bans on imports of elephant trophies from Tanzania and Zimbabwe.

Part 2: The Hunters

Chapter 4: British Trophy Hunters

Malcolm King

Malcolm King is a retired businessman with homes in Gloucester and Jersey. He is one of the world's top award-winning hunters of all time. His extraordinary roll-call of prizes with Safari Club International includes the coveted Hunting Achievement Award (Diamond level) which is presented only to hunters who have 125 of their kills in SCI's Records Book.[415]

In order to win all the SCI prizes to his name, King will have had to kill huge numbers of animals in every corner of the planet. To win the 'Inner Circle Global Hunting Award' at Gold level he will have shot wild animals in a minimum of 5 different continents, each with a minimum number of species: 17 from Africa, 13 from North America, 4 from South America, 6 from Europe, 6 from Asia, and 4 from the South Pacific. To win the 'Inner Circle Animals of Africa Award' (Gold) King will have shot at least 61 different species, including 2 African big cats, an elephant, a rhino, a hyena, a buffalo, a hippo, a wild pig, and a combination of spiral-horned antelopes, oryxes, wildebeest etc.[416]

He has also won the Safari Club International 'Pinnacle of Achievement Award' (Fourth Pinnacle) and its 'Zenith Award', both of which are given only to the world's top trophy hunters. He has won the 'Ullman

---

[415] Safari magazine – Awards 2015, Safari Club International
[416] Safari magazine – Awards 2015, Safari Club International

Award' (Fourth Echelon), a European hunting award, too. A winner must kill at least 40 different species to attain the Fourth Echelon.[417] In 2019, he narrowly missed out on the Weatherby Award, arguably the industry's most coveted award. He was pipped to the post by Spain's Jose 'Pepe' Madrazo, a hunter who has shot 390 different species.[418]

King's other prizes include the 'Africa 15' Continental Award (minimum 15 different African species), the 'Africa 29 Grand Slam' (minimum 29 species), the 'Cats of the World Grand Slam', 'Bears of the World Grand Slam', and the 'Top Ten' award for having 15 entries in the SCI Records Book. He has also won the Animals of Asia Diamond Award (minimum 15 different species), the Animals of Europe Diamond Award (minimum 16 different species), and the Animals of South Pacific Gold Award (minimum 10 different species).[419] (For a full list of Malcolm King's awards, visit the Appendix.)

Carl Knight

Carl Knight was born in Surrey, England, in September 1973. He is the only living British hunter known to have shot both the 'African Big Five' (lion, elephant, leopard, rhino and buffalo) and the "Dangerous Seven" (the African 'Big Five' plus hippopotamus and crocodile).[420] He may be the only

---

[417] Safari magazine – Awards 2015, Safari Club International
[418] https://www.safariclub.org/blog/jose-madrazo-named-2019-weatherby-award-winner
[419] Safari magazine – Awards 2015, Safari Club International
[420] https://www.takeaimsafaris.co.za/

British hunter ever to have done this in the modern era. In all, he has taken part in over 400 big game hunts. He claims to have "personally hunted every African country open to hunting including and south of Tanzania".[421]

He currently lives in Johannesburg, South Africa, where he runs a hunting company during the hunting season and is a real estate agent with Remax in the affluent Johannesburg suburb of Bedfordview for the rest of the year.[422]

He describes himself as "a specialist Southern African big game Hunting Outfitter, Hunting Agent and South African Professional Hunter."[423] His company, Take Aim Safaris, was launched in 2008 and organises trophy hunting trips in South Africa. He operates from two hunting concessions in South Africa, one in Limpopo-Serengeti and the other in Philippolis. The latter is in the Free State – in the centre of the country – while the Limpopo-Serengeti area in the far north-east is approximately 3 hours' drive from Pretoria. He provides 4 and 5-star luxury lodges on site.

The Limpopo-Serengeti concession is 10,000 hectares (25,000 acres) in area – equivalent to 100 square kilometres. There is a gym and swimming pool, and also a helipad and runway for private aircraft.[424] The animals on offer here include rhinos, crocodiles and leopards. Lions can be shot for $20,000.

In Zimbabwe, Knight has a hunting concession next to the Gonarezhou National Park in the south-east, which is adjacent to the Kruger National Park. He has another in the Matetsi

---

[421] https://www.takeaimsafaris.co.za/

[422] https://www.remax.co.za/real-estate-agents/south-africa/gauteng/bedfordview/bedfordview/one-bedfordview-800568/carl-knight-829085/

[423] https://www.takeaimsafaris.co.za/

[424] https://www.takeaimsafaris.co.za/limpopo-serengeti-hunting-area/

area by the Marico-Bosveld Nature Reserve close to Victoria Falls and Hwange National Park - where Cecil was shot in 2015 - in the west of the country. In Matetsi he offers leopard, elephant, lion, hippo, crocodile, zebra, baboon and hyena hunts. Eighteen-day wild lion hunts are available for $75,000, while 14-day leopard hunts cost $27,000.

A 21-day 'Big 4' hunt with Knight for a South African lion and Zimbabwean leopard, buffalo and elephant costs $1,800 per day plus a trophy fee of $20,000 for the lion, $13,000 for the elephant, $5,000 for the leopard and $5,000 for the buffalo. Hippo and crocodile packages are both around the $36,000 mark. Knight also offers special deals on tusk-less elephants, with a 7-day hunt costing just $8,750.

The trophy fees of other animals he has available in South Africa include the African wild cat for $460; Baboons for $200; Crocodiles – $2800 up to 3m, $4200 over 3m; Giraffes for $2400; Hippos for $9000; Jackals for $150; Porcupines for $250; Vervet Monkeys for $200; and Zebras for $1100. In his Zimbabwe concession, Baboons cost just $80, Tuskless elephants $4000, Giraffes $1800, Vervet monkeys $75, Wild cats $250, and Zebras $1200. For rhinos, the price is available on request. (See Appendix for a full list of Carl Knight's hunting packages).

Paul Roberts

"I have in my time owned and parted with many wonderful treasures: superb antique and modern guns; fabulous jewels; Ferraris, Maseratis, Porsches... However, my greatest treasures still remain my hunting memories and some of the trophies that go with them."[425]

---

[425] "Great Hunters – their trophy rooms & collections", volume 3, Safari Press, 2001

Paul Roberts is a British hunter known within the fraternity for having one of the world's most famous collections of hunting trophies. Many of his larger ones are on display at the West Sussex showroom and workshop of the gunmaker company founded by his father, Joseph Roberts. Some can be viewed at the Royal Armouries in Leeds while others are kept at his homes in London and Sussex.[426]

Roberts has been hunting in Africa since the 1970s. He is one of the very few trophy hunters still alive who has hunted in India. He says he is a big fan of African big game species such as the cape buffalo: "The buffalo hunt and the follow-up is still for me the greatest thrill that hunting has to offer."

He also hunts a number of deer species in Dorset and Scotland as well as roe deer near his West Sussex home. He visits Europe to take part in driven boar shoots, including on the estate of Count Jean de Bearn in Normandy, France.[427]

His personal trophy room features a series of shoulder mounts of lions, and various antelope and buffalo horns mounted on wooden plaques. He has a lion rug and a number of large elephant ivory tusks. There are antlers mounted on wooden plaques, skulls, and a mounted partridge in his trophy room.[428]

---

[426] "Great Hunters – their trophy rooms & collections", volume 3, Safari Press, 2001

[427] "Great Hunters – their trophy rooms & collections", volume 3, Safari Press, 2001

[428] "Great Hunters – their trophy rooms & collections", volume 3, Safari Press, 2001

As a gun enthusiast, he uses a number of different rifles on his hunts. "For an African minimal battery, I have found that the .416 Rigby and .300 Winchester Magnum cover everything very well, although I still like to tote the double .470 just in case."[429]

Safari Club International records indicate that Roberts won the Grand Slam 'Africa Big Five' Award in 1989.[430]

Derek Stocker

Derek Stocker runs an African safari hunting company called ProStalk from a village near Glastonbury, England. He has sold monkey hunts for as little as £47, and charged just under £1700 for the right to shoot a giraffe.[431] Stocker, who is in his 60s, has also charged clients £20,000 for elephant hunting trips.[432]

For just over £5,000, Stocker currently lays on a Father and Son 'bonding' holiday where you can shoot impalas, warthogs and jackals at night using a lamp.[433] The fee for shooting zebras starts at £700.[434] Hunting a Scimitar-horned oryx, which is extinct in the wild[435], costs £1700.

---

[429] "Great Hunters – their trophy rooms & collections", volume 3, Safari Press, 2001

[430] Safari magazine – Awards 2015, Safari Club International

[431] https://www.mirror.co.uk/news/uk-news/british-man-running-sickening-safaris-18858959

[432] https://www.mirror.co.uk/news/uk-news/british-man-running-sickening-safaris-18858959

[433] http://prostalksafaris.com/management-safaris/

[434] http://prostalksafaris.com/Animals/

[435] IUCN SSC Antelope Specialist Group. 2016. Oryx dammah. The IUCN Red List of Threatened Species 2016:

Other deals include African wildcats, which are priced at £300, and baboons which are available for £200. An ostrich, meanwhile, costs £285. Additional animals available include porcupines (£50) and jackals (£75). Hippo hunts start at £5500. The cost of a leopard hunt is available on request.[436] The former gamekeeper says that his African safaris are "adventures of a lifetime."[437]

Stocker also organises hunting trips in the UK and across a number of European countries including Germany, Poland, Czech Republic, Hungary and Romania, mainly of deer and wild boar. Moose hunts can be booked via Stocker in Estonia.[438]

David Watt

David Watt is the 'International Booking & Client Coordinator' for Nduna Safaris[439], a company which sells 'canned' lion hunts - including of juvenile lions and lionesses.[440] Nduna Safaris also hosts caracal lynx hunts using packs of dogs.[441] Watt has been safari hunting for

---

e.T15568A50191470.

[436] http://prostalksafaris.com/Animals/

[437] https://www.mirror.co.uk/news/uk-news/british-man-running-sickening-safaris-18858959

[438] http://prostalkeurope.com/

[439] http://www.ndunahuntingsafaris.co.za/team/

[440] http://www.ndunahuntingsafaris.co.za/gallery/nggallery/page/8

[441] http://www.ndunahuntingsafaris.co.za/hunting-packages/caracal-lynx-felis-caracal/

over 20 years, and helps trophy hunters bring in their favourite hunting rifles when travelling to Africa.[442]

The company's website paints an exciting picture of the adventure that awaits its clients. "The call of the wild. The breath taking sunsets, each one as perfect as, yet different from the previous one. Time will seem to stand still as you absorb and appreciate the special part of the world that is Nduna."[443]

Around 40 different species are available to hunt. They include the African 'Big Five', baboons, giraffes, and zebras.[444]

Of its hunts of caracals with packs of dogs it says: "The Caracal can be hunted with dogs in the Eastern Cape. Any .22 centrefire will do for hunting Caracal but larger calibres can also be used. Make the correct choice of bullet if you want to keep the skin."[445] The cost of this hunt is £800.[446]

Trophy fees range from £240 for baboons and ostriches, to £2800 for a giraffe. Zebras are £950.[447] The prices of lions, elephants, leopards and rhinos are available on request.

---

[442] http://www.ndunahuntingsafaris.co.za/team/

[443] http://www.ndunahuntingsafaris.co.za/

[444] http://www.ndunahuntingsafaris.co.za/trophy-hunting-south-africa/

[445] http://www.ndunahuntingsafaris.co.za/hunting-packages/caracal-lynx-felis-caracal/

[446] http://www.ndunahuntingsafaris.co.za/trophy-hunting-south-africa/

[447] http://www.ndunahuntingsafaris.co.za/trophy-hunting-south-africa/

RealTree, a hunting website, describes Watt as "charismatic and a well-travelled hunter. It's easy to see why Nduna chose him to represent them for their international clients."[448] TeamWild, a hunting video channel, adds: "Nduna's International Client Services Representative – David Watt has created a range of affordable safari packages especially for the show."[449]

Aside from booking hunting holidays for Nduna, Watt is also owner of Kingstone Deer Management Services in the UK.[450]

Alex Goss

Alex Goss is a dual British and South African national. He may be the only British owner of a safari hunting company in Africa that currently offers 'canned lion' hunts.[451]

He lives part of the year in Oswestry near Shrewsbury, and spends the hunting season in South Africa[452]. A slight figure with an English accent that gives away no hint of his split citizenship, he hunts and organises hunts on a 50,000 acre hunting estate 40

---

[448] https://www.realtree.com/global-hunting/articles/game-management-in-the-southern-hemisphere

[449] http://www.teamwild.tv/news/2939-check-out-the-awesome-deals-from-nduna-hunting-safaris-this-weekend

[450] https://www.linkedin.com/in/david-watt-14441331/

[451] https://www.dailymail.co.uk/news/article-7170751/British-safari-boss-charging-hunters-thousands-kill-farm-bred-lions-South-Africa-Zimbabwe.html

[452] https://www.dailymail.co.uk/news/article-7170751/British-safari-boss-charging-hunters-thousands-kill-farm-bred-lions-South-Africa-Zimbabwe.html

minutes' drive north of the South African mining town of Kimblerly. The town is in South Africa's Northern Cape province and lies on the outskirts of the Kalahari desert.

He operates under the business name of Blackthorn Safaris and has a wide variety of lions and lionesses available for hunters to choose from. The animals are shot within fenced enclosures. In addition to lion hunts, Goss guides hunters wanting to shoot and take home trophies of elephants, leopards, hippos, and crocodiles. Other hunts on offer include zebras, buffaloes and antelopes.[453]

Andy Denson

Andy Denson is a leading taxidermist to the UK hunting industry. He is also a trophy hunter and claims to have shot every species of wild animal in South Africa's Eastern Cape.[454] In addition, Denson has worked as a broker for a company called Thaba Thala Safaris which is popular among British hunters[455].

Born in February, 1969, he lives in the Lancashire town of Padiham near Burnley and describes himself as a "taxidermist/hunting and African hunting safari agent". He has been working in the industry for 30 years. He says that his best African trophies are a 15-inch Black springbuck, two 17-inch common reedbuck and a 42-

[453] http://www.blackthornsafaris.com/things-to-do/big-game/
[454] https://www.africahunting.com/members/andrew-denson.14212/
[455] https://www.mirror.co.uk/news/uk-news/brit-trophy-hunters-slay-at-20324100

inch Cape Buffalo, all of which he shot in the Eastern Cape. His favourite African trophies are bushpigs. He uses both rifles and bows and arrows on his hunting expeditions.[456]

In the 1980s his family moved to South Africa where his aunt was a manager on one of South Africa's largest private game reserves.[457] Photos have emerged of him with zebra trophies.[458]

Ivan Carter

Ivan Carter is a presenter on the Outdoor Channel. Brought up in Zimbabwe, he is – according to US media reports - a British citizen. He spends much of his time in the Bahamas.

Until recently he was an adviser on trophy hunting to US President Donald Trump.[459] Carter was a member of a controversial White House committee – disbanded after allegations it broke government rules - named the 'International Wildlife Conservation Council'. In contrast to what its name suggests, the committee – comprised almost entirely of trophy hunters and industry

---

[456] https://www.africahunting.com/members/andrew-denson.14212/

[457] https://www.mirror.co.uk/news/uk-news/brit-trophy-hunters-slay-at-20324100

[458] https://www.mirror.co.uk/news/uk-news/brit-trophy-hunters-slay-at-20324100

[459] "Trump Wildlife Protection Board Stuffed with Trophy Hunters", VOA News, 16 March 2018 https://www.voanews.com/usa/us-politics/trump-wildlife-protection-board-stuffed-trophy-hunters

figures - was set up to come up with policy proposals on how the American government could make it easier for hunters to bring home trophies of threatened species into the US. Its remit also included developing a positive image for trophy hunting, including by communicating the purported jobs created by the industry in Africa and elsewhere.

Carter has his own 'conservation' group called the Ivan Carter Wildlife Conservation Alliance which, it says, promotes "true wildlife conservation".[460] His website goes on to claim that "Ivan Carter has become well known in African wildlife circles for his dedication to all manner of conservation and conservation initiatives"[461].

Less well-known, though, is the fact that Carter is also a celebrated hunter and has been a professional hunting guide for the safari hunting industry since 1988. According to one industry website, he "spends over 180 days in the field each year in pursuit of dangerous game". The website goes on to add: "Ivan is a great advocate for sustainable and ethical hunting and truly believes in hunting as a conservation tool."[462]

However there is little conservation or ethical behaviour in evidence in a shocking unlisted video - believed to be the only video in existence showing a British trophy hunter in action - which has recently come to light. It shows Carter shooting wounded lions and

---

[460] https://ivancarterwca.org/
[461] https://www.ivancarter.com/who-is-ivan
[462] https://www.cordobadovehunting.com/the-value-of-game-by-ivan-carter.html

elephants, several hours after shooting them a first time before then leaving them in agony.[463]

The film is a promotional video for a 'double' rifle, which allows hunters to fire off two shots in quick succession. To a background of dramatic music, it contains clips of half a dozen different elephants being shot - some at close range - as well as lions and buffalos being killed by hunters. In one scene early on, Carter urges a fellow hunter to shoot an elephant again and again as it collapses and falls to the ground. He then shoots a lion himself before turning to the camera and saying: "That's why you carry a double rifle."

Carter continues: "If you're going to engage in the pursuit of large dangerous game, the classic rifle that's been built for that is a double rifle." He proceeds to explain in a matter of fact tone why he has chosen the particular brand of double rifle he is advertising.

In almost Blue Peter-style, he then says: "Here's a couple of clips that we've prepared just to show you one of the reasons why you want a double rifle in place of a bolt rifle when you're shooting close up big game." He proceeds to show a hunter using a bolt action rifle shooting a buffalo. The hunter – a client of Carter's - succeeds only in wounding the animal which, despite its injuries, somehow manages to escape into thick bush.

It's quickly followed by a clip featuring a hunter with a double rifle who shoots an elephant standing just a few feet away. Carter can be heard telling him to shoot the animal again. As the elephant collapses to the ground,

___

[463] http://unlistedvideos.com/vm.php?v=youtube-C-WJcYpNR0Q.html

the two joyfully embrace and run together towards the dying animal. "All my life I've wanted to hunt elephant," the euphoric hunter tells the cameraman. "Today was my day."

The film moves onto another elephant hunt. A trophy hunter shoots an elephant that is standing just a few yards away. Carter can be heard off camera saying: "Again in the ear!" As the animal slowly crumbles to the ground, an excited Carter is heard saying: "Look at that brilliant second shot – right in the earhole!"

The next segment is of a buffalo hunt. The animal is shot twice, twisting as it falls. A group of hunters can be heard to whoop and laugh in the background.

Carter takes up commentary again. This time his victim is a lion. "This was a lion we had wounded several hours previously," he says almost breathlessly as he walks through tall grass. Upon locating the injured animal he tells the viewer that "my first shot ... went right in just underneath his chin, it was enough to just turn him." A muted growl can be heard coming from the bush as Carter moves in, and then fires. "The second shot, I got him just on the cheek bone," he says in almost clinical tone.

With a laugh, he then adds: "Without a double gun, I would have been busy reloading as he took off and got on top of me!" He stands over the slain animal, then turns to the camera and says jauntily: "That's why you carry a double rifle!" There's almost a swagger to the delivery.

The video continues, this time with another elephant hunt. "This elephant had been previously wounded," says Carter as he goes up to the animal and shoots it from a distance of just a few inches.

Another elephant is shot, this time a calf. The young animal falls at the hunters' feet. "It was dead, and that's all that matters", says Carter. Yet another scene of an elephant being shot follows, after which Carter brings the film to a close with a segment to camera in which he invokes the merits of shooting with a double rifle.

The video ends with more dramatic music over a rapid succession of clips showing animals being shot.

It is not the only commercial video featuring Carter shooting animals while endorsing a brand of hunting equipment. He also stars in a video for Trijicon, an American manufacturer of rifle sights.[464] It includes a scene in which a leopard is shot out of a tree. At the end, Carter whips around to the camera and says: "I'm Ivan Carter and I use Trijicon. Do you?" The film fades to black amidst a backdrop of dramatic music punctuated by a series of rifle shots in rapid succession.

Safari Club International (SCI) has a Records Book which – among other things – lists the Professional Hunters who have helped their clients acquire the world's biggest trophies. The Records Book is used by many hunters to book themselves into hunts with Professional Hunters who are most likely to land them a listing in the much-coveted book. Ivan Carter features repeatedly within it, including for several of the largest-ever known African elephants as well as the biggest leopards ever shot by trophy hunters. In all, Carter has helped hunters to shoot 37 of the world's biggest

---

[464] https://www.youtube.com/watch?v=xtqNeGslFyE

animals, including 3 record-sized elephants and 2 record-sized leopards. The hunts took place in Zimbabwe, Botswana and Tanzania (for details see Appendix).

Scientists have warned that the deliberate pursuit of record-sized elephants could drive the species to extinction. The average size of elephant tusks is shrinking, a sign of a weakening gene pool indicating elephants are less likely to adapt to environmental challenges such as global warming.

Buffaloes, another of the 'African Big 5', and hippopotamuses are among the other animals to feature in the SCI Records Book alongside Carter's name. Like elephants, buffaloes are also said by scientists to be feeling the effects of 'artificial selection' as a result of trophy hunting. IUCN recently upgraded the extinction threat level of the once-plentiful Cape buffalo from 'Least Concern' to 'Near Threatened'.

For someone who claims to be a 'conservationist', Carter may in fact be helping to make it more likely that some of Africa's most iconic animals could one day disappear.

Chapter 5: European Trophy Hunters

NAME: Michel C Bergerac
NATIONALITY: French

"I, Michel C Bergerac, am an international businessman, a philanthropist, and a Fulbright scholar educated at the Sorbonne, Cambridge, and UCLA. I have been on the boards of Cornell Medical School, CBS, and Chase Bank, among others, and for many years I was chairman of Revlon, Inc., which I sold in 1985. I am currently a director of the World Wildlife Fund, a trustee of the New York Zoological Society, and a member of SCI."[465]

This resume, delivered by Bergerac himself, are his opening remarks in the chapter of a book about some of the world's leading trophy hunters. The former Revlon chief and WWF Director began trophy hunting in Kenya in 1967. He has 'done' the Africa Big Five - twice, in Mozambique as well as in Zambia. He has also hunted in Ethiopia, South Africa, Sudan and the Central African Republic, often accompanied by his wife Alicia.

His trophy room is located within a 16th century villa and includes lions, elephants and many other species including animals that are no longer hunted in the wild because they are now either extinct or down to the very last handful of animals. They include the addax and the

---

[465] "Great hunters: their trophy rooms & collections", Vol. 3, 2001 Safari Press

scimitar-horned oryx plus "the great elephants of the Tana river, and the Iranian ibex and Iranian sheep."

A roaring fireplace takes centre-stage in the room. Behind the sofa which faces the fireplace is a large table with a full lion skin covering it, the head (mouth prised open) at one end. Elephant tusks reach upwards either side. A leopard skin is draped over one sofa, while a rhino's head looks upwards toward the ceiling.

There is a zebra skin rug, and a bear's head mounted on the wall. A large skylight overhead serves to illuminate the room and the trophies within. A puma head/shoulder mount is located to one side of the room in an alcove.

"Though it doesn't make a great difference to me, several are world records, sixteen of which are in the top ten. Others are 'Number 1' because of the unique circumstances that surrounded my taking them.

"My trophies help me recall great memories and great friendships. Good and bad shots. Drinks by the campfire. Super meals in camp washed down with good wine and tall tales."

Bergerac features prominently in Safari Club International's Records Book.[466] His top record trophies include elephants shot in Zambia, Central African Republic, Ethiopia and Mozambique; a lion shot in Botswana; a leopard and a spotted hyena he shot in Tanzania; and a scimitar-horned oryx shot by him in Chad (the species is now extinct). He also has a record

---

[466] SCI Record Book of Trophy Animals – edition IX, Vol 1, Africa Field Edition. SCI, 1997

addax trophy from Sudan - only a few dozen addaxes today remain in the wild.

He has won over 20 prizes with Safari Club International including its Pinnacle of Achievement award, the Grand Slam Cats of the World Award, the Grand Slam Africa 29 Award, the Global Hunting Award, the Hunting Achievement Award, the Animals of Europe Award, and the Animals of Africa Award.[467] (For a full list of his Awards and Records Book trophies see the appendix.)

NAMES: Jacques & Micheline Henrijean
NATIONALITIES: Belgian and Swiss
ESTIMATED KILLS: 240

Hunting expedition highlights:
150 hunts to six continents
The Persian Gulf for a rare Kerman hybrid
The Gobi Desert of Mongolia and the Altai Mountains
The Northwest Territories for polar bear
Afghanistan (Pamirs) for yaks
African Big Five

Jacques Henrijean first learned to shoot birds at the age of eight. In 1958, he went on his first hunt for a chamois near Garmisch Partenkirchen, a German ski resort in Bavaria. According to a book about Jacques and his famous trophy room, "the excitement of this trip encouraged Jacques to take up wild boar shooting". He

---

[467] Safari magazine – Awards 2015, Safari Club International

also began a quest for sheep, starting with the shooting of a Stone sheep in British Columbia in 1970.

In 1972, he went on his first African safari, travelling to the Tsavo National Park, Kenya where he shot a black rhino.

Jacques met Micheline in the US at the launch of Apollo 11. They went on their first hunt together just before their wedding. For their honeymoon, they went hunting at the Royal Reserve near Tehran, Iran, where they shot several rams from a herd of Alborz red sheep. They also visited the Khosh-Yeilagh Wildlife Reserve where they shot a rare Trans-Caspian urial. Among the other sheep they have shot together are Armenian, red, Shiraz and Laristan sheep, all of them in Iran.

Jacques has won the prestigious Weatherby Big Game Trophy Award. He has also won Belgium's clay pigeon shooting championship five times. He was part of the Olympic skeet team and has held the national record for Belgium in skeet since 1966.

Micheline, meanwhile, is a leading trophy hunter in her own right, having shot one of the world's rarest species of sheep, the Kamchatka bighorn that inhabits the Putorona Mountains in north-western Siberia close to the Arctic circle. A story about this hunt was the subject of an article published in the May/June 1992 edition of Sporting Classics magazine. Micheline Henrijean was the first woman in the world to shoot a record-book Marco Polo sheep in the Afghan Pamirs, and she has also shot the No.3 world-record giant forest hog in Ethiopia and the world's No.3 Peters duiker in Cameroon.

As a couple, they were the first and – for a while - the only couple in the world to both be 'Super Slammers', meaning that they had both shot 12 major world sheep 'specimens', in industry vernacular.

The Henrijeans have built a trophy room next to their home which houses 185 of their trophies. More than 150 have since been donated to the Museum of Natural Sciences in Brussels (Institut Royal des Sciences Naturelles de Belgique).

According to a book about their famous trophy collection, "Jacques insured some of the first Toyota cars imported into Europe from Japan, beginning with five or six cars per shipment, growing to nearly 48,000 a year for Belgium within the first decade.

"To relax, Jacques went bird shooting."[468]

NAME: Bela Hidvegi
NATIONALITY: Hungarian
CONFIRMED KILLS: 350

Hungary's Bela Hidvegi is one of the world's top trophy hunters of all time.

He began hunting as a child after being given his first air rifle by his father. His parents were landowners in Nagyszenas. His first hunting trophies were sparrows.

Hidvegi moved to the UK at the age of 20 after the Soviet invasion of Hungary. He studied agriculture and food engineering and then began working for a company

---

[468] "Great hunters: their trophy rooms & collections", vol.6, Safari Press

that developed a process to stop soft drinks cans corroding. He subsequently worked for Nestle and was a marketing executive for companies that sold food processing machines before starting his own company in his native Hungary.

He says that "hunting is in my blood. It is either in you or it is not in you. Nobody but another hunter who has it in his blood can understand."[469] He has an English wife who often joins him on pheasant shoots. He has 45 African safaris under his belt and says his great love is mountain hunting where he shoots wild sheep.

"After I started mountain hunting I got a .257 Weatherby and shot my three markhors with it. For driven boar I have a .300 Winchester and for mountain hunting I now have the .30-378 Weatherby. This is a great, great rifle."

To date, he has shot hundreds of different species in 6 different continents. Within Europe he has hunted in Spain, Austria, the Czech Republic, and the UK. He hunts twice a year in Africa where his favourite species include spiral-horned antelopes. His African hunting expeditions have included Tanzania, Ethiopia, Zimbabwe, the Central African Republic, Cameroon, South Africa and Zambia. He has also hunted in Alaska, the Rocky Mountains, the Hindu Kush and the Himalayas.

His trophy collection includes 150 life-size animals mounted on plinths depicting their natural authentic habitats. Many of his trophies are on display at the

---

[469] "Great hunters: their trophy rooms & collections", vols. 6 & 8, Safari Press

Keszthely Helikon Castle Museum. A new building there was paid for by the European Union and houses 170 of his trophies. There are 350 trophies of his covering more than 70 species which can be viewed at the University of Sopron. The display was opened in 2012 and was attended by Hungary's Deputy Prime Minister. Among his most famous kills is a 176-pound leopard which he shot in Tanzania.

His trophies include one of a polar bear that has been transformed into a rug, complete with head. He has a large number of wall-mounted trophies which are each labelled with a plaque, many of which proudly bear the message 'Gold Medal trophy'. A single elephant ear and tail hang as wall mounts over a leopard floor rug. As with the polar bear, the leopard's head is intact and its eyes and mouth open, almost as if it is gasping for breath. In a wooded scene, a full-size brown bear 'encounters' a pair of wolves.

An archway made of two huge elephant tusks form the entrance to a raised area of the museum which contains the heads and skins of zebras on the walls. Hidvegi also has trophies of tigers, lions, cheetahs, hippos and hyenas.

In 2006, Hidvegi founded the Hungarian chapter of Safari Club International. Hungarian hunters are now killing growing numbers of animals, including lions, each year. He has published a number of books, articles and DVDs about trophy hunting, some of which have been translated into English. They include 'Hunting Dreams' and 'I had a dream'. He has been awarded the Order of Merit of the Hungarian Republic.

He holds the world record for a bay duiker trophy, and has shot a gold medal Mountain Nyala. Among his other industry-recognised kills are a warthog with 18 inches tusks, a Marco Polo ram with 62.5-inch horns, and three subspecies of the endangered markhor. Twenty-five of his trophies are listed among SCI's 'Top Ten'.

He is a Life Member and Honorary International Director of Safari Club International. In 2007, Hidvegi was awarded SCI's most prestigious prize, the World Hunting Award Ring. He has also won awards for his sheep and goat hunting exploits, won the Carlo Caldesi Award (twice) and the Ullman Award.

"I have hunted in jungles, on savannahs, in pine forests, over tundra, in swamps, in groves, and on plains," he says. "In fact, I have been everywhere in the natural world where it is possible to hunt legally. As I think back over the past decades, memories of my hunts flash before me. There were so many great experiences with their joyous highs."[470]

He has been awarded around 40 of Safari Club International's top prizes, including the Pantheon Award - which has only ever been given to fewer than a dozen trophy hunters.[471] (For a full list, visit the Appendix.)

---

[470] "Great hunters: their trophy rooms & collections", vol.6 & 8, Safari Press

[471] Safari magazine – Awards 2015, Safari Club International

NAME: Dr Egon J Lechner
NATIONALITY: German

Germany, after the US, provides the world's largest source of globe-trotting trophy hunters. Lechner is one of Germany's, and the world's, all-time top safari hunters.

An economist by profession, he is author of a number of books about hunting and has led several regional and international hunting organisations. He has gone on more than 150 hunting expeditions around the world – some to places he says are now closed and/or unknown to foreigners.

Born near Munich, he claims to be a descendent of a long line of Bavarian-Tyrolean hunters. He also claims to have opened up hunting for bear and bezoar-ibex in Turkey, Sind ibex in Pakistan, and to have discovered a population of Nubian ibex between the Nile River and Egypt's Red Sea in 1986 which was previously thought to be extinct.

He was the first hunter in the modern era to have hunted Marco Polo sheep in the Pamir mountains of Tadzhikistan in 1987, and was also the first foreign hunter to shoot saiga antelope in Kazakhstan and brown bear on the Pacific side of Kamchatka.

According to a book recording his exploits, Lechner "fulfilled his life-dream" by bagging a desert bighorn sheep in Mexico's Sonora desert, said to be the best ram ever measured from Sonora by the SCI record book.[472]

---

[472] "Great hunters: their trophy rooms & collections", vol.1, 1997 Safari Press

He is a member of Safari Club International and the International Professional Hunters Association. He also claims to be a member of WWF.

Lechner's trophy room features an inside balcony that overlooks cougars, leopards, a large bear and an even larger polar bear. Alongside the balcony is a wall which features the heads of multiple wild sheep and goats. Among other trophies, he possesses a zebra skin rug.[473]

Lechner features in SCI's Records Book for having shot some of the world's biggest-ever animals including a record-size leopard and spotted hyena.[474] (See Appendix for details.)

NAME: Tony Sanchez-Arino
NATIONALITY: Spanish
CONFIRMED KILLS: 4,044

Hunting career highlights:
1,317 elephants
340 lions
127 black rhino
167 leopards
2,093 buffaloes

Tony Sanchez-Arino may be the world's biggest living trophy hunter. Only 12 hunters in history have shot more than 130 lions, and only 13 have killed more

---

[473] "Great hunters: their trophy rooms & collections", vol.1, 1997 Safari Press

[474] SCI Record Book of Trophy Animals – edition IX, Vol 1, Africa Field Edition. SCI, 1997

than 1000 elephants. Tony Sanchez-Arino is thought to be the only man ever to have done both.

Sanchez-Arino hails from Valencia, Spain and is a personal friend of former Spanish King Juan Carlos, himself a keen elephant hunter. He says that "hunting is an art." He has also admitted, however, that hunting could cause the extinction of the elephant: "it has become quite clear that the African elephant has suffered enormous and irremediable losses, and it is apparent that unless these activities cease, the African elephant will be hunted to extinction in the wild within our lifetime, to the shame of humanity". He has also written about his regret that "the long tuskers have long ago vanished forever, and only by extremely good luck can the hunter come across a good trophy."[475]

He went on his first elephant hunt in Gabon in 1952 and started guiding hunts in 1960, which he has continued to do into his 80s. He hunted extensively for ivory throughout what was then French Equatorial Africa, the Belgian Congo, Cameroon, Sudan, and Somalia. Sanchez-Arino hunted in Kenya until trophy hunting was banned there in 1977, and more recently has hunted and guided hunters in Zambia, Uganda, Angola, Sudan, Zimbabwe, Botswana and South Africa.

Even in his 80s he spends as much as 8 months of the year hunting elephants and other 'African Big Five' animals. Since 2014 alone he has killed 13 elephants, 10 buffaloes, 1 lion and 2 leopards.

---

[475] "Elephants, Ivory & Hunters" Tony Sanchez-Arino, Safari Press Inc, 2002

Fellow trophy hunter Robert Wilson, writing in the introduction to Sanchez-Arino's 2002 book 'Elephants, Ivory & Hunters', says: "There is not a single country in Africa in which he has not hunted. If Tony Sanchez-Arino is not the greatest elephant hunter of them all, he shares the title with a handful of the very best. If Tony Sanchez-Arino is not a hero for our time, or of any time, who is?," he adds.

Few people had heard of Sanchez-Arino when he came out in public defence of beleaguered Spanish King Juan Carlos in 2012 after photos of the monarch emerged showing him killing elephants in Botswana. In an interview for Spanish TV, he said that people opposed to trophy hunting should also oppose abortion: "You cannot talk about killing," he said. "Killing is a disgusting act; hunting is an art. If you are sensitive to elephant hunting, I suppose (you) will also be sensitive to the thousands of abortions that are taking place in Spain."[476]

The king was forced to step down as President of WWF-Spain and abdicated from the throne two years later. However Sanchez-Arino says he still takes gifts of buffalo and antelope meat to the ex-king whenever he returns from his African hunting trips.[477]

---

[476]
https://www.telecinco.es/elprogramadeanarosa/corazon/antonio-sanchez-marino-cazador-amigo-rey-defiende-la-caceria-elefantes_0_1398075718.html

[477] https://www.levante-emv.com/comunitat-valenciana/2012/06/18/rey-caza-legalmente-paga-alto-precio-piezas/897849.html

Sanchez-Arino started hunting young and acquired his first fire-arm at the age of 9, a single barrelled shotgun. At the age of 13 he shot 14 rabbits with a 20-guage in the space of a single day. At the age of 17, he killed 54 rabbits in one morning.

In an article written in 2016, 'The 13 hunters of the 1000 elephants',[478] he talks about the 13 hunters who have reached the 1000 elephant tally as a "brotherhood" who between them had taken a total of 22,300 elephants.[479] He also boasts about the size of some of the tusks he has obtained: "Among the trophies I got 43 elephants with tusks exceeding one hundred pounds (45 kilos) with my best example a pair of (tusks) with 132 and 129 pounds (59.8 and 58.4kg) followed by another of 127 and 123 pounds (57.5 and 55.7kg) in addition to a single-(tusked animal) of 131 pounds (59.3kg).

"Numerically my personal record was 20 in 75 minutes!", he adds excitedly.[480]

Writing in 'Elephants, Ivory & Hunters', Sanchez-Arino talks of his good fortune to have been able to earn a living as a hunter. "For the last 49 years I have constantly been hunting elephant and conducting safaris

[478] "The 13 hunters of the 1000 elephants", by Tony Sanchez-Arino https://cazawonke.com/c28-internacional/65584-los-trece-cazadores-los-mil-elefantes-iv-tony-sanchez-arino

[479] "The 13 hunters of the 1000 elephants", by Tony Sanchez-Arino https://cazawonke.com/c28-internacional/65584-los-trece-cazadores-los-mil-elefantes-iv-tony-sanchez-arino

[480] "The 13 hunters of the 1000 elephants", by Tony Sanchez-Arino https://cazawonke.com/c28-internacional/65584-los-trece-cazadores-los-mil-elefantes-iv-tony-sanchez-arino

in the most diverse parts of Africa, covering practically the whole of the continent.

"I consider myself to be one of the few lucky mortals who has managed to make a profession of his greatest love, arriving in Africa still in time for the cream of the hunting."

NAME: Marcial Gomez Sequeira
NATIONALITY: Spanish
CONFIRMED KILLS: 2,000

Hunting career highlights:
400 different species in approximately 500 hunting trips across 5 continents
His Spanish hunting trophies number approximately 2,000 animals, including 120 gold, 110 silver and 122 bronze medal trophies
14 elephant trophies, at least 6 of which are record book-class
40 species of wild sheep, 29 wild goats, 14 wild oxen.

Fellow Spaniard Marcial Gomez Sequeira was born in Madrid in 1940. He studied medicine at University and took his first Africa safari in 1971 in Angola. Since then he has been on more than 50 African hunting expeditions in over 15 different countries, some of which no longer allow trophy hunting.

In 1987 he travelled to Australia and New Zealand where in the space of 31 days he shot every species permitted. Shortly after, he spent 21 days in North America where he shot the last 7 of the animals he lacked to complete the list of all species it is permitted to hunt in the US and Canada. His North America trophy collection now totals 60 species and 55 exotics. He has hunted in the Philippines where his sambar deer trophy is thought to have been the first entry of this new species in SCI's Records Book

His trophy collection is so voluminous that he has had to enlarge his trophy room on a number of occasions. Sequeira has hunted elephants with his 10 year-old daughter Marta, but says he has now stopped hunting elephants because "his elephant tally was already sufficient."[481]

Sequeira has won all of Safari Club International's prestigious 'Inner Circle Awards' at Diamond level – the highest level possible – as well as SCI's Grand Slam Awards. In all he has received approximately 50 awards from SCI.[482] He also has over 70 entries in SCI's Record Books that come in the Top Ten. His top records include elephants shot in the Central African Republic, Sudan, and Mozambique; white rhinos shot in South Africa; a lion he shot in Botswana; leopards shot in Zimbabwe and the Central African Republic; and a spotted hyena killed in Mozambique.[483] (See the appendix for a full list of Sequeira's awards and records.)

Sequeira's personal trophy room resembles a warehouse in both appearance and size. It features row upon row of mounted heads and skulls. One wall alone

---

[481] "Great hunters: their trophy rooms & collections", vols. 2 & 5, Safari Press

[482] Safari magazine – Awards 2015, Safari Club International

[483] SCI Record Book of Trophy Animals – edition IX, Vol 1, Africa Field Edition. SCI, 1997

has over 40 deer heads and skulls. There are also heads of hippos, rhinos and bears. In one long room, there are several bodies of bears and multiple leopards, pumas, a lion and even a tiger. Other trophies include a polar bear and an arctic fox. There are countless antlers, and the bodies of wild goats, leopards, jaguars, leopard skin rugs, and lions. The heads of mountain sheep and goats with impressive curled horns feature prominently.

Other species include lynxes, various smaller wild cats, and a wolf. A pair of large elephant tusks are mounted on pedestals. Crocodiles mingle with wild boar. A pair of leopards have been placed on rock ledges which are embedded into a wall. An elephant's head can be seen with its trunk rearing up over a large white fireplace. A solitary turtle sits next to a bear skin rug.

Sequeira has announced plans to open the world's largest hunting museum in Madrid in order to display his trophies.[484]

NAME: Sergey Yastrzhemskiy
NATIONALITY: Russian
CONFIRMED KILLS: 251

Hunting career highlights:
180 hunts on 6 continents and in 44 countries
251 species of animals
250 trophies listed in the SCI Records Book

---

[484] https://www.thetimes.co.uk/article/disgust-over-world-s-largest-museum-of-hunting-trophies-jqlsbbx9z

Sergey Yastrzhemskiy is a familiar name among seasoned international media correspondents. As a former Moscow correspondent of The Times put it, Yastrzhemskiy is Russia's "voice of power. For 10 years, including Putin's first 8 as President, he was the Kremlin's best-known spokesman in the west... He was spokesman for Boris Yeltsin at his most inebriated, adviser and spin-doctor in chief for Putin in the darkest days of the Chechen war and Russia's special envoy to Europe at a time (2004-8) when Russia's relationship with Europe was crashing on the rocks of the Ukrainian revolution and the murder of a prominent Putin critic in the middle of London."[485] Yastrzhemskiy has also served as a Russian Ambassador.

What is less well known is that he is also one of the world's leading trophy hunters.

Yastrzhemskiy went on his first African safari in 1997, flying to Tanzania's famous Selous Game Reserve.[486] When he returned to Africa some years later, however, he said things had changed dramatically. Whereas on his first trip he saw large groups of elephants every day, "it was different in 2013... First there was a large number of hyenas, for two weeks I did not see a single living elephant. Hyenas multiplied due to the fact that there was just a massacre, the mass destruction of elephants. During this period, the number of animals of Tanzania decreased dramatically – from

---

[485] "Sergey Yastrzhemskiy: from the Kremlin to Africa", The Times, October 30 2014, Giles Whittell

[486] "Great Hunters – their trophy rooms an collections", volume 8, Safari Press, 2017

100,000 to 12-15,000."[487] He points the finger of blame solely at poachers, though.

Among his list of hunting trophies are the African 'Big Five'. He has killed hippos and crocodiles, and has likened his new past-time to a drug. He has built a trophy building adjacent to his home 60 km outside Moscow which has been described as being "a cross between being in the middle of Africa and being in a natural history museum".[488] He designed it with the help of his wife, Anastasia. "Our idea was to combine four stand-alone areas into one big room: a museum, an office, a kitchen, and a cozy 'restaurant' for friends... and we succeeded!

"Our trophy room soon became the hub of our domestic life. That was where we celebrated all the major holidays and filmed my TV hunting shows. That was also a place where my younger children, Anissia and Milan, began to play.

"This is one of my favourite places in life. Every time I see those magnificent creatures of nature, my eyes light up, for they remind me of the vivid experiences I have had, and adrenaline starts coursing through my blood."[489]

Inside there are certificates and plaques on glass shelves; commemorative plates, bronze statues and framed diplomas. There are bodies of bears, boars, antelopes, deer, hyenas, lions and a polar bear. The skin of a crocodile hangs from a wall. Wolves have been

[487] interview with Lina Sarimova, www.Realnoevremya.com

[488] "Great Hunters – their trophy rooms an collections", volume 8, Safari Press, 2017

[489] "Great Hunters – their trophy rooms an collections", volume 8, Safari Press, 2017

transformed into rugs, zebra skins into stool covers. Shoulder mounts of animals are packed together with some fifty on one wall alone. An eagle 'flies' suspended from the ceiling over the fireplace. There is a family of 3 wolves - their eyes make them look eerily alive; one has its paws crossed in an almost nonchalant manner. There are life-size lynxes, caracals and pumas too.

An elephant head, complete with ears and trunk, contrasts with the small body of an otter. Four elephant tusks hang suspended over a table carved in the shape of the African continent. A rhino's head occupies centre stage, hung over an elegant stone and wood fireplace. There are endless rows and columns of animal heads including zebras and antelopes. A lion 'leaps out' by a set of stairs.

Yastrzhemskiy has won almost 40 awards with SCI, including some of its most prestigious prizes such as the Pinnacle of Achievement Award, Zenith Award, Grand Slam Cats of the World Award, Grand Slam Bears of the World Award, Grand Slam Africa 29 Award, the African Big Five and the Hunting Achievement Award.[490] (For a full list see the Appendix.)

---

[490] Safari magazine – Awards 2015, Safari Club International

Chapter 6: American Trophy Hunters

NAME: Steven Chancellor
CONFIRMED KILLS: 482[491]

Hunting career highlights:[492]
Six elephants, two rhinos, 18 lions (Botswana, Zambia and Tanzania), and 13 leopards (eleven in Botswana, one in Zambia, one in South Africa)
Five Argentinean pumas In South America using a handgun

Steven Chancellor and his wife Terri are multi-award-winning hunters[493] and generous donors to the trophy hunting industry.[494] Steven Chancellor is also a major donor and fundraiser for US President Donald Trump.[495]
Until recently, he sat on a White House committee to advise President Donald Trump on relaxing national and international hunting restrictions.[496] A long-time

---

[491] "Trophy Madness", HSUS, HSI & Shield Political Research; September 2015 https://www.hsi.org/wp-content/uploads/assets/pdfs/trophy-madness-report.pdf

[492] "Trophy Madness", HSUS, HSI & Shield Political Research; September 2015 https://www.hsi.org/wp-content/uploads/assets/pdfs/trophy-madness-report.pdf

[493] Safari magazine – Awards 2015, Safari Club International

[494] The Chancellors are major donors to Safari Club International Foundation

[495]
https://eu.indystar.com/story/news/politics/2017/04/19/here-hoosiers-who-gave-big-trumps-inauguration/100654958/

Republican[497], Chancellor is chairman of a company called the American Patriot Group based in his home state of Indiana which includes a company that supplies ready meals to the US military.[498]

Chancellor was represented by Conservation Force when he sought to bring home trophies of a lion from an endangered population in Zimbabwe. There was a US import ban in place at the time.[499] He has donated up to $49,000 to Safari Club International's Foundation (SCIF) as well as to its "Hunter Legacy 100 Fund", which SCI describes as comprising members who "have given generously to endow the SCIF for generations to come."

Craig Packer, a lion researcher, has calculated that Chancellor has shot approximately 50 lions. Many of them can be seen at his home in Indiana.[500] Humane Society International estimates that he has killed up to 500 animals, including a large number of leopards, elephants and rhinos.

Until recently, a lion shot by Chancellor in Chobe, Botswana was credited as being the biggest lion ever to have been killed by any trophy hunter. Chancellor's other Record Trophies include lions shot in Tanzania,

[496] https://www.wideopenspaces.com/trumps-wildlife-conservation-board-packed-with-hunters/

[497] https://www.nydailynews.com/news/politics/trump-wildlife-protection-board-packed-trophy-hunters-article-1.3876922

[498] https://www.bloomberg.com/profile/person/17961362

[499] "Trump wildlife protection board stuffed with trophy hunters", AP, Mar 15, 2018

[500] "Who would want to kill a lion? Inside the minds of trophy hunters", Elle Hunt, Guardian/Observer, 4 November 2018

Zambia and Botswana's Linyanto Delta; African elephants and white rhinos shot in South Africa; and leopards shot in Botswana, Zambia and South Africa. His wife Terri also appears in the Records Book courtesy of lions and leopards she shot in Botswana.[501]

Between them, the couple have won over 40 major hunting prizes with Safari Club International including SCI's International Hunting Award, the World Hunting Award, the Pinnacle of Achievement award, the Crowning Achievement Award, the Hunting Achievement Award, the Top Ten Award, the Grand Slam Cats of the World Award, and the Grand Slam Bears of the World Award. Both of them have won SCI's Africa Big Five Award.[502] (For a full list of records and awards see the Appendix.)

The Weatherby Foundation recently presented Steven Chancellor with the Weatherby Magnum Award, a newly-created prize given for the very first time and designed "to recognize individuals who have made exceptional and unusual contributions to the sport of hunting and conservation".[503]

---

[501] SCI Record Book of Trophy Animals – edition IX, Vol 1, Africa Field Edition. SCI, 1997

[502] Safari magazine – Awards 2015, Safari Club International

[503] http://huntingreport.com/fedrico-sada-recipient-of-2006-weatherby-conservation-award/

NAME: CJ McElroy
CONFIRMED KILLS: approx. 450

Key Awards:
The Weatherby Award
The NRA 'Silver Bullet' Award
The Shikar Asiatic Big Game Trophy
The Air France Trophy
The SCI International Hunting Award

CJ McElroy is arguably one of the most colourful as well as influential figures in the world of trophy hunting in recent times. He single-handedly founded Safari Club International, which is today's largest and most powerful trophy hunting organisation. One of SCI's top hunting prizes was named in his honour, and he was inducted into the Safari Club International Hall of Fame in 1982.

Born in 1913, he began his professional career as a night-club 'bouncer' and carpet layer. At the end of World War II he ran a bar with his wife Alvie and built cabins in California's Big Bear Lake area. He went on to own Los Angeles' biggest flooring business.

McElroy went on his first African safari in 1959, travelling to Kenya where he hunted with famed professional hunting guide Glen Cottar. He subsequently went on hunts in 50 countries on 6 continents over a 50 year period, including 75 African safaris, 41 hunting expeditions in Europe and Asia, and 62 hunts in various parts of North America. He accumulated hundreds of record trophies, many of which are still in SCI's all-time top 20%.

The SCI Records Book contains no fewer than 354 entries from McElroy, of which 92 animals are in the Top Ten. He has shot elephants, walruses, rhinos, hippos, polar bears, leopards, wolves and lions. He has killed tigers in India, jaguars in Mexico, sheep and goats on every continent, and shot many of the largest Scimitar-horned oryxes on record, three of them featuring in SCI's all-time top 10.

He once said that he started hunting at the age of 8 when he obtained his first rifle, a .22 Hamilton rifle. He began trapping then too and by the following year had his own string of 40 traps.

Photographs of his personal trophy room show huge tusks forming an archway in front of a long sofa and coffee table. Every inch of the room's stone wall is filled with mounts of animals. An elephant's head is sat on a wall overlooking the room. An upright polar bear stands next to a bear while a zebra looks on from within a large in-set alcove.[504]

Interviewed in 1996 by John J Jackson III, who was then SCI's President, McElroy said: "I personally think that the hunting of elephant is probably the greatest sport in all of hunting, and as you know, I have done it all."[505]

McElroy's top Records Book trophies include lions shot in Zambia and Tanzania; leopards shot in Kenya and Angola; black rhinos and elephants killed in Kenya; white rhinos shot in South Africa; scimitar-horned

---

[504] "Great hunters – their trophy rooms and collections", vol. 1, 1997 Safari Pres

[505] "Elephant hunting – absolutely the greatest hunt in the world", SAFARI Magazine January/February 1996

oryxes, Dama gazelles and addaxes killed in Chad; and hyenas from Zimbabwe.[506]

McElroy's Records Book Trophies

Africa – total: 216 top ten: 53
Asia – total: 39. Top 10: 20
North America – total: 54. Top 10: 5
Europe: total: 24. Top 10: 7
Exotics – total: 9. Top 10: 3
South America – total: 6. Top 10: 4
South pacific – total: 6.

Grand total: 354 of which 92 are 'Top 10' Trophies.

(For a full list see the Appendix).

NAME: John J Jackson III

"I can plainly see the African lion that has leaped into the air the moment its head snaps backward and explodes with smoke from my bullet" – John J Jackson III[507]

John J Jackson III is arguably the most influential person in the world of trophy hunting today.

---

[506] SCI Record Book of Trophy Animals – edition IX, Vol 1, Africa Field Edition. SCI, 1997

[507] "Great hunters – their trophy rooms and collections", vol 1, 1997 Safari Press

His grandfather John Jackson Sr was New Orleans' police chief while his father John J Jackson Jr - who taught his son about firearms - was a New Orleans murder detective. However it was his uncle who taught him to hunt.

John J Jackson III became a big game hunter in the 1970s. At the same time he also undertook *pro bono* legal work helping hunters to bring trophies back into the US if they were blocked by the authorities. He went on to become President of Safari Club International where he radically revamped the organisation's legal and lobbying operations. He subsequently set up 'Conservation Force' to lobby governments and international institutions such as CITES to remove restrictions on the hunting of endangered species.

In a recent interview for National Geographic, Jackson described elephant hunting as "the most intimate, real relationship one can have with elephant. Nothing else in life is more satisfying than an elephant hunt."[508] In fact Jackson has often expressed his love of elephant hunting. When he was President of SCI, he wrote: "Many hunters, including me, have found it to be so far superior an activity as to overshadow all other hunts... Believe me, there is no greater hunt on the face of the earth than that quest for a trophy elephant.

"If he can afford it, every hunter owes it to himself to become one of those who really know the elephant. On my own tombstone I want but these few words: 'Here lies John J Jackson III. He knew the African elephant'."[509]

---

508 "Controversy swirls around the recent US suspension of sport-hunted elephant trophies", blog.nationalgeograophic.org, May 6, 2014 – by Christina Russo

His trophies include those of polar bears and several record-breaking lions, elephants and leopards.

His wife Chrissie – a former yacht broker - is also a keen hunter and has served as Vice-President of Safari Club International's Executive Committee. She was previously President of SCI's Louisiana Chapter. She has joined her husband on many of his hunting expeditions, and helped him to found Conservation Force. She is a Life Member of Dallas Safari Club and the NRA. She holds several world fishing records including for tarpon and barracuda, and has shot a number of animals which appear as world records with the Boone & Crockett Club (antelope) and the bow-hunting Pope & Young association (elk, elephant and Cape Buffalo).

She has been quoted as saying: "Few things in all the world are equal to letting an arrow fly at a reeking bull during the rut high in the Rockies. I've made it a permanent part of my life by going every year, as I have Africa 44 times. Nothing offers my husband and me more as a couple or awakens my senses more as an individual."[510]

SCI's Record Books show that Jackson has shot some of the world's largest animals including African elephants in Tanzania and Ethiopia; lions and leopards in Tanzania; and a hyena in Ethiopia (for details see Appendix).[511] Despite this, Jackson has been able to

---

[509] "Elephant hunting – absolutely the greatest hunt in the world", John J Jackson, Safari magazine, January/February 1996

[510] https://www.conservationforce.org/chrissie-jackson

[511] SCI Record Book of Trophy Animals – edition IX, Vol 1, Africa Field Edition. SCI, 1997

become a member of the inner circle of a number of international organisations that set hunting and conservation policies. He sits on a number of committees of the IUCN, the world conservation organisation, and his group Conservation Force has acquired official Observer status within CITES and the United Nations.[512]

NAME: Mark Sullivan

Mark Sullivan is a Professional Hunter who runs a safari business called Nitro Express Safaris. He has also produced a series of controversial DVDs about his hunting expeditions which some have likened to 'snuff movies'.

In a printed promotional catalogue, one such film – entitled "Death Rush" - is described as "hands down… Sullivan's finest movie ever featuring the absolute best life and death, kill or be killed footage of his career… Perfectly filmed and beautifully edited, this movie has over-the-top adrenaline." Another film, 'Sudden Death', features a hunt for a wounded lion.

'Africa's Black Death' is called "the movie that has become a Legend… Over 20 buffalo shot on camera plus three great maned lion." 'Simba', meanwhile, is said to be "the finest lion hunting movie ever made. Follow Sullivan and his clients as they stalk and kill four great maned lion. The farthest shot, just 38 yards away. The closest, a mere 28 yards. Thrill as massive monster lion are taken right before your eyes".

---

[512] www.conservationforce.org

There are many more. 'Death on the run' is full of "non-stop life and death action... Unquestioningly one of the greatest movies ever made". Another, 'm'Bongo – Africa's Deadliest game', is "pure heart-pounding Cape Buffalo action unlike any you've ever seen. Eighty gun shots in 62 minutes. Viewers are advised to wear ear protection when watching this movie. Marvel as huge bulls get pulverised with .416s, .458s, and the ultimate nail-pounder the .577 Nitro Express."[513]

In one scene, a hunter is heard to say: "we can shoot him right now or we can let that buffalo decide how it's gone (sic) die".

His hunting lodge is famous for dressing up African staff in colonial-era dress as they wait on (white) clientele. Sullivan is adamant that he is an animal-lover: "People think Hunters are from a different planetary system, that we have no love, no compassion for the beauty around us. But if the truth be known, we love animals more than so called animal lovers themselves".[514]

Sullivan says his videos are popular among visitors to Safari Club International's conventions. An American newspaper once accompanied Sullivan on a hunt for a lion and recorded what happened: "The great beast has a quizzical expression on his face, blinking lazily at the actions of these strange, mostly hairless bipeds. He turns slightly and ruffles his long, blond mane, which encircled his head like an oversize crown. There is no sign he recognises the danger...

---

[513] www.marksullivanhuntingvideos.com
[514] https://www.africahunting.com/threads/listen-to-mark-sullivans-disgusting-words.4055/

"The first shot hits the lion in the neck, the impact of the blow forcing all 450 pounds of muscle, fur and teeth to cartwheel head over hindquarters. He roars. Then comes the second shot. And the third. The creature rolls into its side, and with a last shudder, dies. It is all over - except for the congratulations.

"'You've just shot a great lion,' Sullivan exclaims, grasping the man's hand. 'Look at this beautiful, beautiful mane. This will look excellent in your trophy room!' The man grins in triumph at the video camera that is recording the event."[515]

NAME: Chuck Adams

Major Awards:
More than 100 Pope and Young bow-hunting trophies
The only bowhunter to complete five 'Grand Slams' on American deer

Chuck Adams' list of records is one of the most extraordinary in the hunting world. He holds at least 5 bowhunting world records. He has the most Pope & Young World Records. He is the first bowhunter ever to kill all 27 species of North American big game animals. He has twice as many bowhunting record trophies as any other bowhunter in history, with 122 confirmed and another 36 pending confirmation.

---

[515] 'The noble hunter safari guide Mark Sullivan', Darrin Hostetler, Phoenix New Times, July 17, 1993

In all he has a total of 189 archery animals in SCI's bowhunting record book – more than any other bowhunter in history. He has killed 73 records book-eligible deer, more than any other hunter. During one 12-month period alone, Adams killed 13 official Pope & Young record book-size animals.

He is the youngest person ever inducted into the 'big three' bowhunting halls of fame – SCI's Bowhunting Hall of Honor, the National Bowhunters Hall of Fame, and the Archery Hall of Fame. Industry insiders say that Adams may be the most accomplished bowhunter on the planet. He regularly appears on the Outdoor TV Channel and on the 'Easton Bowhunting' TV show.

"As soon as I could walk I was trying to toddle along hunting behind my dad and grandad," he says. He was 12 years old when he began deer-hunting in California. "I love elk because a big bull is difficult and the most exciting animal I've ever bowhunted.

"I think you need to belong to organisations like Rocky Mountain Elk Foundation, the NRA and North American Hunting Club – any organisation that is pro-hunting and makes a difference, I think everybody should support."

He claims to feel bad when he kills animals and says he feeds wild rabbits in his back garden. "I feel sad for every animal that I kill to this day. They're beautiful. I love animals. In Wyoming, Gretta and I have about 40 cottontail rabbits that come out on the lawn every night. We feed them carrots, and I wouldn't think of shooting one of those rabbits.

"And yet, that's the ironic part about hunting. I'm designed to hunt. I'm a predator with my eyes in the front of my head for good depth perception, like a coyote or a wolf or a bear or a mountain lion. I'm designed from one end to the other to launch a projectile of some sort and take down game. I don't fight that. I figure it's in my genetics and in the way I was raised.

"I love to hunt. I love to hunt more than anything. I hunt for the challenge. I hunt for the love of the outdoors. I hunt for physical activity. I love to climb the mountains. And, if anything, I don't get to hunt as much as I want."

He is enthusiastic about young children being involved in trophy hunting. "I do my best to take kids hunting… if you can, get active in a big brother program and take a kid hunting."[516]

---

[516] "Chuck Adams: his side of the story", The Rub Tree, P J DelHomme www.rubtree.com

Chapter 7: Hunters from around the world

NAME: Japto Soerjosoemarno
NATIONALITY: Indonesian

Japto (sometimes spelt Yapto) Soerjosoemarno is a keen pro-am golfer. The Indonesian Golf Club of the USA has a tournament named after him.[517] He is listed as a member of the PGA Tour Indonesia's board of advisors and has hosted several tournaments in Southern California. He has been the amateur partner of a number of PGA Tour pros and has played several times in the Coachella Valley, formerly known as the Bob Hope Classic which has been sponsored by the Clinton Foundation.

He is also leader of a notorious political group known to have operated as a paramilitary death squad.

Soerjosoemarno heads up Pemuda Pancasila, also known as Pancasila Youth (PY), a group described by the Financial Times as "one of Indonesia's biggest paramilitary organisations".[518] Joshua Oppenheimer's award-winning 2012 film, 'The Act of Killing', tells the story of how groups such as the Pancasila Youth helped the Indonesian army kill more than one million alleged communists, ethnic Chinese and intellectuals. Pancasila

---

[517] https://www.facebook.com/IGCUSA2015/
[518] 'It was wrong but we had to do it' - Ben Bland, Financial Times, June 21 2013 https://www.ft.com/content/c0980a8c-d763-11e2-8279-00144feab7de

Youth is described as "one of the main paramilitary groups involved in the genocide".[519]

At the beginning of the film is an extraordinary scene filmed on a golf course in which the interviewer tries to ask Soerjosoemarno about his role in the genocide: "How did Pancasila exterminate the communists?" he asks. Soerjosoemarno calmly replies: "We killed them all. May I hit the ball now?" Soerjosoemarno then calmly takes his shot.[520]

Media reports also describe Soerjosoemarno as "a self-professed 'gangster'."[521] Despite this, he has been given multiple awards by Safari Club International.[522] He has also been an official SCI Master Measurer and his name features a number of times in SCI's Records Book for white rhino, lion and leopard trophies.[523]

His SCI awards include the African Big Five, the Grand Slam Dangerous Game of Africa Award, the Global Hunting Award, and the Hunting Achievement Award. (For a full list of his SCI prizes and records see Appendix).

---

[519] https://pov-tc.pbs.org/pov/downloads/2014/pov-theactofkilling-discussion-guide-print.pdf

[520] "Why Does A Leader Of The Indonesian Genocide Get To Play In So Many PGA Tour Pro-Ams?", Patrick Redford, Deadspin 1/24/19 https://deadspin.com/why-does-a-leader-of-the-indonesian-genocide-get-to-pla-1831995150

[521] "Why Does A Leader Of The Indonesian Genocide Get To Play In So Many PGA Tour Pro-Ams?", Patrick Redford, Deadspin 1/24/19 https://deadspin.com/why-does-a-leader-of-the-indonesian-genocide-get-to-pla-1831995150

[522] Safari magazine – Awards 2015, Safari Club International

[523] SCI Record Book of Trophy Animals – edition IX, Vol 1, Africa Field Edition. SCI, 1997

NAME: Ron Thomson
NATIONALITY: Zimbabwean
CONFIRMED KILLS: 5,930

One hunter alone is credited with shooting 5000 elephants as well as 800 buffalo, 50-60 lions, 30-40 leopards, and some 50 hippos.[524] Ron Thomson, from Zimbabwe, is reputed to have once killed 32 elephants in the space of just 15 minutes.[525]

He was born in 1939 and began work as a park ranger in what was then Rhodesia in the late 1950s. He was regularly called on to kill animals of which he later said: "It was a great thrill to me, to be very honest... Some people enjoy hunting just as much as other people abhor it. I happened to enjoy it."[526] Thomson also told newspapers: "I didn't have any sentiment. I'm totally unrepentant, a hundred – ten thousand – times over for any of the hunting I've done."[527]

---

[524] "Hunter who has killed at least 5,000 African elephants and hippos says he has no regrets", Jane Dalton, The Independent, 8 April 2019
https://www.independent.co.uk/news/world/africa/hunter-elephants-hippos-buffalo-lions-leopards-wildlife-africa-a8860291.html

[525] "Who would want to kill a lion? Inside the minds of trophy hunters", Elle Hunt, The Observer 4 November 2018
https://www.theguardian.com/environment/2018/nov/04/trophy-hunters-who-would-kill-lion-elephant-big-game-hunting

[526] https://www.mirror.co.uk/news/uk-news/worst-trophy-hunter-whos-killed-14267723

[527] https://www.thesun.co.uk/news/8820919/hunter-ron-thomson-killed-5000-elephants-and-60-lions-no-regrets/

In a survey about attitudes towards elephant hunting conducted by Safari Club International, Thomson responded: "Hunting the African elephant is the ultimate experience for all serious hunters. Why this should be so is most easily explained – without uttering a word – by the experience itself... No-one can define the rush of adrenaline that sends the pulses racing but the hunter, himself; the goose-pimples that run up and down his arms, and along the length of his back, erecting the hair on the nape of his neck... Then to manoeuvre myself into a position to be able to place a bullet – smaller than two digits of a man's little finger – into the elephant's brain! A brain that is no bigger than a football. A brain that is hidden away in some secret place in a huge head that, in size, is more than a yard cube.

"Bang! The die is cast. For a brief instant in time, I am struck with the thought, 'What will be, will be'. Sluck! The sound of the bullet hitting its target. The elephant throws its head up, its trunk rising high... It is the elephant's final salute. Its hind quarters collapse first – then it falls sideways to the ground, its large brown eyes already staring into the great hereafter.

"Then the shaking begins, not from fear, but the release of it! Not from excitement, but from the expiring of tension. The smile on my face is painful. The exhilaration is complete.

"Surely there can be no more thrilling experience for the serious hunter than to have hunted the biggest quarry on the earth - and to have killed it with one clean shot. Sadly, those who are not hunters at heart will never understand the feeling of accomplishment, of utter fulfilment that comes with the satisfying of this, the greatest of man's instincts."[528]

In 1971, Thomson and two other hunters halved the elephant population in Zimbabwe's Gonarezhou national park in a matter of minutes. They killed 2,500 animals using military NATO-7.62 mm semiautomatic rifles. "The three of us were able to kill between 30 and 50 elephants stone dead with brainshots in less than 60 seconds," he later said. "We did the job that had to be done, without any emotion and without any blood loss, and we did it exceptionally well."[529]

Awards received from Safari Club International, Conservation Force and other hunting groups:

The SCI Conservation Trophy

Associate Life Membership of the International Professional Hunters Association

The Technical Prize, International Council for Game and Wildlife Conservation

Namibian Conservation Medal, The Namibian Professional Hunters Association

Natal Conservationist of the Year Award, Natal Hunters and Game Conservation Association, South Africa

Golden Award, The Confederation of Hunters' Associations of South Africa

---

[528] "Elephant hunting – absolutely the greatest hunt in the world", John J Jackson, SAFARI magazine, January/February 1996

[529] "Who would want to kill a lion? Inside the minds of trophy hunters", Elle Hunt, Guardian/Observer, 4 November 2018

Honorary Membership of the SA Hunters Association, South African Hunters and Game Conservation

Certificate of Achievement, Conservation Force

The Order of the Bateleur 2012, South African Hunters and Game Conservation Association[530]

Thomson's book 'Mahohboh' has been acclaimed as "the most definitive work on elephant hunting ever written (and) contains some of the author's most exciting elephant hunting stories."[531]

He has recently been vocal in his support for the reintroduction of elephant trophy hunting in Botswana, and has also said that around 90% of Kruger National Park's elephants should be shot.[532] When Japan recently walked out of the International Whaling Commission, Thomson penned an open letter of congratulations: "I'm elated and congratulate Japan on its guys in making this decision now."[533]

Leading African conservationist and writer Don Pinnock has suggested that Thomson be "tried for crimes against nature".[534]

[530] https://www.ronthomsonshuntingbooks.co.za/awards.html

[531] "Ron Thompson Trophy Hunter of 5000 elephants applauds President Masisi", GMERL, 4 March 2019

[532] "Kruger should cull 88% of its elephants, says Ron Thomson" – africageographic.com 30 October 2017

[533] "Congratulations Japan on your guys' resignation from the IWC", Ron Thomson December 28 2018. www.mahohboh.org

[534] http://elephantnews.org/pipermail/african-elephant_elephantnews.org/2019-April/012791.html

NAME: Hossein 'Soudi' Golabchi
NATIONALITY: Iranian
CONFIRMED KILLS: 400

'Soudi' (sometimes spelt 'Soudy') Golabchi was born in Iran in 1941, one of four brothers. He began hunting in his teens in the foothills of the Alborz Mountains, about an hour's drive from Tehran, a place he describes as a sheep hunter's 'paradise'. As a young child he learned to hunt by shooting at sparrows and pigeons using a homemade slingshot made out of the inner tube of a bicycle tyre.

After finishing High School he was sent first to England and then to the US where he went to university in Oklahoma. He returned to Iran in the late 1960s to help run the family business, subsequently setting up a company manufacturing tractors. This allowed him to pursue his love of hunting sheep in his spare time.

"I collected all the sheep of Iran – several times," he says. "Besides these well-known species of Iranian sheep, it is worth mentioning that Iran is rich in other game too: maral, goitered gazelle, brown and black bear, roebuck, wild ass, five kinds of wild cats including cheetah and Asian leopard, hyena, fox, jackal, birds, and of course Persian ibex and bezoar goat."[535]

He returned to the US in the 1980s and launched a construction company in Augusta.

He currently goes on around 10-12 hunting trips every year and has amassed a trophy collection of 400 animals

---

[535] "Great hunters – their trophy rooms and collections", vols. 1 & 6, Safari Press

covering 250 different species which are on display in his trophy room. Around half are life-size animal mounts, including 50 sheep and ibex. He has recreated mountainsides teeming with animals crowded onto rock ledges. Along the bottom are bear skins complete with the animal's head, their mouths prised open.

He keeps his African haul in a separate room. Here there is an elephant's head, a full rhino body, lion and zebra rugs, a leopard on a ledge, an ostrich, and a seemingly endless row of antelope heads interspersed with those of zebras and warthogs.

His first trophy room, built in 1982, was 1,000 square feet in size. By 1985, however, it was full. A further 2,000 square feet was added, which was extended by an additional 4,000 square feet in 1990. "Today this room is 7,000 square feet, and I have no space left either on the walls or on the floor, and I am still hunting just as much."

He courted controversy recently when photos emerged of him with what appeared to be a dead snow leopard draped across his shoulders. A Care2 petition was launched by animal welfare and conservation group TERA International which condemned the killing of the rare animal.[536] Newspapers – which said he had killed hundreds of animals on six continents – reported that he had brought the snow leopard's remains to Germany. He claims to have then had it shipped to Mexico.

Following the intervention of his lawyers, some newspapers subsequently printed the following

---

[536] https://www.thepetitionsite.com/en-gb/111/531/275/bring-hossein-quotsoldyquot-golabchi-the-us-snow-leopard-poacher-to-justice/

clarification: "Since first publication of this article we have been contacted by Mr Golabchi's representatives who have confirmed that the hunt took place 30 years ago at a time when it was permitted by the Mongolian government. The Mongolian government issued permits for snow leopard hunts and provided government guides".[537]

Golabchi wrote about the hunt in his book 'Obsessed! Hunting Mountain Game in North America, Asia and around the world.' The publishers, Safari Press, wrote the following review: "If ever there was a man obsessed with sheep hunting, it is Soudy… he has hunted sheep in just about every conceivable place on earth, and he holds a number of world records as well as numerous top-ten heads. Soudy has close to 100 wild sheep hunts to his name… Whether it is the North American Grand Slam of Sheep, the huge argali rams of Central Asia, or the urials of his native Iran, Soudy has hunted them all as well as most ibex and chamois. This is a phenomenal story of a single-minded obsession that has taken the author more than 4 decades to fulfil. There are simply so many hunts and so many stories that Soudy's accomplishments are unlikely to be equalled soon."[538]

In 2015, Golabchi was given SCI's Pantheon Award, described by Safari Club International as "the most prestigious quantifiable big game hunting award in the world."[539] Only 7 hunters had ever been presented the

---

[537] https://www.dailymail.co.uk/femail/article-5054315/Wealthy-hunter-posed-body-rare-snow-leopard.html

[538] https://www.safaripress.com/books/safari-press-publications/obsessed-trd-l.html

[539]

award before him. His other SCI Awards include the World Hunting Award, The Pinnacle of Achievement Award, the Crowning Achievement Award, the Grand Slam Cats of the World Award, the Grand Slam Bears of the World Award, the African Big Five Award, the Grand Slam African 29 Award, the Global Hunting Award, and the Hunting Achievement Award.[540]

Several of Golabchi's trophies are listed in the SCI Records Book, including a white rhino shot in South Africa and two lions, both of which he shot in Tanzania. (For full details see Appendix).

https://www.legacy.com/obituaries/birmingham/obituary.aspx?n=dennis-charles-campbell&pid=188084962&fhid=19975

[540] Safari magazine – Awards 2015, Safari Club International

Chapter 8: The Five Hundred Hunters who've been given SCI's "Africa Big Five" Award

The Africa Big Five is considered by many within the hunting world as the 'gold standard' of the industry's prizes. It requires a hunter to kill at least one lion, elephant, leopard, rhinoceros and buffalo.

The number of hunters recognised by SCI for having completed is going up rapidly. Between 1986-1995, 80 hunters were given the award. By 1996-2005 the figure had shot up to 187. In the following decade between 2006-2015, it rose further still to 227. An additional 23 hunters are recognised as having completed it before 1986.

Since the mid-1980s, the award has been presented to a total of 515 hunters – two of whom completed it with both rifle and bow and are thus recognised twice by Safari Club International.[541]

A.
Simon Char Abdala; Robert S. Adams; Ronald G. Adams; Paul E. Adams; Hal Ahlberg; James R. Ake; Chester Aleksandrowicz; Patrick C. Allen MD; Arnold Alward; David G. Anderson; Dennis Anderson; Lee "Andy" Anderson Jr.; Lee R. Anderson Sr.; Roger L. Anderson; Edwin G. Andrew; Herb Atkinson; Larry

---

[541] Safari magazine – Awards 2015, Safari Club International

Atkinson; Pamela S. Atwood; Stanford Atwood; David G. Aul; Armen Avedissian; Xavier Aznarez

B.

Luis L. Bacardi; William D. Backman Jr.; Dennis G. Bailey; Rex Baker; Dr. Jorg Bankmann; L. Irvin Barnhart; Kenneth L. Barr; Ron Bartels; Jerry Barth; Keith Bates; Charles "Chip" Bazzy; Charles "Chuck" Bazzy; Carroll D. Beaman; Jeffery Thomas Becks; Kenneth E. Behring; Eugene Bell; Angiolo Bellini; James A. Beman; Robert M. Bensinger; Michel C. Bergerac; Van C. Bethancourt Jr.; Olle Bexander; David Bickel; Oliver R. Biggers MD; Bradford T. Black MD; Chuck Blalock; Johnny Bliznak MD; Jerry Bofferding; Wade Boggs; Gary Bogner; Greg Bond; Jim Boulton; Lee Branch; Christian Brendel; Suzie Brewster; William S. Bricker DDS; William Brisben; Ralph Brockman; Thomas F. Brodesser Jr.; Walter F. Broich III; Irvin Brown; Michael G. Brown MD; Dr. Leon Brumen; Ronald Brunsfeld; Duncan M. Burkholder; Henry Bynum

C.

Mary Cabela; Ms. Elizabeth Caddell; Isabel Cadenas; Dennis Campbell; Jose M. Carbonell; Roger Card; Rick Cassidy; Maurice A. Cattani; Juan Antonio Cedillo; Edward Cerkowski; Arturo Cernuda; Steven E. Chancellor; Terri L. Chancellor; Jeffrey K. Chaulk MD; Jose Luis Chavez Ramos; Gregory R. Cheek; James D. Chen; Albert A. Cheramie; Richard Childress; Alan Chopp; Mike Christianson; Gene P. Ciafre; David R. Clark; Kerry Lewis Clary; Brett Coleman; Robert L.

Coleman; William Coppola; Ann Cornell; Harry Cornell Jr.; William Corrigan; Martin B. Cotanche; John C. Crawford; William H. Crawford; Bob Crupi; Vincent E. Cucci Jr.; Deb Cunningham; Ralph S. Cunningham

D.
Serge M. d'Elia; Dewey M. Dalton; John M. Daly; Danny Danell; Farley R. Daniels; Prince R. d'Arenberg; Carlos Davidov; Pemble Davis; Steve Davis; Jonathan W. Davis; Abigail Day; Dr. Adrian de Villiers; Brown Delozier; Valeriy Dema; Robert G. Deveny; Roman A. DeVille; James DiFrancia; James L. Digristina; Jack Dodds Jr.; Anne Dodgson; James Domokos; Lloyd Douglas; Palle C. Drescher; Roy A. Duddy; Bob DuHadaway; Jan E. Duncan; Scott D. Duncan; Bruce R. Dunn; Roy Durbin; Tom Dyer

E.
Patrick J. Early; Robert Eastman; Jim Eckles; Richard Edelen; Vern Edewaard; Alexander Egorov; Dave Elkins; David Elua; Anders N. Engstrom; James B. Estes; John L. Estes

F.
Frank L. Fackovec; Robert B. Fay Jr.; Jo Ann C. Ferre; William D. Figge; Dr. William Don Firman; Joseph Fiske; Bryan L. Fitzgerald; Peter Flack; Dave Florance; Eduardo Negrete Franco; Nicolas Franco; Lawrence A. Franks; Tommy E. Freestone; John D. Freitag; Dick Fruchey; Sandi Fruchey; Stephen Fullmer

G.

Siddharth Singh Garha; Roberto Garza Delgado; John Gebbia; Patrick Gentil; Dr. Gerald Max Koppes; Henry W. Gerber; Frank Giacalone; Jodie J. Gilson; Tony Gioffre; Michael Gitlin; Hossein Golabchi; Arnold Goldschlager MD; Ramon E. Gonzalez III; Joan V. Gordon; Dee Gratrix-Mobley; Larry Green; Sandra Green; Joseph Greenfield Jr. MD; James R. Grimm; Richard Gronblom; James E. Guist; Arthur J. Gutierrez Jr.; Arturo J. Gutierrez

H.

H. Andrew Hansen II MD; Terry D. Hagman; W. Laird Hamberlin; Thomas J. Hammond; Gary Hansen; Marc Hansen; James A. Hanson; Robert H. Hanson; Dorothy Harber; Dr. T. Dewey Harden; George Harms; Tom Harrison; Duane L. Hart; Don Harter; Mary Harter; John I. Harvill; Darryl Hastings; Vern Haugen; William C. Hayes; Don Headings Jr.; Jerry Heiner; Nelson Hendler; Lonnie Henriksen; Richard Hensley; Terry K. Herman; Jose F. Herrera; William L. Heubaum; Thomas Hewlett; Bela Hidvegi; Larry Higgins; Marvin D. Hill Sr.; John R. Hollenbeck; Hanne Homaizi; Peter L. Horn II; Randy House; Leon E. Houser; Jeffery A. Hunter; Frank Huschitt; Mike Hutchins; Gerhard Huttel; Rick Lee Hunt

I.

Gary R. Ingersoll; Don Ingram; Joseph A. Iorio

J.

Hugh B. Jacks; Dale Jacobs; Gregory B. Jacobs; Sheldon K. James; Kris Johnson; Beth Jones; Jeffrey D. Jonson; Antanas Jurcius

K.

Lawrence S. Katz; Yawan Kayali; Robert S. Keagy; Bruce R. Keller; Edward L. Keller; George E. Keller; I Lionel Kelley; Vincent Kelly; John Kemhadjian; Dr. Donald B. Kettelkamp; Valeriy Khodus; Bob Killett; Lane J. Kinney; George Kishida; Rodney A. Klein; Alexey Klevtsov; Mechislav Klimovich; Steve Kobrine; Bart Koontz; Anatoliy Kovalenko; Andrew D. Kranik MD; Ronald P. Krueger; Evgeny Kurgin; Dr. Bob Kurtz; Alexander Kuznetsov

L.

Edward Lamolinara; Donald Larsson; Igor Ledecky; Harold F. Lee; Richard H. Leedy; Werner Lettl; Bruce Leven; Dennis Leveque; Tom Lillibridge; Ancil L. Lindley III; Dave Liniger; Gail Liniger; Jack Link; Jay E. Link; Lee Lipscomb; Ramon Llano; John Lochow; M. William Lockard DDS; Michael D. Lockhart; Robert J. Lodge; Torry D. Lofgreen Jr.; Gary C. London DDS; Ricardo Longoria; Dr. William W. Lossius; Rodolfo B. Lozano Jr.; Jason Luquire; Sergey Lyapuntsov; John B. Lynch Jr.; Wayne G. Lyster III

M.

Dr. L. W. Mack Jr.; Luis F. F. Madeira Rodrigues; Jose Madrazo; Alan W. Maki; Oleg Mamatchenko; Ronald Mancuso; Raymond Mancuso Sr.; Wayne F

Manis; Ralph M. Marcum; H. Bradley Martin; James L.
Masten; Chuck Matthews; Matt Matthews; Agostino
Marron Mattoli; Robert J. Matyas; David M.
Mausenbaum; Terry M. Mayer; Page Mays; Dr. John A.
McCall Jr.; Robert McCarthy MD; James D. McChesney
MD; Fred E. McDonald III; Lt Col Pat McMahon; Butch
Meilinger; Dr. Lloyd F. Mercer; Jeffery L. Meyerl;
Harold Meyers; Ron Mika; Stephen H. Miller; Molly
Millis-Hedgecock; Dr. Werner Milota; Edwin Minges,
Jr.; Francisco Minieri; Tom Miranda; Lou Misterly Jr.;
Chester Mjolsness; Igor Mochaev; Carl B. Molander;
John R. Monson; Tom Montgomery; Craig M. Morgan;
James D. Morgan; Ray M. Morgan; Brian K. Mortz;
Alexander Moshkalov; Leon J. Munyan; Steve Murnan;
Greg Murtland

N.
Carlos Nachon; Peter C. Nalos; James H. "Booty"
Nance; Jeff C. Neal; Archie Nesbitt; Phillip J. Netznik;
William B. Newlin; Mike Nice; Mike Nicholas; Lucky
Nightingale; Richard B. Nilsen; Bill Nye; Peter M.
Nyman

O.
Gary Oberer; Juan M. Olabarria; Valeri Ostretsov

P.
Frank D. Paino; Pete Papac; Gary D. Parker; Dr.
Michael A. Parnell; Charles D. Patterson; William A.
Paulin; Ronald J. Pavlik; Theodore J. Pawlias DDS;
Melanie Pepper; Will C. Perry; Scott Petty, Jr; Charlotte
Peyerk; Danial A. Peyerk; Helmuth Pfennig; Dmitry

Piskunov; Hampton Pitts; Tom Place; Wayne Pocius; Jeffery M. Ponder; Randy Pope; Konstantin Popov; Bill Porteous; John Pouleson; John Dale Powers; Michael C. Powers; Thomas Price; Ted Priem; Caroline Pruitt

R.

Carlos Humberto Ramirez; Glenn Rasmussen; Cecil Redstrom; William F. Reeves; Deborah A. Remillard; Robert P. Remillard; Fred Rich; George Riley; Philip P. Ripepi MD; Utz Rittmeier; Paul Roberts; Larry C. Rogers MD; Michael Runyan; William Rypkema

S.

John M. Saba Jr.; Alan Sackman; Barbara Sackman; MaryAnn Sackman; Warren A. Sackman III; Federico Sada; Byron Sadler; Sandra Sadler; Antonio Sainero; Manuel Salazar; Ildefonso Salido; Andrew A. Samuels Jr.; S.R. Sankowski; Andres Sarri; Franz Scheffer; Lotte Scheiber; Peter Scheuermann; Eugene Weston Scott; D. L. Seals; John M. Searles; Juan Renedo Sedano; Ben L. Seegmiller; Perry Segura; Fernando Seixas; Dr. M. Gomez Sequeira; Stefan Serlachius; Thomas Shaffer; Rahmat Shah; John C. Shaw; Virginia Shawver; Viktor Shiganov; Jim Shockey; Steven E. Shull; Morgan D. Silvers; Mike Simpson; McKenzie Sims; James Sink MD; Stephen C. Slack; Robert H. Sliwoski; Brent E. Smith; Daniel Smith Jr.; J. Alain Smith; Steve Smith; Alexander Smuzikov; Renee Snider; Thornton N. Snider; Japto S. Soerjosoemarno; Fernando Soler; Robert Spangler Jr.; A J. Arnie Spiess; Frank B. Sprow; Dr. Robert R. Spurzem; John Ed Stepan; Bill Stratton;

Jose J. Suarez; Dr. Juan B. Suarez; Joseph A. Susi MD; Thomas E. Swift III

T.

Robert Talley; G. Kelley-Kines Taylor; George Kines Taylor; Debbie Thames; Earl K. Thompson; Lynn C. Thompson; Hubert Thummler; J.B. Tinney; Ry Tipton MD; Reginald W. Titmas Jr.; David Tofte; Robert J. Tonti; Bill Treichel; Alexei Troinkov; Ted Allen Trout; Antanas Truskauskas; David Tuttle

U.

Russell H. Underdahl; Ali Haydar Ustay

V.

Robert Van Horn; Jorge A. M. Vasques; William F. Vigor; Vitaly Vinogradov; Fernando Viyella; Mike Vogel; Michael J. Vorst; Damir Vrhovnik

W.

David Wahl; Gary R. Walker; Charles D. Wall; Jed Wall; Matt Ward; Michael T. Warn; Gerald L. Warnock MD; Ewald Warzecha; Marc Watts; Dr. Heinz Weber; Roger A. Weidner; Arno Weiss Jr. MD; Robin Wendland; M. Craig West; Sidney Ross Wilhite; Fred Williams; Gregory S. Williamson; Michael J. Wilmet; Ken Wilson; Kenneth T. Winters

Y.

Dr. R. Douglas Yajko; Eugene W.C. Yap; Jim Yarborough; Sergey Yastrzhembskiy; Edward D. Yates; Gary D. Young; Fausto Yturria Jr.; Jesus Yuren

Z.

Mohamed Y. Zahid; Richard W. Ziminski; Karin Zinn; Richard Zinn; Leonard M. Zullo

Part 3: What's wrong with trophy hunting?

Chapter 9: Why do people kill animals for trophies?

"Kill 'em all, let God sort 'em out!... Did you ever get up feeling like you just HAD to kill something?"[542]

"Over the years I've been wonderfully successful in taking some awesome trophies. Now my trophy room is full. Ok I could squeeze in a couple of European mounts of tiny antelope but that's about it. Now what? Hunt long enough and every hunter will eventually have the same problem. I am absolutely not ready to stop hunting. However I don't see the point on hunting trophies when I can't display them."[543]

When defending trophy hunting in the media, hunters often claim it has conservation or job creation benefits. However when describing the hunts in industry journals and online forums, there is rarely if any mention of this. Instead, hunters' accounts often include graphic details of the shocking injuries and suffering experienced by animals, and focus on the sheer thrill of the hunt.

In an article about a lion hunt in South Africa, a hunter's wife – who has accompanied him - writes: "My heart was pounding at an excessive pace, my clothes

---

[542] "African Hunter Magazine – Campfire Tales, vol 1", African Hunter, 2009 (Mag-Set Publications)

[543] https://www.africahunting.com/threads/out-of-space-for-trophies-advice-suggestions.47788/

were soaked through. How the human body jolts to life when all senses are simultaneously alive. To say I was fevered with excitement would be a vast understatement."[544]

Another story describes in horrific detail a hunt for a leopard which goes badly wrong. The animal is left seriously wounded but somehow manages to evade capture. The hunt goes on for 3 days, with various attempts to shoot it dead. On the third day, the leopard finally succumbs to its injuries in a cave after various failed attempts to 'smoke it out'. One of the attempts nearly ends in disaster when a pack of dogs are brought in: they become stuck in the mouth of the cave.

At the end, the hunter writes in almost dismissive tone: "The leopard was a big female. I was not disappointed in the least about it being a female. After all the time and effort that we put into getting the cat, it will always be one of my most rewarding and prized trophies."[545]

In his book "Killing for Profit – exposing the illegal rhino horn trade", Julian Rademeyer tells the story of the excruciating suffering of a rhino that has just been shot by a trophy hunter. "A terrible, almost indescribable keening cuts the air, like a baby crying out or a pig being slaughtered. It is a sound you don't easily forget."

---

[544] https://www.africahunting.com/threads/south-africa-update-hunt-report-on-lion-hunt-in-south-africa-with-umlilo-safaris.39173/

[545] "The Cave Leopard", Richard Vallecorsa in "African Hunter magazine – Campfire tales, volume one", Mag-Set publications, 2009

The animal tries desperately to escape, but in vain. "It rolls onto its side, feet thrashing wildly as it battles to stand." The animal is shot a second time, then a third. And a fourth. "The rhino runs a few paces and collapses under the tree. Mewling in agony, it tries to rise up on its haunches, then topples over." Its cries decrease in volume, but it is still alive. "The rhino isn't dead yet. Blood oozes from flared nostrils. An eye stares glassily into the middle distance. Its right hind leg twitches. Ragged breaths displace scrub and dust near its head."[546]

In another account of a rhino hunt, Rademeyer writes: "Forty meters away, a white rhino lets out a high-pitched squeal, falls – legs thrashing – and bleeds out into the dust. The young woman poses for photographs with her kill, arms held rigidly at her sides, her head bowed. She doesn't smile." The woman is in fact a Vietnamese peasant who has been flown out to hunt rhinos on behalf of a Far Eastern wildlife trafficking ring.

CJ McElroy, founder of Safari Club International, once wrote a detailed piece about a hunt for a jaguar. "In a single fast flow of motion, I moved the rifle, found the cat's chest across my open sights, and triggered an explosion that shattered the stillness. The jaguar reeled back, the same way any animal will recoil when hit in the chest at close range. But he didn't go down. He staggered, then recovered and started running across the small clearing, heading for thick jungle to my right."

McElroy shoots him again. However the animal manages to find cover in the undergrowth as McElroy

---

[546] "Killing for Profit – exposing the illegal rhino horn trade", Julian Rademeyer, Zebra Press, 2012

fires off a third shot. "The blood trail was easy to follow. The spots of red glistened like jewels in our flashlight beams." McElroy eventually locates him. "The tigre (as he calls it) was still bleeding quite heavily, and his trail led out of the grass and into thick jungle."

McElroy fires off a fourth shot. "The bullet slammed into his neck. He collapsed in a spotted heap." He runs forward to inspect the dead animal. "I examined the cat carefully and discovered that my first two bullets, fired from the machan, had slammed into him at my precise points of aim. The first had opened a gaping hole in his chest, and the second had broken up on his massive shoulder bone."

He discovers afterwards that the cat was a new world record jaguar trophy. "I had the animal mounted in a full lifelike pose. He is now the feature attraction in my trophy room".[547]

'20 Great Trophy Hunts – personal accounts of hunting North America's Top Big Game Animals' is a book which contains a number of personal accounts, including one of a hunt for a bear.

At the beginning of the story, on locating their quarry, the hunter's partner urges his friend to "take him in the throat and break his neck". He describes what happens after firing the first shot as follows: "I heard my slug slam into the animal with a distinct 'Whomp!'. What happened next just didn't make any sense at all. That bear went into a rage. He acted as if the bullet never

---

[547] C J McElroy, 'The Tigre is behind us', in "20 Great Trophy Hunts – personal accounts of hunting North America's Top Big-Game Animals", edited by John O Cartier. David McKay Company Inc

fazed him. He started smashing branches in all directions. He grabbed a limb as big as my arm in his jaws and snapped it like a dry twig. I was dumbfounded. I decided a neck shot wouldn't do the job; I'd have to shoot him in the lungs and bleed him to death."

The second bullet, fired into the bear's lung, appears to have little effect, however. The hunter fires yet another bullet into the lungs, but the bear is still thrashing around. Eventually it collapses. A pack of hounds then moves in. "The dogs were all over him when he smacked the ground. There was a violent uproar of barking and snarling."[548]

In 2009, African Hunter magazine published a series of short stories entitled 'Campfire Tales'. It includes a detailed account of a hunt for a buffalo. "The tranquillity of the glorious African morning was shattered by the ear splitting roar of the .375. He collapsed in a massive heap of muscle and mayhem."

However the animal is still alive. The hunter's companion urges him to "keep shooting into his chest til he stops moving!" Several more rounds are fired at virtually point blank range. The satisfied hunter exclaims: "Finally the valiant warrior was vanquished. I had at last been worthy of him. Now I was officially inducted into the brother hood of African Hunter".[549]

Another story in the same edition tells the following tale of a hunt for a bushbuck, a species of antelope

---

[548] "20 Great Trophy Hunts – personal accounts of hunting North America's Top Big Game Animals", edited by John O Cartier. David McKay Company Inc

[549] "African Hunter Magazine – Campfire Tales, vol 1", African Hunter, 2009 Mag-Set Publications

present in sub-Saharan Africa. "The bullet holes were clearly visible in the neck and centre of the shoulder... I set off to fetch the vehicle, fairly bursting with joy at a wonderful culmination to a hunt which had gone just about perfectly."

However the hunter then notices that the animal is still alive; shortly after it somehow manages to run off into the bush. He eventually finds it again and shoots it once more. "The ram was lying on its side apparently dead bar a tremor."

The hunter leaves and returns 30 minutes later on to find the bushbuck has gone. The hunter goes off again, this time to get a pack of dogs to try and hunt it down, which he eventually succeeds in doing. He signs off the article with the words: "What an exciting hunt. Sometimes the Lord does bless fools."[550]

AfricaHunting.com is a popular forum for trophy hunters. In February 2019, it carried a contributor's account of a gazelle hunt in which the hunter used a bow and arrow. After hitting the animal, the animal runs but eventually stops. "He swayed back and forth a bit and then turned and I saw the blood pouring out of his nose. He took a few steps away from the blind and then began turning in circles slowly as he began to suffer the effects of heavy haemorrhaging. I watched as he staged in a circle about five times with a steady stream of blood coming out of two holes and his nose and mouth."

The hunter concludes the article: "After the photos, we head back to the skinning shed."[551] Readers posted

---

[550] "African Hunter Magazine – Campfire Tales, vol 1", African Hunter, 2009 Mag-Set Publications

comments including "awesome hunt", "great adventure", "congratulations on a fantastic stalk on a unique animal", and "you are the man".

In his excellent book 'Cuddle me, Kill me – a true account of South Africa's captive lion breeding and canned hunting industry', author and film-maker Richard Peirce tells a haunting story about how captive lion cubs are often 'recruited' into the industry.

"The lioness and her cubs were shut in a small barred cage that opened onto a large enclosure surrounded by an electrified fence. Four days earlier she had given birth to three cubs, which had just finished the latest in a round-the-clock succession of feeds. The cubs slept, and she dozed. The largest of the cubs was a light-coloured male and he slept sprawled across her throat with a tiny paw dangling near one of his mother's half-closed eyes.

"The noise of an engine approaching meant little because vehicles often passed the enclosure, so the lioness took no notice of it at first. But then it stopped only a few metres from her cage, and she raised her head. The cub fell off her neck and squirmed briefly in protest before cuddling up to its sisters and going back to sleep.

"A man and woman dressed in khaki shorts and shirts got out of the vehicle's cab; they went to the open back and lowered the tailgate. The man leaned in and dragged out a bloody chunk of meat – part of a donkey's leg.

"The meat hit the dry ground with a thud and threw up a small cloud of dust. The lioness was on her feet,

---

551 Posted on www.africahunting.com by 'mrpoindexter (an AH fanatic)' on February 27 2019

standing in the doorway of her cage as the tempting meal landed less than 20 metres away. She knew what it was and she leapt in one bound and was onto the meat.

"Behind her there was a loud clang: metal struck metal as the door of her cage crashed shut. She had fallen for the cruellest of tricks: the cubs were on one side of the bars and she was on the other. She knew what had happened: perhaps it had happened to her before. Instinct made her hang onto her meal as she ran, so she dragged the meat back to the cage gate.

"She then watched as the last of her three cubs was picked up by the woman and handed to the man who carried it to join the others, which were already in a small cage in the back of the pick-up truck. At only four days old, the tiny, pale-coloured male lion and his sisters still had their eyes tightly closed.

"The engine started and they were on their way into a life that would involve exploitation, sadness, cruelty and suffering.

"The lioness' eyes were filled with a terrible anger and despair as the paced the fence and cried out for her cubs being driven away, and gradually the sound of the engine faded to nothing."[552]

The 'right' to use and kill animals for sport and trophies is partly drawn from an interpretation of Biblical teachings which asserts that God created man in his own image and gave man dominion over all living things. Under this world view, the world was made for the enjoyment and benefit of man; animals are not

---

[552] "Cuddle me, Kill me – a true account of South Africa's captive lion breeding and canned hunting industry", Richard Peirce, 2018

endowed with souls, and man is free to use and consume animals as he sees fit. In the words of former US President Theodore Roosevelt, arguably the architect of the 20th century hunting industry: "all of nature's needs are still subservient to the well-being of man. Nature is there for the benefit of the people."[553]

However, Matthew Scully, an American conservative and former speech-writer for President George W Bush, strongly contests this interpretation in his book 'Dominion'. In a review published in the New York Times, Scully's argument is summarised: "When our cruelty expands and mutates to the point where ... we insist on an inalienable right to stalk and slaughter intelligent, magnificent creatures like elephants or polar bears for the sheer, bracing thrill of it - and today's moneyed big-game hunters do just that - then we debase ourselves."[554]

Scully directly challenges the interpretation of the Bible used by trophy hunters to justify their sport: "My copy of the Good Book doesn't say 'Go forth to selleth every creature that moveth'. It doesn't say you can baiteth and slayeth and stuffeth everything in sight, either. Oddly enough, no mention here of the 'Big Four' either, or of Inner Circles and Pinnacles of killing achievement and competitive hunting as godly pursuits. Believe it or not, nowhere in all of God's holy word did He even think to mention the 'point size' of any creature."[555]

---

[553] "Very Best of enemies – Man, Lion and their Eternal Conflict", BB Slater, 19 Juliet Publishers, 2017

[554] https://www.nytimes.com/2002/10/27/books/the-most-compassionate-conservative.html

But what actually prompts some people to kill animals for 'sport' and souvenirs? Some scientists believe trophy hunting is a form of sexual gratification. According to one academic paper: "individual infliction of pain on an animal or another person has given rise to sexual excitement. We have noted elsewhere the connection between strong emotional and sexual stimulation".[556]

Dr Joel R Saper of the University of Michigan agrees that hunting "may reflect a profound yet subtle psychosexual inadequacy", while clinical psychologist Margaret Brooke-Williams believes that "hunters are seeking reassurance of their sexuality. The feeling of power that hunting brings temporarily relieves this sexual uneasiness."[557]

Craig Packer, a lion researcher who has written about the impacts of trophy hunting, was recently interviewed by The Guardian. He stated: "Many hunters model themselves on the Marlboro man, the stereotypical of masculinity" – or what he calls 'toxic masculinity'.[558]

A 2016 study of trophy hunting by Darimont et al. says that men use hunting to send signals about their

[555] "Dominion: The Power of Man, the Suffering of Animals, and the Call to Mercy Paperback" by Matthew Scully, Souvenir Press Ltd, April 2011

[556] "Abnormal Psychology and Modern Life": James N. Carson, Robert C.; Mineka, Susan; Butcher; Allyn & Bacon; 11th edition (2000)

[557] http://www.wordsonlife.co.uk/hunting-is-a-cowards-pastime/

[558] "Who would want to kill a lion? Inside the minds of trophy hunters". Elle Hunt, Guardian/Observer, 4 November 2018

fitness to rivals and potential mates. "By sharing images of their trophies on social media, hunters can now trumpet messages about their personal wealth and social status to a global audience."[559]

The trophy serves the function of 'bragging rights'. It is "a sign of the hunter's social position. There should be no pretence that this type of hunting is a means of survival: trophy hunting is a means of dominance."[560]

An article in Psychology Today agrees that trophy hunting is used to show off wealth to one's peers, commenting that "trophy hunters, whether they like it or not, are likely hunting for status. It's like driving a luxury car, though in this case the lives of animals are taken."[561]

Exhibitionism, and what scientists call 'costly signalling', is a key element of the trophy hunting experience. A number of companies offer professional film and photography services to hunters. Got The Shot Productions, for instance, "captures your African safari with professionalism and pride... You can't bring along all your hunting buddies but you can take your safari back to them by sharing your video."[562]

---

[559] "Hunting big game – why people kill animals for fun", Mindy Weisberger, Scientific American, May 28, 2017

[560] "Can trophy hunting ever be justified?", Prospect Magazine, February 2018
https://www.prospectmagazine.co.uk/philosophy/can-trophy-hunting-ever-be-justified

[561] "Why men trophy hunt: showing off and the psychology of shame", Psychology Today. Marc Bekoff. March 28 2017

[562] https://www.johnxsafaris.com/partners/

Tinashe, a leading safari hunting company, has its own in-house DVD and video production team. "Trained to not only take the kill-shot, the incredibly talented crew is skilled at capturing every moment that makes your heart beat faster in close-up detail. Shot from multiple angles, your safari can be captured in time in full HD... The team is happy to meet your special requests, and will gladly deliver your photos and video in formats suitable for social networks."[563]

The 'selfie' is a key part of the ritual too. Ray Cartonia, a hunter, has written a book in which he offers advice to other hunters about the photographic 'ceremony'. He advises fellow hunters to "take pictures immediately after the kill and prior to field dressing the animal. Be sure the animal's tongue is in its mouth and that any significant amounts of blood are cleaned away from the face and hide. If possible, pose the animal in a way to hide any wounds."

He adds: "Be sure to get several different views of the antlers and body paying special attention to any important aspects of the trophy. The backdrop behind the antlers should be free of clutter to ensure a good view of the rack."[564]

William Shuster, meanwhile, gives the following guidance to fellow hunters: "One of the best ways to preserve the fond memories of a successful black bear hunt is to have some photographs made of the hunter with his trophy. If possible, have photographs taken in

[563] https://www.tinashegroup.co.za/p31/hunting/dvd-and-video-productions-by-tinashe-outfitters.html

[564] "A practical strategy for trophy big game hunting", Ray Cartonia, 2010

the field before the bruin is dressed. Photos taken at or near the kill site when the carcass is still fresh and limber often look the best. If a bear goes down in the open where there's good light, that's great."

"Try to position a bear for photographs to eliminate most, if not all, blood from view and make sure the animal's tongue isn't hanging out of its mouth. It is usually possible for the hunter to stand or kneel next to the carcass to block blood from view. When this isn't possible, frame pictures in the camera's viewfinder that exclude bloody portions of the carcass." [565]

The trophy room is also central to the purpose of trophy hunting, of course. It was formerly known as the 'Game Room' when it first originated in Britain at around the time the empire was expanding into India and Africa, and a new class of industry leaders sought to use their wealth to emulate the nobility.

An industry book which celebrates the trophy rooms of top hunters from around the world tells how "once the United States became an industrial superpower, its hunters took the British concept of a game room and transformed it into gargantuan galleries of heads and full-size mounts, called trophy rooms."[566]

Many trophy hunters today go to extraordinary lengths and expense to create world-leading trophy rooms to house and display the evidence of their successful kills. Just as 'Hello' magazines feature celebrities photographed at home, the hunting industry

[565] "Hunting trophy black bear (Hunter's information series)", Richard P Smith, North American Hunting Club, 1990

[566] "Great Hunters – their trophy rooms & collections", volume 3, Safari Press Inc, 2001

publishes books with the world's greatest trophy rooms together with their proud owners often striking casual poses amongst a litany of animal bodies.

In his introduction to one such book, record-breaking hunter and Conservation Force director Chris Klineburger writes: "Trophy rooms are magical... Unlike most tourists, (trophy hunters) are the paramount collectors."[567]

There are several books which give hunters detailed hints and tips as to how to best display their hard-earned trophies to best effect. In his book 'Hunting Big Game Trophies'[568], trophy hunter and writer Tom Brakefield gives the following advice to fellow big game hunters: "A good trophy room will be both striking and tasteful in appearance. It will project a unique yet traditional masculine character that is attractive to both men and women of varied backgrounds."

He goes on to give advice about room location, ceiling height, humidity, and the location of fireplaces and doorways. "Many sportsmen like to have a door open from their trophy room onto a patio for entertaining or just for general convenience on warm still evenings. This does create an agreeable option."

A recent thread on hunting forum Africahunting.com posed a direct question to trophy hunters: 'Why do you hunt?' It was started on January 22, 2019 by a trophy hunter identifying himself as 'AH Veteran'.[569] A

---

[567] "Great Trophy Hunters – their trophy rooms & collections", volume 7, Safari Press Inc, 2013

[568] "Hunting Big Game Trophies – a North American Guide", Tom Brakefield, An Outdoor Life Book/Times Mirror Magazines Inc, 1976

contributor named 'JakeH' soon answers as follows: "I enjoy providing my family with the bounty that God had provided us… I also hunt as an escape. When I'm out hunting it is me and nature, and me and nature alone. No work, no wife, no kids, no bills, no stressors".

Another, 'Shootist43', writes: "Hunting takes me back to a point in time where life was much simpler. It enables me to forget about the fast paced dog eat dog world we live in. Time away from the rat race allows me to rationalize about what is important in my life."

A couple of contributors attempt to equate trophy hunting with subsistence hunting. However, as one former hunter has pointedly written: "You could live on filet mignon for what shooting a deer costs (in license fees, equipment, ammunition and time)."[570] 'Tarbe', meanwhile, says: "in the final analysis, I have to say that I hunt because I am a hunter. I love guns, shooting, handloading, planning trips… I think hunting is just natural to many of us, and we refuse to deny its expression in our lives." The contribution of 'Bruce' is short and to the point: "Because I can."

There are a couple who claim that trophy hunters are actually providing an altruistic or humane 'service'. In the words of 'Sgt_zim': "There is no old folks home for

[569] https://www.africahunting.com/threads/why-do-you-hunt.47574/

[570] "Hunting linked to psychosexual inadequacy and the 5 phases of a hunter's life of sexual frustration", Brent Lambert, November 7 2016
https://www.feelguide.com/2016/11/07/hunting-linked-to-psychosexual-inadequacy-the-5-phases-of-a-hunters-life-of-sexual-frustration/

wild animals. The prey animals meet their end at the fangs and claws of predators if they're lucky. If they're not lucky, they linger on for days or weeks with a fatal disease, or perhaps they simply and slowly starve to death." 'Njc110381' makes a similar claim: "I put myself in their shoes and ask myself what I would want? Given the options available, I'd take a bullet for sure."

Elsewhere, the killing of the animal in order to turn it into a trophy is sometimes presented as a 'venerable act' by hunters: "Then the moment arrives and when the hunter takes it upon himself to end that magnificent life, the animal is celebrated in a way that the millions of animals which have died in obscurity in the bush will never be. This particular lion… will be mounted in its glorious entirety. It will have pride of place in his home, not to be sneered at, and not to have its memory maligned, but to be admired and respected."[571]

The desire to hunt is also talked about by some as being akin to an addiction: "The deep, innate, primitive desire to hunt an animal is rather an urge. It begs to be satisfied. It is calmed by a successful hunt when dopamine, that delicious secretion, flushes through the hunter's body."[572]

One seasoned trophy hunter delves further into the theme: "Somewhere along the way, I lost the great thrill of hunting. You know what it developed into? A job. Being a top professional at it. And don't get me wrong. Hunting as we know it, trophy hunting, is a great

---

[571] "Very Best of Enemies – Man, Lion and their Eternal Conflict", BB Slater, 19 Juliet Publishers, 2017

[572] "Very Best of enemies – Man, Lion and their Eternal Conflict", BB Slater, 19 Juliet Publishers, 2017

competition… I had to get there first, shoot the animal first, and make sure it was the biggest. And when it lay on the ground, if it wasn't within the top ten, I didn't feel the old adrenaline that I used to feel when I got something down. It had disappeared. A person gets on that glory road and God help him. He's lost the thrill of just going on a hunt for the sake of going. Christ! Once I'd go on a hunt and be gone six or seven days, climb up and down the mountains and come home with nothing and be very happy. But not anymore. I've got to go with the best possible guide I can find, the best possible place, be sure of access, and try to get the big one."[573]

Back on the hunting forum thread, 'BC.Pat' is the most honest contributor: "I think there are lots of reasons to substantiate why we hunt. But in the end its because we/I enjoy it!" 'Lpace' concurs: "Lots of secondary reasons, most of which are rationalisations. At the end of the day, I hunt because I enjoy the hell out of it!"

At the end of the day, this is the 'bottom line'. 'Conservation' and 'poverty alleviation' don't get a single mention. Whatever the secondary embellishments, they are just that. In December 2018, TV presenter Piers Morgan interviewed Steve Jones, President of the London chapter of Safari Club International on ITV's 'Good Morning Britain' show. In a clip that was to go viral, Morgan repeatedly presses Jones about the trophy hunter's real motives. After attempting several times to side-step the question, Jones is finally forced to concede: "Because they enjoy it."[574]

---

[573] "Bloodties – Nature, Culture and the Hunt", Ted Kerasote, Kodansha America Inc, 2013

[574] https://www.youtube.com/watch?v=cAy4YVBNJPk

Cliched as it may seem, the 'thrill of the kill' and the subsequent social signalling through awards, records, selfies/videos and the trophy itself is what drives some men (and women) to go on long trips at exorbitant expense in which they take the life of a sentient being. As a recent article in the hunters' magazine 'Shooting Times' notes, renowned hunter-writers such as Ruark and O'Connor emphasised "how much fun it all was."[575]

The enjoyment of killing is almost always visible in the film clips of trophy hunting that have occasionally made their way into the public domain. A newspaper report describes how a trophy hunter shoots a crocodile after shouting: "Let me put my beer down... Oh yeah mother......"[576]

Mark Sullivan, an American professional hunter who specialises in lion and buffalo hunting, says: "Nothing else can bring out the senses in you and make the blood run through your veins." He goes on to add: "Safari is like no other experience or adventure that is available to us on planet Earth."[577]

The marketing of hunts mirrors and reinforces this – because this is what the client is after. Outfitters do not sell 'conservation'. Similarly, no trophy hunter embarked on their 'career' having studied biology and

[575] https://www.shootingtimes.com/editorial/big-game-hunting-fun-and-games-or-a-lifetime-calling/330394

[576] https://www.dailymail.co.uk/news/article-5092193/Documentary-shows-big-game-hunters-kill-African-beasts.html

[577] https://www.phoenixnewtimes.com/news/the-noble-huntersafari-guide-mark-sullivan-believes-that-to-preserve-the-earths-greatest-beasts-some-of-them-must-die-6425832

concluding that a lifetime of sport hunting was the means to achieve their professional goal. "Nothing beats the adrenalin rush of finally having the trophy buck of your dreams step into your shooting lane," says Rack Ranch.[578] "Experience the adrenaline pumping through your body as you scope out some of the most exciting trophies you'll ever find," Tinashe Outfitters adds.[579]

As an article in the journal Psychology Today – entitled *"Trophy Hunters' smiles show how much they like to kill"* – reminds us: "'pleasure smiles' are greater when hunters pose with large 'dangerous' corpses".[580]

---

[578] "Trophy hunting by the numbers – the United States' role in global trophy hunting", HSI-HSUS, February 2016

[579] https://www.tinashegroup.co.za/

[580] https://www.psychologytoday.com/gb/blog/animal-emotions/201511/trophy-hunters-smiles-show-how-much-they-kill

Chapter 10: A Question of Ethics

"Unleash the beast and let the predator/prey games begin!" - Ted Nugent[581]

IUCN scientists recently concluded that trophy hunting is unethical.

In a damning, if not entirely surprising report, IUCN's ethics committee strongly criticised the claims of those who promote trophy hunting as the 'sustainable use' of wildlife saying this is incompatible with IUCN's mission.

The report was directed at least in part at a group within IUCN which promotes trophy hunting as a form of 'sustainable use' of wildlife. The ethics committee conducted their study in the wake of an application by a 'sport shooting' group to join IUCN - which was supported by some IUCN members. Around the same time, there were attempts by some within IUCN to block the International Fund for Animal Welfare from joining.

In their report, the committee concluded unequivocally: "The critical question is whether trophy hunting as it is practiced by individuals and promoted by certain hunting organizations may be consistent with IUCN's general objectives... This is clearly not the case. Any other view would threaten IUCN's credibility for providing moral and ethical leadership in conservation

---

[581] "The Journal of the Texas Trophy Hunter", November/December 2017, volume 42 no.6

policies. It would certainly undermine the many efforts of IUCN members to promote a just and sustainable world."[582]

In possibly the most comprehensive scholarly review of the ethics of trophy hunting to date, Batavia et al (2018) state: "Compelling evidence shows that such animals have intelligence, emotion, and sociality (DeMello, 2012), all of which are profoundly disrupted by the practice of trophy hunting (Muposhi, Gandiwa, Makuza, & Bartels, 2016; Sogbohossou et al., 2014). However, nonhuman animals are not only physically, socially, and emotionally disrupted, but also debased by the act of trophy hunting. Commoditized, killed, and dismembered, these individuals are relegated to the sphere of mere things when they are turned into souvenirs, oddities, and collectibles."

The scientists add: "nonhuman animals are not mere objects but living beings with interests of their own, to whom we owe at least some basic modicum of respect (Regan, 1983). To transform them into trophies of human conquest is a violation of duty and common decency; and to accept, affirm, and even institutionalize trophy hunting, as the international conservation community seems to have done, is to aid and abet an immoral practice."

The paper concludes: "For a Western hunter to pay for the privilege of killing an animal, and to then take its body as a trophy of conquest, is alarming and morally reprehensible."[583]

---

[582] "Compatibility of Trophy Hunting as a Form of Sustainable Use with IUCN's Objectives", IUCN WCEL Ethics Specialist Group, Fri, 27 Sep 2019

Scientists have recently demonstrated the physical and biological impacts on animals of being hunted. A study of cougars in simulated hunts assessed stress levels resulting from the chase by measuring cortisol production.[584] Behavioural ecologist Anne Engh conducted a study on baboons who had lost close female relatives by analysing the hormones in faecal samples. Her findings, reported in Proceedings of the Royal Society B, showed that females had significant increases in stress hormones called glucocorticoids.[585]

There is ample scientific evidence of animals grieving and mourning the loss of fellow creatures. Writing in The Smithsonian, Jessica Pierce points to how animals such as elephants, chimpanzees, magpies and wild pigs are aware of death and will mourn their dead, often performing intricate rituals.[586] Barry Yeoman of the National Wildlife Federation has described how a giraffe stood vigil over the body of her calf for several days without eating or drinking. Scientists, he says, have identified mourning-like behaviours in cetaceans, turtles, bison and birds.[587]

[583] "The elephant (head) in the room: A critical look at trophy hunting", Chelsea Batavia Michael Paul Nelson Chris T. Darimont Paul C. Paquet William J. Ripple Arian D. Wallach, Conservation Letters, 2018
https://conbio.onlinelibrary.wiley.com/doi/full/10.1111/conl.12565

[584] https://mountainlion.org/us/ut/library/UT-R-Harlow-et-al-1992-Stress-response-of-cougars-to-nonlethal-pursuit-by-hunters.pdf

[585] https://www.ncbi.nlm.nih.gov/pmc/articles/PMC1560071/

[586] https://www.smithsonianmag.com/science-nature/do-animals-experience-grief-180970124/

In fact, some of this has been known for many years. Charles Darwin observed this phenomenon in 1871: "The lower animals, like man, manifestly feel pleasure and pain, happiness and misery," he wrote in *'The Descent of Man'*. "So intense is the grief of female monkeys for the loss of their young, that it invariably caused the death of certain kinds."[588]

In his book *'Lion Hearted'*, Andrew Loveridge writes of how many mammals and birds "show behaviour and have cognitive function not very different from our own. They experience fear, recognise friends and enemies, care for their offspring, make sacrifices for their social group and close kin, and form and maintain strong social bonds."

He adds: "In the case of lions, the removal of older males who control prides may result in the influx of younger male animals and a consequent rise in infanticide, which may have serious welfare impacts for cubs and the adult females who care for them, and may severely disrupt social cohesion and population stability."

When male lions were killed by trophy hunters, he saw 2 lion prides undergo a change of males 4 times in the space of 5 years. A total of 19 cubs were thought to have been lost due to infanticide as a result.[589]

---

[587] https://www.nwf.org/en/Magazines/National-Wildlife/2018/Feb-Mar/Animals/When-Animals-Grieve

[588] https://charles-darwin.classic-literature.co.uk/the-descent-of-man/ebook-page-47.asp

[589] "Lion hearted – the life and death of Cecil and the future of Africa's iconic cats", Andrew Loveridge, Regan Arts, 2018

A large number of animals hunted for their trophies are not killed instantaneously and suffer extreme cruelty as a result. A significant proportion cannot subsequently be located after being hit by a bullet. A study by the Ohio Department of Natural Resources investigated what happened immediately after the killing of a deer by a trophy hunter. It found that, on average, deer travelled 74 yards before finally dying. The animal would be severely wounded and in severe pain and distress for a considerable period.[590] In some cases, it took more than an hour for the hunter to finally locate the animal.

A report by the Montana Dept. of Fish Wildlife and Parks showed wounding rates of 51%; an identical figure has been reported by the Texas Parks and Wildlife Department, while a figure of 58% is recorded by the Michigan Dept. of Natural Resources. In Vermont, the rate is 63%.[591]

Those animals that are not recovered and killed immediately will in all likelihood experience prolonged pain and suffering caused by septic infection, peritonitis, blood loss and other complications. However Safari Club International awards prizes for hunters who accomplish

---

[590]

http://wildlife.ohiodnr.gov/Portals/wildlife/pdfs/publications/hunting/Pub%205304_DeerSummary_R0916.pdf

[591] "Preliminary Archery Survey Report", Montana Dept. of Fish Wildlife and Parks; "Archery Wounding Loss in Texas", Texas Parks and Wildlife Department; "Deer Hunting Retrieval Rates", Michigan Pittman-Robertson Report, Michigan Dept. of Natural Resources; "Bow hunting for Deer in Vermont: Some Characteristics of the Hunters, the Hunt, and the Harvest", Vermont Fish and Game Department.

the 'African Big Five' and other categories using just a bow and arrow, crossbow, or muzzle-loader. Some hunting associations, such as Pope and Young, only award prizes for hunters using bows and arrows. This increases the likelihood of wounding, and reduces the likelihood of instantaneous death.

Because one of the objectives of trophy hunting is to secure an attractive trophy for display, brain-shots - which are most likely to result in instantaneous death - are often avoided. Instead, shooting guides for different species (including big cats) tend to recommend a heart-lung shot through the shoulder. This is a very difficult shot to achieve even in optimum conditions – for instance, with no wind and with the animal standing absolutely still. It is also often the case that hunters shoot from considerable distances of 200 metres or more.

Hunter publications are frequently filled with accounts of long, slow deaths of a range of animals – including lions, leopards, zebras and sheep – as well as accounts of animals that could not subsequently be found despite having been severely wounded.

A number of companies organise hunts with packs of hounds, including for leopards. Many dogs are killed or suffer horrifying injuries during these hunts. In Canada, hounds equipped with GPS collars are used to chase and tree bobcats, lynxes and cougars. "There are glaring ethical issues," say local conservationists. "The use of hounds to hunt wild cats can separate mothers from their young; puts the dogs at unnecessary risk of injury or death and ultimately provides an unfair advantage that should not fall under the category of fair-chase.

"While it's illegal to kill a mother cougar in the presence of her kittens, killing a mother while she has left her kittens in the safety of a nursery or rendezvous site is legal. Orphaned kittens are often left to starve or are attacked by other predators and rarely survive," they add.[592]

Trophy hunting of great apes or dolphins is generally considered unacceptable because of their intelligence and their close genetic similarity to humans. Yet trophy hunting of other primate species with whom we share almost the same amount of DNA is conducted with few if any restrictions. Hunting trophies of some 39 different species of primate have been lawfully traded since CITES came into force.

Trophy hunting throws up a fundamental paradox: whether an elephant is killed by a poacher or by a trophy hunter, the end result is the same – at least insofar as the elephant is concerned. So why, then, is one considered 'bad' (unlawful) and the other 'good' (lawful)? Killing a wild cat for a trophy or for pleasure is permitted: however killing a domestic cat for the same reason attracts severe punitive sanctions. Yet genetically the two are virtually identical.

In a letter published by The Times in February 2020[593], a group of Members of Parliament from 9 different political parties make the following argument: "Trophy

---

[592] www.wildlifedefenceleague.org

[593] "Trophy Hunting" – Letter to the Editor, The Times, published 24 February 2020. Signatories: Lisa Cameron (SNP), Stephen Farry (Alliance), Sir Roger Gale (Con), Claire Hanna (SDLP), Wera Hobhouse (Lib Dems), Caroline Lucas (Green), Luke Pollard (Lab), Liz Savile-Roberts (Plaid Cymru), Gavin Robinson (DUP)

hunting is often framed as a conservation issue. It certainly has strong ramifications for conservation, with studies showing that trophy hunting has had devastating impacts on many species' populations, and led to the extinction of some. 'Artificial selection' – hunters singling out and killing the biggest animals – weakens the gene pool and leaves species less able to adapt to and survive threats such as climate change. Research has also shown populations have made remarkable recoveries where trophy hunting has been suspended.

"Trophy hunting is also presented as a socio-economic issue. Rightly so, as a recent study by a leading South African foundation showed that switching from trophy hunting to nature tourism could create over 11 times as many jobs in that country alone.

"However, trophy hunting is above all a question of ethics. A 2020 YouGov poll commissioned by Humane Society International/UK and the Campaign to Ban Trophy Hunting reflects the strong public view that trophy hunting is morally unacceptable. When asked to what species a UK ban on trophy imports and exports should apply, 76% of respondents said 'all species'. Only 14% responded that it should apply just to threatened or endangered species, and a mere 2% said the government should not bring in any restrictions.

"Fundamentally, trophy hunting lacks respect," the group of MPs conclude. "It lacks respect for wild animals, for the communities that live alongside them, and for the scientists and organisations who dedicate themselves to their conservation.

"A complete ban … is the only way for the UK to take the appropriate moral stand against this archaic practice," they conclude.

Chapter 11: Is Trophy Hunting 'Murder'?

"Dragging a squealing and gutted duiker across the ground to a tree where it was wired up (still alive) to attract a leopard to shoot after dark (also illegal), diesel used to pour into warthog holes where a wounded leopard had run, and then set on fire; over 200 rounds of gunfire shot into a palm island where they thought a male lion was holed up, but ended up shooting his pride and eight cubs, and then later, setting the palm alight to 'smoke the sucker out' – are all testaments to the atrocities. The male was wounded so couldn't escape and burned to death, but the hunters logged it up to an accident and went on to shoot his brother… (I) heard the hunters tell the stories with no remorse afterwards around the campfires. Well-known local professional hunters were nicknamed 'Matches xyz' and 'Fireman xyz' for burning the swamp to attract the rare sitatunga to kill".[594]

"The trophy hunters' transgressions were all caught on tape — capturing baby zebras, running over an impala with a truck, watching wildebeests writhe and bleed before killing them, letting children participate in the hunt."[595]

---

[594] "Dereck Joubert sets the record straight about trophy hunting impact on lions and refutes claims of so-called benefits", Africa Geographic, 6 February 2019

[595] "Tanzania gives hunting permit to a firm despite video of animal abuse", Kevin Sieff, Washington Post, June 29, 2016

There is virtual unanimity in scientific circles that trophy hunting is unethical. And it is clear that it is cruel and that animals can suffer greatly when they are targeted by trophy hunters. Even some of its defenders have been forced to admit that it is "repugnant".[596] But does trophy hunting constitute 'murder'? And are there links between trophy hunters, violent crime and indeed serial killing?

Dr Marc Bekoff, a Professor at the University of Colorado, describes trophy hunting as an act of "gratuitous violence", saying that "an animal is killed in the same manner for which it is declared that a human has been murdered." He argues that calling trophy hunting anything other than murder represents "sanitizing the killing".[597]

Criminologist Dr Xanthe Mallett agrees: "the failure to use the word 'murder' for nonhumans is due to a misleading extension of the 'them' versus 'us' way of thinking, one that is, or should be, long gone, and a view that ignores who other animals truly are – their cognitive and emotional lives and capacities – based on large amounts of detailed empirical research. While we surely are different from other animals, we also share many traits that make us all very similar to the magnificent animals who are routinely hunted as trophies."[598]

---

[596] https://science.sciencemag.org/content/365/6456/874/tab-e-letters

[597] https://www.psychologytoday.com/gb/blog/animal-emotions/201510/the-psychology-and-thrill-trophy-hunting-is-it-criminal

[598] https://www.psychologytoday.com/gb/blog/animal-

Graham Collier, a contributor to *Psychology Today*, describes how 'thrill killing' of humans is "clearly considered to be aberrant and criminal behaviour that rightfully is called murder" and that the same approach should be taken with regards to trophy hunting: "The bottom line is that anyone who thrill kills should be punished regardless of whom the victim is."[599]

Kirk Robinson, executive director of the Western Wildlife Conservancy, agrees with the parallel: Trophy hunting "is done with planning (premeditation) and without provocation or biological justification. The animals are entirely innocent creatures killed only for ego-gratification and fun." He adds that trophy hunting is "a gratuitously violent act."[600]

In an essay entitled '*Is Trophy Hunting a Form of Serial Killing?*', lion expert and conservationist Gareth Patterson argues that "trophy hunting – the repeated killing of wild animals – should surely be viewed as serial killing." He says that "killing innocent animals for self-gratification is no different from killing innocent people for self-gratification".[601]

---

emotions/201510/the-psychology-and-thrill-trophy-hunting-is-it-criminal

[599] https://www.psychologytoday.com/us/blog/the-consciousness-question/201302/animals-and-hunting

[600] https://www.psychologytoday.com/gb/blog/animal-emotions/201510/the-psychology-and-thrill-trophy-hunting-is-it-criminal

[601]

https://exposingthebiggame.wordpress.com/2015/08/05/trophy-hunter-serial-killer/

"Trophy hunters are mostly 'repeat' killers," he notes. "Trophy hunters often hire a cameraperson to film their entire hunt in the bush, including the actual moments when animals are shot and when they die. These films are made to be viewed later, presumably for self-gratification and to show to other people – again the need to feel 'important'? Other serial killers have tape-recorded the screams of their victims, which were kept for later self-gratification."

"Like the serial killer, the trophy hunter plans his killing with considerable care and deliberation. Like the serial killer he decides well in advance the 'type' of victims – i.e. which species he intends to target. Also, like the serial killer, the trophy hunter plans with great care where and how the killing will take place – in what area, with what weapon."

Colin Wilson and Donald Seaman, writing in '*The Serial Killers*'[602] - a book on the psychology of violence – also remark on the similarities between serial killers and trophy hunters. Both have a 'compulsion' to collect 'trophies' or 'souvenirs' from their killings. They tell the story of Robert Hansen, an Alaska businessman and trophy hunter, who hunted naked prostitutes through the snow as though they were wild animals before shooting them dead. Hansen would point a gun at his victim, order her to take off all her clothes, and then tell her to run. He would give his victims a 'head-start' before stalking them.

---

[602] "The Serial Killers: A Study in the Psychology of Violence", Colin Wilson and Donald Seaman, Virgin Books, 2007

The authors remark on the similarities between the 'thrill' of stalking his victim with comments often made by trophy hunters who say 'No, hunting isn't just about killing,' 'It's also about the stalk, the build-up to the kill.' Hansen was a celebrated trophy hunter feted for shooting a Dall sheep using a crossbow and whose home contained several trophies of elk and bears. He also took items of jewellery from his victims as 'trophies' which he hid in the attic away from his family.

Scientists have also found that trophy hunters are particularly inclined towards what they call 'dominionism' – the ultimate need to control.[603] Albany killer Stephen Francis Kuber, 20, exemplified the concept of dominionism when he murdered Kimberly Jaye Decker on July 10, 1990: "You know how you drag a deer by the horns or the neck? That's how I dragged her," he told New York State Police investigator James Horton. "You know how you kill a sunfish? You really have to pound. That's how I had to pound on her. She wouldn't die."[604]

Arthur Shawcross, a notorious serial killer, was an active hunter. When he was released from prison, where he served a sentence for raping and murdering two children, he went on to kill a further 11 women.[605] High

---

[603] Heberlein, T. cited in Clifton, M. (2003). https://www.animals24-7.org/1994/03/17/new-york-state-statistics-show-link-hunters-and-molesters/
[604] Clifton, M. (2003). https://www.animals24-7.org/1994/03/17/new-york-state-statistics-show-link-hunters-and-molesters/
[605] Clifton, M. (2003). https://www.animals24-7.org/1994/03/17/new-york-state-statistics-show-link-hunters-and-

School shooter Jaylen Fryberg, given a gun for his 14th birthday, "bragged about hunting and posted gruesome photos of the animals he'd killed on his social media accounts, with captions such as 'oooo kill 'em'."[606]

Wilson and Seaman point out that Jack the Ripper also collected trophies from his victims, such as the nose, breasts and strips of flesh from the thighs of his victims which he displayed on his bedside table, while another serial killer skinned his victim and turned it into a waistcoat.

Other scientists have written about the 'dominionistic attitude' toward animals, characteristics of which are that the individual's primary satisfaction derives from "mastery and control over animals", and found that the same attitude extended to how they view women and children.[607]

Doctors have reported increased incidences of domestic violence the day before the start of the hunting season.[608] Researchers recently discovered the startling statistic that children in upstate New York counties, an area that has one of the highest number of hunters per capita, are three times more likely to be sexually

---

molesters/

[606] https://www.peta.org/blog/youth-hunting/

[607] Kellert, S.R. and Felthous, A.R. (1985). Childhood cruelty towards animals among criminals and non-criminals. Human Relations, 38, 1113-1129.

[608] "Hunting linked to psychosexual inadequacy and the 5 phases of a hunter's life of sexual frustration", Brent Lambert, November 7, 2016
https://www.feelguide.com/2016/11/07/hunting-linked-to-psychosexual-inadequacy-the-5-phases-of-a-hunters-life-of-sexual-frustration/

assaulted than children in the crime-ridden Bronx district of New York City.[609]

Renowned psychiatrist Dr Karl Menninger, who was awarded the Presidential Medal of Freedom by President Jimmy Carter in 1981, wrote that trophy hunting represented a socially acceptable form of sadism in which the "destructive and cruel energies of man (are) directed toward more helpless creatures."[610]

Alan Felthous of the University of Texas Medical Branch and Stephen Kellert of Yale University carried out a major study in which they interviewed over 150 prisoners. In their subsequent paper, *Cruelty toward Animals among Criminals and Non-criminals*[611], they write how violent offenders were much more likely to have carried out acts of cruelty towards animals when they were children.

Studies indicate that children who are shown that violence and abuse towards living creatures is acceptable are more likely to commit acts of bullying, hurt animals, pick fights, and engage in theft, vandalism, and arson as they grow older.

---

[609] https://www.animals24-7.org/1994/03/17/new-york-state-statistics-show-link-hunters-and-molesters/

[610] "Hunting Linked To Psychosexual Inadequacy & The 5 Phases Of A Hunter's Life Of Sexual Frustration", Brent Lambert. 'Neuroscience, Psychology, Society', November 7, 2016
https://www.feelguide.com/2016/11/07/hunting-linked-to-psychosexual-inadequacy-the-5-phases-of-a-hunters-life-of-sexual-frustration/

[611]
https://journals.sagepub.com/doi/10.1177/001872678503801202

They are also more likely to display other forms of empathy deficit, lack of remorse and callousness[612]. A study of children aged 10-15 who were exposed to sport hunting showed they were more abusive, more likely to commit crimes, showed signs of depression, hit out at their own parents, and were more likely to abuse drugs and alcohol.[613]

FBI agents who have examined the backgrounds of serial and sexual killers found that animal cruelty frequently appeared in their childhoods. "Murderers … very often start out by killing and torturing animals as kids," says R.K. Ressler, who developed profiles of serial killers for the FBI.[614] Infamous American serial killers including Ted Bundy, Jeffrey Dahmer, and the 'Son of Sam' killer David Berkowitz. Dennis Rader (the so-called 'BTK' killer – BTK stood for 'bind, torture, kill') and spree killer Boyd Malvo also all committed acts of cruelty against animals when they were younger.[615]

The Columbine High School killers and Jon Venables, the 'dominant' child of the two boys who killed Jamie Bulger, had previous histories of animal

[612] N. Taylor & T.D. I. Signal (2005). Empathy and attitudes to animals. Anthrozoös., 18(1), 18-27.

[613] Nikela https://www.nikela.org/unlikely-trophy-hunting-victims-children/

[614] Ressler, Robert K.; Burgess, Ann W.; Douglas, John E. (1988). Sexual Homicide Patterns and Motives. New York, NY: Simon and Schuster. ISBN 9780669165593.

[615] Daniel Goleman (1991) "Experts See Parallels Between Dahmer, Previous Serial Killers," New York Times News Service. Aug.11.

abuse, as did notorious murderers Ian Brady and Ian Huntley, the Soham killer.

There is now a growing trend within the hunting industry to encourage young children to go trophy hunting. Industry lobbyists are pushing hard for the minimum age of legal hunting to be lowered in US states. There are youth 'hunting camps' at which hunting groups hand out 'goody bags' with hunting paraphernalia. Some researchers fear that this could lead to an increase in violent and anti-social behaviour.

Children learn acceptable behaviours from adult models such as parents, TV characters, peers, and teachers, and will imitate approved behaviour, says researcher and author Penny Morgan: "If a child witnesses a model being reinforced/rewarded for her behaviour, he/she will be more motivated to copy her. This is vicarious reinforcement. Similarly, if the child observes the model being punished, he/she would be less motivated to copy her. This is termed vicarious punishment. In other words, the child learns by observing the consequences of the models' behaviour."[616]

She points to a number of examples of how trophy hunting is promoted – and rewarded – among children. "The state of South Dakota has a program that pays children in order to incentivise them to kill animals. The website of Texas Hunt Lodge reads: 'We love to have 1st time hunters join us. We take great pride in helping to educate children and beginner hunters about the responsibilities of hunting.'"[617]

---

[616] pers. Comm.

[617] https://www.texashuntlodge.com/hunting-packages

She says that scientists[618] have shown that normalising violent behaviour can have long-term effects on children, including "aggressive behaviours, aggressive thoughts, angry feelings, arousal levels. This is crucial for considering the impact of early exposure to trophy hunting".

Other scientists say that witnessing or being forced to commit animal abuse constitutes a form of abuse in itself[619] and that abused children often grow up to be abusers themselves.[620] In a 2016 study, Plant et al. state: "We found not only have most animal abusers been exposed to violence and abuse, but that this has resulted in reduced empathy and a normalisation of aggression".[621]

The FBI now classifies animal abuse as a Grade A felony. "The FBI's decision will not only be a way to stop cases of animal abuse but also can help to identify people who might commit violent acts," according to a recent analysis of the decision. "Psychological studies show that nearly 70 percent of violent criminals began by abusing animals, and keeping statistics on such cases

---

[618] Bushman, B.J. & Heusmann, R. (2006). Short-term and long-term effects of violent media on aggression in children and adults. Arch. Pediatr. Adolesc. Med. 160(4), 348-352.

[619] Schafer, K. D. (2007). Cruelty to Animals and the Short- and Long-Term Impact on Victims. Journal of Emotional Abuse, 7(3), 31-57.

[620] Murrell, A.R., Christoff, K.R. & Henning, K.R. (2007). Characteristics of domestic violence offenders: Associations with exposure to violence. Journal of Family Violence, 22, (7), 523–532.

[621] Plant, M., van Schalk, P., Gullone, E. (2016). "It's a Dog's Life": Culture, Empathy, Gender, and Domestic Violence Predict Animal Abuse in Adolescents—Implications for Societal Health. J. Interpersonal Violence. 34(10).

can help law enforcement track down high-risk demographics and areas."[622]

Trophy hunting may not be classed in law as murder – at least not yet. But the parallels are clear, as are the very real risks to society of indulging it.

[622] "The FBI Now Considers Animal Abuse a Class A Felony", Vice News, January 7 2016
https://www.vice.com/en_us/article/wjazgy/the-fbi-now-considers-animal-abuse-a-class-a-felony

Chapter 12: What do Western voters – and Africans – really want?

"I think sometimes we need to take step back and just remember we have no greater right to be here than any other animal" – Sir David Attenborough[623]

A number of polls have been carried out in Britain on people's attitudes towards trophy hunting and what they want the government to do about it.

The first such survey, carried out in July 2019 by Survation[624], asked people the following: "To what extent do you support or oppose a ban on trophy hunters bringing back hunting trophies of wild animals to the UK?"

The results were:

Support: 75%

Oppose: 15%

Neither support nor oppose: 9%

Don't know: 2%[625]

---

[623] "Sir David Attenborough: my wild life", The Times, September 16 2017 https://www.thetimes.co.uk/article/sir-david-attenborough-my-wild-life-including-how-to-train-a-dragon-5xpqtlqst

[624] Commissioned by the Campaign to Ban Trophy Hunting

[625] The total adds up to 101% as individual percentages are rounded up/down

A poll 6 months later by YouGov[626] asked a similar question: "To what extent, if at all, would you support or oppose a ban on imports and exports of hunting trophies?" The results were, if anything, stronger:
Support: 80%
Oppose: 10%
Neither support nor oppose: 5%
Don't know: 4%

In September, 2019, Survation carried out a new poll[627]. This time the question asked was: "Which of the following statements is closest to your view?"
Trophy hunting should be universally banned: 86%
Trophy hunting should not be universally banned: 8%
Don't know: 6%

The January 2020 YouGov poll put a further question to respondents: "If the government were to bring in restrictions on imports and exports of hunting trophies, to which types of animal should they apply?" The response was unequivocal:
Threatened or endangered species only: 14%
All species: 76%
The government should not bring in any restrictions: 2%
Don't know: 8%

Detailed analysis of each of these polls also shows there to be very little difference in people's views

---

[626] Commissioned by Humane Society International/UK and the Campaign to Ban Trophy Hunting
[627] Commissioned by the Campaign to Ban Trophy Hunting

according to what political party they support, what part of the country they come from, their age, income or educational qualifications, or even how they voted in the EU Referendum.

Across the board, the message is clear: people want to see an end to trophy hunting, and they want Britain to ban all imports and exports of trophies - not just those of endangered species.

The current position of the UK government and main opposition parties is that there should be a ban on body parts of endangered or threatened species. But voters do not see this as a conservation issue. They see it primarily as a moral imperative. Trophy hunting is a social evil that should be abolished. Britain, they believe, should take a lead and implement a comprehensive ban.

Opposition to trophy hunting is not restricted to the UK. In the US, nearly 70% of voters oppose it and almost 80% are against imports of trophies from species such as lions and elephants.[628] Surveys suggest similar numbers want to see a change in the law even in countries where there are powerful hunting lobbies such as Germany.

There is – perhaps unsurprisingly - little support for trophy hunting within African communities. In 2019, Mucha Mkono – a leading academic - conducted extensive analysis of comments posted by Africans on news sites and social media platforms. "The dominant pattern was resentment towards what was viewed as the neo-colonial character of trophy hunting, in the way it

---

[628] "Lion hearted – the life and death of Cecil and the future of Africa's iconic cats", Andrew Loveridge, Regan Arts, 2018

privileges Western elites in accessing Africa's wildlife resources," she reported.[629]

Paula Kahumbu is one of Africa's best-known conservationists. Writing shortly after the killing of Cecil the lion, she said the issue "has revealed the deep grieving and heartbreak across Africa" and that "there is also revulsion at the whole idea of killing animals for pleasure, something that is completely alien to the African tradition of respect for wildlife."

She added: "Trophy hunting is, and always has been, a rich white man's sport. For Africans, it is a symbol of colonial oppression. The idea that trophy hunting benefits African economies is also a myth – or more accurately a lie. Trophy hunting generates lots of money for a few people, most of whom are already rich. Local people in Africa are being expelled from their lands to make room for private game reserves."[630] She called for "an end to (the) whole barbaric practice of trophy hunting".[631]

When US President Donald Trump lifted the ban on trophy imports from elephant hunting, one of the loudest voices of protest was that of Botswana's President Ian

---

[629] Mucha Mkono (2019): "Neo-colonialism and greed: Africans' views on trophy hunting in social media", Journal of Sustainable Tourism, 27:5, 689-704, DOI: 10.1080/09669582.2019.1604719

[630] "Justice for Cecil", Paula Kahumbu with Andrew Halliday, The Guardian, 30 July 2019
https://www.theguardian.com/environment/africa-wild/2015/jul/30/justice-for-cecil

[631] "Justice for Cecil", Paula Kahumbu with Andrew Halliday, The Guardian, Thu 30 Jul 2015
https://www.theguardian.com/environment/africa-wild/2015/jul/30/justice-for-cecil

Khama. He condemned the decision "in the strongest possible terms", accusing the US government of undermining Botswana's efforts to protect elephants: "How do you explain the import of elephant trophies from Botswana while we have a ban on hunting?"[632]

In April 2019, The Guardian newspaper published a letter calling on Britain to stop imports from trophy hunting. Among the dozens of signatories to the letter were some of Africa's leading conservationists, scientists and NGOs.[633] A letter published by The Times on January 11, 2020, had an even longer list of scientists and conservationists from around the world, many of them from Africa.[634]

South Africa's Parliamentary Portfolio Committee on Environment Affairs has called for an outright ban on captive lion breeding. In a report entitled *"Captive Lion Breeding for Hunting in South Africa: Harming or Promoting the Conservation Image of the Country"*, they wrote that the canned lion hunting industry "undermines South Africa's tourism brand value" and threatened to make the country an "international pariah". Their report adds: "It is obvious in this instance that hunting of

[632] "To kill or not to kill - Parliament to decide the fate of Botswana's elephants", Thobo Motlhoka, The Independent, Monday 30 July 2018
https://www.independent.co.uk/voices/campaigns/GiantsClub/Botswana/to-kill-or-not-to-kill-parliament-to-decide-the-fate-of-botswanas-elephants-a8470551.html
[633]
https://www.theguardian.com/environment/2019/apr/12/ban-the-import-of-hunting-trophies
[634] https://www.thetimes.co.uk/article/times-letters-private-drama-played-out-on-a-global-stage-fh0ldwflw

captive-bred lions might have done irreparable damage to the reputation of South Africa, especially considering the negative global publicity."[635]

Prince Buthelezi, the longstanding leader of South Africa's Inkatha Freedom party, is among many African politicians to have been a strong vocal critic of the industry.[636]

Those living in areas where trophy hunting takes place are candid about how they believe they have been lied to by companies and officials who promised they would benefit from trophy hunting. Mkono dismisses the claims that trophy hunting is necessary for funding conservation and that local communities benefit from trophy hunting as a "myth" and says that trophy hunting's economic importance is "overstated".[637] She accuses hunting lobby groups of having "built a narrative where hunting is the only viable means of financing sustainable conservation in Africa."[638]

In an address to MPs and peers in the British Parliament in January 2020, South African economist and wildlife policy analyst Dr Ross Harvey said: "The idea that local communities in rural Africa desire trophy

[635] "SA calls for all-out ban on canned lion breeding", News24, 2018-11-15 https://www.news24.com/Green/sa-calls-for-all-out-ban-on-canned-lion-breeding-20181115

[636] https://www.youtube.com/watch?v=jumvAW4ki9A

[637] "Trophy hunting is not the solution to Africa's wildlife conservation challenges", Muchazondida Mkono, QuartzAfrica May 16, 2019 https://qz.com/africa/1621198/trophy-hunting-cant-fix-africas-wildlife-conservation-challenge/

[638] Mucha Mkono (2019): "Neo-colonialism and greed: Africans' views on trophy hunting in social media", Journal of Sustainable Tourism, 27:5, 689-704, DOI: 10.1080/09669582.2019.1604719

hunting, or that it is nasty but necessary for conservation, is fanciful propaganda. It ignores the fact that economic alternatives exist. It ignores the fact that those alternatives may create up to 11 times more jobs per hectare than trophy hunting. It ignores the fact that killing the biggest and best elephants or lions destroys genetic strength and ecological integrity, the very bedrock of future photographic tourism."

Harvey has studied the parallels between the arguments used by supporters of trophy hunting today and those deployed by defenders of the Atlantic slave trade in the 18th century. Proponents of slavery claimed that abolition would "involve both master and slave in one common destruction." In a refrain familiar to those who have heard the industry's attacks, slavery may be morally repugnant but there was no economic alternative. To act against it therefore would "imperil the welfare" of slaves.

Politicians then, as now, dithered in the face of this moral blackmail. The abolition of slavery took a further 50 years to come about. In the aftermath of the killing of Cecil, the British government announced it would ban lion trophy imports if there were no improvements in the industry. Nothing, arguably, has changed within the industry. Despite this, the government dropped its pledge.

The lives of some 50 lions could have been saved had they kept their promise.

Chapter 13: A New Contract with Nature

"The big question is, why are you shooting a lion in the first place? I'm honestly curious to know why a human being would be compelled to do that. How is that fun?" - Jimmy Kimmel, US TV talk show host

"The time will come when they will cease to sneer, when they will understand that the animal world was placed... under our protection and not at our mercy; that animals have as much right to live as we have, and that our right to take their lives is strictly limited to our right of defence and our right of existence. The time will come when the mere pleasure of killing will die out in man. As long as it is there, man has no claim to call himself civilised, he is a mere barbarian." - Axel Munthe, 'The story of San Michele'[639]

Society has banned many forms of animal cruelty and blood-sports such as bear baiting and dogfighting. However trophy hunting has so far escaped. We have banned the trafficking of trophies, but not the killing of animals for trophies. We have legislated against killing endangered animals for their meat, but we allow the same endangered animals to be shot for entertainment. We hand out stiff penalties to those who kill domestic

---

[639] 'The story of San Michele', Axel Munthe, John Murray Publishers, 2004

cats for pleasure, but killing wild cats can merit the perpetrator highly prestigious prizes. We have given farmed animals some modest welfare protections, but none to wild animals who often die in agonising circumstances.

When Jimmy Kimmel expressed his astonishment at the killing of Cecil, he spoke for millions of people who honestly believed the world had moved on from such colonial pastimes. We – perhaps naively - think that as a modern civilisation we have laws and institutions that prevent such barbarity. The reality is that the world's richest and most powerful people are (still) allowed to murder living creatures for their pleasure.

In his epic work 'Half-Earth', Edward O. Wilson says that "only a major shift in moral reasoning… can meet the greatest challenge of the century."[640] The consequences of our current approach towards nature are plainly visible. WWF's latest Living Planet Report (2018) tells us that we are living in a period of "unprecedented planetary change".[641] People in developed nations enjoy a lifestyle that, were it to be replicated by every person on earth, would require three planets to satisfy our desires (and absorb our waste). Our ecological footprint has increased by almost 200% in the last 50 years. There has been a 60% decline in the population sizes of vertebrates over an equal period.[642]

---

[640] "Saving half the planet for nature isn't as crazy as it seems", National Geographic, Simon Worrall

[641]

https://wwf.panda.org/knowledge_hub/all_publications/living_planet_report_2018/

[642]

"Treating the planet as a commodity became firmly established as the norm in the Western World with the advent of the Industrial Revolution," says Polly Higgins, a prominent environmental lawyer. She has called for the crime of 'ecocide' to be recognised under international law.[643] Is the African elephant "to be looked upon as a resource, like coal or coffee beans? (or)… does it have a right to exist?", asks James Clarke, author of 'Overkill', a book which charts the calamitous collapse of wildlife populations due to human exploitation.[644]

We have known since the time of Aristotle that animals experience pain, fear and loss. Chimpanzees mourn. Cheetahs cry out in distress when they lose their companion. Elephants cover the bodies of their dead with dirt and sticks. As we learn more about animals – their intelligence, their capacity for feeling emotions similar to those of humans – the case for fundamental change in how we engage with the natural world becomes ever stronger.

In her introduction to 'Animal Wise', Virginia Morrell writes: "Hardly a week goes by that doesn't see a study announcing a new discovery about animal minds: 'Whales Have Accents and Regional Dialects', 'Fish Use Tools', 'Squirrels Adopt Orphans', 'Honeybees Make Plans', 'Sheep Don't Forget a Face', 'Rats Feel Each

---

https://wwf.panda.org/knowledge_hub/all_publications/living_pla net_report_2018/

[643] Eradicating Ecocide – laws and governance to prevent the destruction of our planet", Polly Higgins, 2010. Shepheard-Walwyn (Publishers) Ltd

[644] "Overkill – the race to save Africa's wildlife", James Clarke, 2017, Struik Nature/Penguin Random House South Africa

Other's Pain', 'Elephants See Themselves in Mirrors', 'Crows Able to Invent Tools'".

In 'The Inner Life of Animals', Peter Wohlleben similarly reveals new insights into the creatures that we share the Earth with. "Roosters that deceive their hens? Mother deer that grieve? Horses that feel shame? … True love among ravens? No question. Squirrels who know the names of their close relatives? That's been documented for a long time. Wherever you look, animals are out there, loving each other, feeling each other's pain and enjoying each other's company."[645]

He shows how wild boar can recognise distant relatives, that bees remember individual people ("They will attack people who have annoyed them in the past, and allow people who have left them in peace to venture much closer") and tells how pigeons can memorise hundreds of cards with different patterns. He recounts how boar in southern France learnt to swim across the river at the start of the hunting season into neighbouring Geneva where hunting was banned.

He concludes by asking: "Has Creation really engineered a unique biological path for us? Are we the only ones guaranteed a life of self-awareness and satisfaction?" Theologian and animal advocate Andrew Linzey poses a similar question: "How likely is it that a God who creates millions, if not billions, of species only cares for one of them?"[646]

---

[645] "The Inner Life of Animals: Love, Grief and Compassion – Surprising Observations of a Hidden World", Peter Wohlleben, The Bodley Head, 2016

[646] "Creatures of the Same God: Explorations in Animal Theology", Andrew Linzey, New York: Lantern Books, 2009

Or as South Africa's Archbishop Desmond Tutu puts it: "it is a kind of theological folly to suppose that God has made the entire world just for human beings, or to suppose that God is interested in only one of the millions of species that inhabit God's good Earth."[647]

In the 18th century, the philosopher Jean-Jacques Rousseau issued a robust challenge to the traditional order. Denouncing the unbridled supremacy of ruling elites, he called for a new 'social contract'. In the 21st century, the time has come for us to challenge the traditional order once again. The view of unbridled human supremacy within the natural world must be discarded, for all our sakes.

The Covid-19 global pandemic – whose origins lie in the wildlife trade - is nothing if not a call to action. The creatures with whom we share this earth are not mere objects of 'trade' or 'sport'. They are sentient and sapient creatures.

It is time for a new contract with nature.

[647] https://www.aswa.org.uk/campaigns/archbishop-desmond-tutu-speaks-out/

Epilogue: Some of the things they say…

"Britain should ban the import of animal trophies" – The Times[648]

"This industry is rife with cruelty, corruption and illegality. It plays no part in conservation and brings shame on all who participate in it. Whilst we cannot stop this barbaric industry, we can make sure that the U.K. is not complicit. And it is." – Lord Ashcroft[649]

"The day may come when the rest of animal creation may acquire those rights which never could have been withholden from them but by the hand of tyranny." - Jeremy Bentham, The Principles of Morals and Legislation

"Trophy hunting isn't just appalling for the beautiful creatures concerned; it also does something terrible to our common humanity." - Shadow Attorney General Baroness Shami Chakrabarti

"What century are we living in? How can we call ourselves a civilisation if we think murdering animals for a laugh is OK? Trophy hunters are spoilt little brats; haven't they got enough toys to play with? They're

---

[648] "The Times view on importing animal trophies into Britain: Killing for Sport", leading article, May 25 2020

[649] Open letter to Defra Secretary Rt Hon Michael Gove MP, 29 April 2019

wiping out wildlife. Soon there will be nothing left. How are we going to explain that to future generations?" – Liam Gallagher

"I find it amazing that anyone would take any kind of pleasure from shooting one of these magnificent creatures such as elephants, lions, even rhinos. It makes no sense to me at all at any level." – Lord Zac Goldsmith

"Trophy hunting is utterly cruel, utterly unnecessary and utterly disastrous from a conservation perspective. It inflicts pain and suffering on animals for no other reason other than to boast of some ephemeral 'prowess'. There is no material human need met by it: it is a hobby, pure and simple, and a deeply wrong one at that." – Jane Goodall

"Making money by slaughtering endangered wildlife for entertainment is a Victorian concept which – following a hundred years of discovery about the natural world – the majority of educated people are no longer willing to tolerate." - Mark Hilety, Director, National Park Rescue

"Trophy hunters are shooting some of the world's most vulnerable wildlife. Virtually all animals targeted by the industry are seeing dramatic falls in numbers. It's a disgraceful activity and needs to be banned now." – Stanley Johnson

"When a man wantonly destroys one of the works of man, we call him a vandal. When he destroys one of the works of God, we call him a sportsman." - Joseph Wood Krutch

"It is not constitutionally allowable to kill or mistreat animals for the sole purpose of recreation. Animals are not things, they are beings with feelings." - Colombian magistrate Antonio Jose Lizarazo[650]

"Trophy hunting is ethically and morally unacceptable. We still hear those involved in this so-called 'sport' trot out the tired old lie that it is all about conservation. But it's not – it's just another way for them to try to justify their desire to kill for pleasure." – Chris Packham

"The time is overdue for individuals, civil society and governments to recognise animals as complex, living beings, rather than as tools, objects and trophies." – Michele Pickover, EMS Foundation

"There is no justification for trophy hunting. We must ban this vile practice. We should all do everything we can to rid ourselves of this disgusting so-called sport." – Peter Shilton

"My sons love hunting, I don't." – President Donald J Trump

---

[650] "Colombia to ban sport hunting", phys.org, February 7, 2019

APPENDIX

Trophy Hunters' Records & Awards

Malcolm King's Safari Club International hunting awards

4 Safari Club International 'Continental Awards':
"South Pacific 8" (minimum 8 different species)
"Asia 8" (minimum 8 different species)
"Europe 12" (minimum 12 different species)
"Africa 15" (minimum 15 different species)

7 Safari Club International 'Grand Slam Awards':
"Africa 29" (minimum 29 different species)
"Dangerous Game of Africa" (minimum 5 different species)
"Cats of the World" (minimum 4 different species)
"European Deer" (minimum 9 different species)
"Bears of the World" (minimum 5 different species)
"North American wild sheep" (minimum 4 different species)
"Moose of the World" (minimum 4 different species)

25 Safari Club International "Inner Circle Awards":
Hunting Achievement Award (Diamond - minimum 125 SCI Record Book entries)
Global Hunting Award (Gold - minimum 50 different species)
Top Ten Awards (15 entries)

Predators of the world (Diamond - minimum 15 different species)

Animals of Africa (Gold - minimum 61 different species)

Animals of Asia (Diamond - minimum 15 different species)

Animals of Europe (Diamond- minimum 16 different species)

Animals of South Pacific (Gold - minimum 10 different species)

Antlered Game of the World (Gold - minimum 30 different species)

Antlered Game of the Americas (Bronze - minimum 12 different species)

Spiral horned Antelopes of Africa (Diamond - minimum 17 different species)

Chamois of the World (Diamond - minimum 6 different species)

Desert Game of the World (Diamond - minimum 22 different species)

Gazelles of the World (Diamond - minimum 11 different species)

Introduced Animals of North America (Gold - minimum 15 different species)

Introduced Animals of Africa (Copper - minimum 4 different species)

Ibex of the World (Diamond - minimum 6 different species)

Mountain Game of the World (Diamond - minimum 24 different species)

Red deer/wapiti of the World (diamond - minimum 8 different species)

Wild pigs/peccaries of the world (diamond / minimum 7 different species)

Pygmy antelope of the world (Diamond - minimum 15 different species)

Ring horned Antelopes of Africa (Diamond - minimum 33 different species)

Wild sheep of the world (Diamond - minimum 12 different species)

Wild oxen of the world (Diamond - minimum 8 different species)

Wild goats of the World (Diamond- minimum 12 different species)

Carl Knight's hunting holiday packages & fees

South Africa

Limpopo-Serengeti Trophy fees (professional hunting guide: $400/day):
African wild cat: $460
Buffalo: $9000-11,000
Baboon: $200
Bush pig: $550
Civet cat: $1000
Crocodile: $2800-4200
Giraffe: $2400
Hippo: $9000
Porcupine: $250
Rhino: POA
Vervet monkey: $200
Zebra: $1100

Philippolis Trophy fees (professional hunting guide: $450/day):
Buffalo: $11,000
Giraffe: $3900
Ostrich: $550
Warthog: $500
Zebra: $2500

Zimbabwe

The cost of hunting packages at Matetsi:
Lion - $57,750
Elephant - $40,000
Leopard - $32,000
Hippo - $25,000
Crocodile - $25,500

Trophy fees for other animals here:
Baboon $80
Giraffe $1800
Hyena $700
Porcupine $300
Vervet monkey $75
Wild cat $250
Zebra $1200

The cost of hunting packages in Gonarezhou:
Lion: $48,600
Elephant: $29,700
Leopard: $18,200
Hippo: $11,300
Crocodile: $10,500

Trophy fees for other animals:
Baboon $100
Giraffe $1750
Honey badger $250
Hyena $750
Impala $450
Jackal $150
Wild cat $400
Zebra $1100

Ivan Carter's Record trophies with clients

African Elephants

Date shot: September 2010
Location: Botswana, CT2
Trophy score: 119

Date shot: May 2013
Location: Botswana, Maun
Trophy score: 139

Date shot: August 2013
Location: Botswana, Maun
Trophy score: 120 ½

Leopards

Date shot: May 2008
Location: Zimbabwe
Trophy score: 16 7/16

Date shot: October 2011
Location: Tanzania, Msima
Trophy score: 14 10/16

Cape buffaloes

Date shot: April 2008

Location: Zimbabwe
Trophy score: 109 6/8

Date shot: October 2011
Location: Tanzania, Msima
Trophy score: 106 4/8

Date shot: October 2013
Location: Tanzania, Rungwa
Trophy score: 101 4/8

Date shot: October 2013
Location: Tanzania, Rungwa
Trophy Score: 121 4/8

Hippopotamuses

Date shot: October 2011
Location: Tanzania, Msima
Trophy score: 61 4/16

Date shot: October 2011
Location: Tanzania, Msima
Trophy score: 62 5/16

Michel Bergerac's record trophies & SCI awards

African elephants

Date: 8/73.
Location: Zambia, Kafue.
Hunting company/guide: Doug Stephenson, Zambia Safaris.
Tusk weights: 94 lb, 85 lb.
Trophy score: 179.

Date: 7/79.
Location: CAR, Chinko.
Hunting company/guide: Daniel Henriot/Haut Chinko Safaris.
Tusk weights: 63 lb, 61 lb.
Trophy score: 124.

Date: 3/88.
Location: Ethiopia, Bebeka.
Hunting company/guide: Col Neguissie Eshete/Rocky Mountain Outfitters.
Tusk weights: 60 lb, 62 lb.
Trophy score: 122.

Date: 8/71.
Location: Mozambique, Tete.
Hunting company/guide: Gilberto Lobo/Safrique.
Tusk weights: 50 lb, 50 lb.
Trophy score: 100.

Lion

Date: 7/91.
Location: Botswana, Okavango.
Hunting company/guide: Ron McFarland, Vira
Safaris.
Skull length & width: 15 1/16", 9 11/16".
Trophy score: 24 12/16

Leopard

Date: 1/93.
Location: Tanzania, Masailand.
Hunting company/guide: Mike Branham/Tanzania
Safaris.
Skull length & width: 8 15/16", 5 6/16"
Trophy score: 14 7/16.

Spotted hyena

Date: 9/93.
Location: Tanzania, Rukwa.
Hunting company/guide: Mike Branham/Tanzania
safaris.
Skull length & width: 11 13/16", 6 8/16".
Trophy score: 18 5/16.

Scimitar horned oryx

Date: 3/67.
Location: Chad, Oum Chalouba.
Hunting guide: Claude Vasselet.
Length & circumference of horns at base: 40 6/8" &
40 6/8", 6 6/8" & 6 6/8"
Trophy score: 95

Addax

    Date: 6/81.

    Location: Sudan, NW desert.

    Length & circumference of horns at base: 38 2/8" &
38 2/8", 6 7/8" & 6 5/8"

    Trophy score: 90.

(note: biggest ever recorded addax trophy; 'picked up')

Bergerac's Safari Club International's awards:

    Pinnacle of Achievement - Fourth Pinnacle (1998)

    Grand Slam Cats of the World Award (1998)

    Grand Slam North American Wild Sheep (1998)

    Grand Slam Africa Big Five Award (1994)

    Grand Slam Africa 29 Award (1998)

    Grand Slam Dangerous Game of Africa Award
(1998)

    Spiral-horned Antelopes of Africa Award – Diamond
(1995)

    Chamois of the World Award - Silver (2002)

    Global Hunting Award - Silver (2002)

    Gazelles of the World Award - Gold (1998)

    Hunting Achievement Award - Gold (2002)

    Ibex of the World Award - Copper (2002)

    Red Deer/Wapiti of the World Award – Copper
(2002)

    Wild Pigs and Peccaries of the World Award - Bronze
(2002)

    Pygmy Antelope of Africa Award - Diamond (1998)

    Animals of Europe Award - Copper (2002)

Animals of Africa Award - Gold (1998)
Wild Oxen of the World Award - Copper (2002)
Wild Sheep of the World Award - Bronze (1998)
TopTen Award (1995)
Animals of North America Award - Copper (2002)
Animals of South Pacific Award - Copper (2002)
Wild Goats of the World Award - Bronze (2002)

Bela Hidvegi's SCI Awards

World Conservation and Hunting Award (2016)
The Pantheon Award.
SCI Major Awards Honor - ASIA (4th) Punjab Urial
131 2/8
Pinnacle of Achievement - Fourth Pinnacle (2004)
Crowning Achievement Award (2006)
North American 12 (2010)
Grand Slam Cats of the World Award (2004)
Grand Slam White-tailed Deer Award (2006)
Grand Slam European Deer Award (2004)
Grand Slam Bears of the World Award (2006)
Grand Slam North American Wild Sheep (2008)
Grand Slam Africa Big Five Award (2004)
Grand Slam Moose of the World Award (2006)
Grand Slam North American Caribou Award (2006)
Grand Slam North American Deer Award (2006)
Grand Slam Indigenous Animals of South America
Award (2006)
Grand Slam Africa 29 Award (2004)
Grand Slam Dangerous Game of Africa (2001)
Spiral-horned Antelopes of Africa Award - Diamond
(2002)
Chamois of the World Award - Diamond (2006)
Desert Game of the World Award - Diamond (2011)
Global Hunting Award - Diamond (2006)
Gazelles of the World Award - Diamond (2006)
Hunting Achievement Award - Diamond (2004)
Introduced Animals of Africa Award - Diamond
(2004)

Mountain Game of the World Award - Diamond (2008)

Red Deer/Wapiti of the World - Diamond (2006)

Wild Pigs and Peccaries of the World Award - Diamond (2004)

Predators of the World Award - Diamond (2006)

Pygmy Antelope of Africa Award - Diamond (2006)

Animals of Asia Award - Diamond (2006)

Animals of Europe Award - Diamond (2004)

Animals of South America Award - Diamond (2006)

Animals of Africa Award – Diamond (2004)

Wild Oxen of the World - Bronze (2006)

Wild Sheep of the World Award - Diamond (2008)

Antlered Game of the World Award - Diamond (2006)

TopTen Award - Diamond (2004)

Animals of South Pacific Award - Diamond (2006)

Wild Goats of the World Award - Diamond (2006)

Egon Lechner's SCI Record Book trophies

Leopard
Date: 10/90.
Location: RSA Transvaal
Professional guide: Piet Otto.
Skull length & width: 9 12/16", 6 5/16"
Trophy score: 16 1/16

Spotted hyena
Date: 6/89.
Location: Zambia, Rufunsa.
Professional guide: Self-guided.
Skull length & width: 11 4/162, 6 14/16".
Trophy score: 18 2/16.

Marcial Gomez Sequeira's SCI awards

Predators of the World Award - Diamond
World Hunting Award (1995)
SCI World Conservation & Hunting Award (2006)
SCI Major Awards Honor – EUROPE: Iberian
Mouflon (7th)
Pinnacle of Achievement - Fourth Pinnacle (1993)
Zenith Award (2011)
Crowning Achievement Award (1993)
African 15 SCI Continental Award (2012)
North American 12 Award (2011)
Grand Slam Cats of the World Award (1986)
Grand Slam White-tailed Deer Award (1986)
Grand Slam European Deer Award (1995)
Grand Slam Elk of North America Award (2000)
Grand Slam Bears of the World Award (1993)
Grand Slam North American Wild Sheep (1985)
Grand Slam Africa Big Five Award (1984)
Grand Slam Moose of the World Award (1993)
Grand Slam North America 29 Award (1993)
Grand Slam North American Caribou Award (1993)
Grand Slam North American Deer (1986)
Grand Slam Indigenous Animals of South America
Award (2012)
Grand Slam Africa 29 Award (1995)
Grand Slam Dangerous Game of Africa (1998)
Inner Circle Award - Antlered Game of the Americas
(Diamond) (1993)
Spiral-horned Antelopes of Africa Award (Diamond)
(1993)

Chamois of the World Award -Diamond (1995)
Desert Game of the World - Diamond (2011)
Global Hunting Award - Diamond (2000)
Gazelles of the World Award - Diamond (1997)
Hunting Achievement Award - Diamond (1993)
Introduced Animals of North America Award - Diamond (1993)
Ibex of the World Award Recipients - Diamond (1995)
Mountain Game of the World Award - Gold (2011)
Red Deer/Wapiti of the World Award - Diamond (1993)
Wild Pigs and Peccaries of the World Award - Diamond (1997)
Predators of the World Award - Diamond (2011)
Pygmy Antelope of Africa Award - Diamond (1995)
Ringed-horn Antelope of Africa Award - Diamond (2012)
Animals of Asia Award - Diamond (1993)
Animals of Europe Award - Diamond (1993)
Animals of South America Award - Diamond (1993)
Animals of Africa Award - Diamond (1993)
Wild Oxen of the World Award - Diamond (1993)
Wild Sheep of the World Award - Diamond (1993)
Antlered Game of the World Award - Diamond (1993)
TopTen Award - Diamond (1993)
Animals of North America Award - Diamond (1993)
Animals of South Pacific Award - Diamond (1993)
Wild Goats of the World Award - Diamond (1993)

Marcial Gomez Sequeira's SCI Records Book trophies:

African elephants

Date: 5/73.
Location: CAR, Bangassou.
Hunting guide: Jose Moreno.
Tusk weights: 71 ½ lb, 86 ½ lb.
Trophy score: 158.

Date: 5/77.
Location: Sudan, Yambio.
Hunting guide: Miguel Guerra.
Tusk weights: 75 ½ lb, 80 lb.
Trophy score: 155

Date: 11/71.
Location: Mozambique, Marromeu.
Hunting guide: Jose Simoes.
Tusk weights: 74 ½ lb, 72 ½ lb.
Trophy score: 147 lb.

Date: 4/74.
Location: CAR, Vovodo River.
Hunting guide: Jose Moreno.
Tusk weights: 71 lb. 69 lb.
Trophy score: 140.

Date: 5/73. CAR, Vovodo River.
Hunting guide: Jose Moreno.
Tusk weights: 65 ½ lb, 69 lb.
Trophy score: 134 1/2.

Date: 4/74.
Location: CAR, Vovodo River.
Hunting guide: Jose Moreno.
Tusk weights: 55 lb, 54 lb.
Trophy score: 109.

White Rhinos

Date: 7/77.
Location: RSA.
Hunting guide: Antonio Moreno.
Horn lengths & circumferences at base: 25 2/8" & 13 2/8", 22 3/8" & 19 2/8"
Trophy score: 81/8.

Date: 7/77.
Location: RSA.
Hunting guide: Antonio Moreno.
Horn lengths & circumferences at base: 24 1/8" & 10 2/8", 21" & 20 4/8".
Trophy score: 75 7/8.

Lion
Date: 5/79.
Location: Botswana.
Hunting guide: Mark Giorgou.
Skull length & width: 15 2/16", 11 1/16"
Trophy score: 26 3/16.

Leopards

Date: 7/82.
Location: Zimbabwe, S.
Hunting guide: self.
Skull length & width: 10 12/16", 7"
Trophy score: 17 12/16.

Date: 4/88
Location: CAR Ouanda Djalle.
Hunting guide: Antonio Ferreira.
Skull length & width: 9 12/16", 5 14/16"
Trophy score: 15 10/16.

Spotted hyena

Date: 9/71.
Location: Mozambique.
Hunting company/guide: Simoens/united safaris.
Skull length & width: 10 9/162, 6 7/162.
Trophy score: 17.

Sergey Yastrzhemskiy's SCI Awards

Magnum Ullman Award
Animals of Africa Award recipients - Diamond
Pinnacle of Achievement - Fourth Pinnacle (2009)
Zenith Award - (2011)
Asia 8 SCI Continental Award (2014)
European 12 SCI Continental Award (2014)
South American 8 SCI Continental Award (2014)
Grand Slam Cats of the World Award (2002)
Grand Slam European Deer Award (2008)
Grand Slam Bears of the World Award (2003)
Grand Slam Africa Big Five Award (2003)
Grand Slam Indigenous Animals of South America Award (2014)
Grand Slam Africa 29 Award (2006)
Grand Slam Dangerous Game of Africa Award (2003)
Spiral-horned Antelopes of Africa Award - Gold (2014)
Chamois of the World Award - Diamond (2014)
Desert Game of the World Award - Gold (2014)
Global Hunting Award - Silver (2014)
Gazelles of the World Award - Diamond (2014)
Hunting Achievement Award - Diamond (2009)
Introduced Animals of Africa Award - Bronze (2014)
Ibex of the World Award - Diamond (2008)
Mountain Game of the World Award - Silver (2015)
Red Deer/Wapiti of the World Award - Diamond (2015)

Wild Pigs and Peccaries of the World Award - Diamond (2014)

Predators of the World Award - Diamond (2009)

Pygmy Antelope of Africa Award - Diamond (2011)

Ringed-horn Antelope of Africa Award - Diamond (2014)

Animals of Asia Award - Diamond (2006)

Animals of Europe Award - Diamond (2003)

Animals of South America Award - Diamond (2014)

Animals of Africa Award – Diamond (2015)

Wild Oxen of the World Award - Diamond (2014)

Wild Sheep of the World Award - Gold (2014)

Antlered Game of the World Award - Silver (2015)

TopTen Award - Diamond (2008)

Wild Goats of the World Award - Diamond (2014)

Steven & Terri Chancellor's record trophies and SCI hunting awards *(Steven Chancellor unless otherwise stated)*

Lions

Date: 4/95.
Location: Botswana, Chobe.
Hunting company/guide: Jeff Rann, Jeff Rann Safaris.
Skull length & width: 16 8/16", 10 14/16".
Trophy score: 27 6/16

Date: 9/85.
Location: Tanzania, Rungwa.
Hunting guide: Jeff Rann.
Skull length & width: 15 12/16", 9 10/16".
Trophy score: 25 6/16.

Date: 4/94.
Location: Botswana, Linyanto Delta.
Hunting company/guide: Jeff Rann, Rand Hunting
Skull length & width: 14 12/16", 9 4/16"
Trophy score: 24

Date: 8/86
Location: Zambia, Luangwa.
Hunting guide: Jeff Rann
Skull length & width: 14 7/16", 8 14/16"
Trophy score: 23 5/16

Terri L Chancellor:
   Date: 4/94.
   Location: Botswana, Linyanti Delta.
   Hunting company/guide: Jeff Rann/Rand Hunting.
   Skull length & width: 14 3/16", 9 2/16"
   Trophy score: 23 5/16.

African elephant
   Date: 3/83.
   Location: RSA Letaba.
   Hunting guide: John Coleman.
   Tusk weights: 65 lb, 65 ½ lb.
   Trophy score: 130 1/2.

White Rhino
   Date: 7/83.
   Location: RSA, Vryburg.
   Hunting guide: Paul Vimercati.
   Horn lengths & circumferences at base: 29 4/8" & 6
1/8", 30 4/8" & 26 4/8"
   Trophy score: 92 5/8.

Leopards

   Date: 5/94.
   Location: Botswana, Linyanto Delta.
   Hunting company/guide: Jeff Rann, Rand Hunting.
   Skull length & width: 10 1/16", 6 5/16
   Trophy score: 16 6/16.

Date: 8/86.
Location: Zambia, Luangwa.
Hunting guide: Jeff Rann.
Skull length & width: 9 12/16", 6 3/16
Trophy score: 15 15/16.

Date: 6/82.
Location: RSA, Letaba.
Hunting guide: John Coleman.
Length & width of skull: 8 14/16", 5 7/16".
Trophy score: 14 5/16.

Date: 7/89.
Location: Botswana, Kalahari Desert.
Hunting company/guide: Jeff Rann, Rand Hunting.
Skull length & width: 8 12/16", 5 8/16"
Tropy score: 14 4/16.

Date: 4/95.
Location: Botswana, Kalahari.
Hunting company/guide: Jeff Rann, Jeff Rann Safaris.
Skull length & width: 8 12/16", 5 5/16"
Trophy score: 14 1/16.

Terri Chancellor:
Date: 4/92.
Location: Botswana, Okavango.
Hunting compny/guide: Jeff Rann/Rand Hunting.
Skull length & width: 6 2/16", 9 12/16"
Trophy score: 15 14/16.

SCI Awards (Steven Chancellor unless otherwise stated)

International Hunting Award (2006)
World Hunting Award (1999)
SCI World Conservation Hunting Award (2006)
Pinnacle of Achievement - Fourth Pinnacle (1998)
Crowning Achievement Award (1998)
Grand Slam Cats of the World Award (1996)
Grand Slam White-tailed Deer Award (1996)
Grand Slam European Deer Award (1997)
Grand Slam Elk of North America Award (1999)
Grand Slam Bears of the World Award (1995)
Grand Slam North American Wild Sheep Award (1987)
Grand Slam Africa Big Five Award - Steven E. Chancellor (1984); Terri L. Chancellor (2000)
Grand Slam Moose of the World Award (1995)
Grand Slam North America 29 Award (1994)
Grand Slam North American Caribou Award (1995)
Grand Slam North American Deer Award (1984)
Grand Slam Africa 29 Award (1998)
Grand Slam Dangerous Game of Africa Award (1998)
Inner Circle Antlered Game of the Americas Award - Diamond (1999)
Spiral-horned Antelopes of Africa Award - Diamond (2002)
Chamois of the World Award - Diamond (2000)
Desert Game of the World Award - Diamond (2002)
Gazelles of the World Award - Diamond (1999)

Hunting Achievement Award – Copper: Terri L. Chancellor (1996); Diamond: Steven E. Chancellor (1998)

Introduced Animals of North America Award - Diamond (1997)

Ibex of the World Award - Diamond (1999)

Red Deer/Wapiti of the World Award - Diamond (1998)

Wild Pigs and Peccaries of the World Award - Diamond (2002)

Pygmy Antelope of Africa Award - Diamond (1998)

Animals of Asia Award - Diamond (2001)

Animals of Europe Award - Diamond (1998)

Animals of South America Award - Diamond (1999)

Animals of Africa Award – Diamond (2000)

Wild Oxen of the World Award - Diamond (1999)

Wild Sheep of the World Award - Diamond (1998)

Antlered Game of the World Award - Diamond (1997)

TopTen Award – Bronze: Terri L. Chancellor (1996); Diamond: Steven E. Chancellor (1997)

Animals of North America Award - Diamond (2002)

Animals of South Pacific Award - Diamond (1997)

Wild Goats of the World Award - Diamond (1998)

CJ McElroy's Records Book trophies

Lions

Date: 8/73
Location: Zambia, Luangwa River.
Professional guide: Adrian Carr.
Length & width of skull: 14 12/16", 10 7/16"
Trophy score: 25 3/16

Date: 9/62
Location: Tanzania, N'Kululu River.
Professional guide: Glen Cottar.
Length & width of skull: 14 15/16". 8 13/16".
Trophy score: 23 12/16.

Leopards

Date: 9/71
Location: Angola, Cubango.
Professional guide: Alfredo Ferreira.
Length & width of skull: 10 4/16", 7 5/16"
Trophy score: 17 9/16"

Date: 1/60.
Location: Kenya, Kajiado.
Professional guide: Glen Cottar.
Length & width of skull: 9 11/16", 5 13/16"
Trophy score: 15 8/16.

African elephants

Date: 5/66.
Location: Kenya, Athi River.
Professional guide: Mike Horsley.
Tusk weights: 118 lb, 108 lb.
Trophy score: 226.

Date: 1/60.
Location: Kenya, Tana River.
Professional guide: Glen Cottar.
Tusk weights: 81 lb, 82 lb
Trophy score: 163

Black Rhino
Date: 1/60.
Location: Kenya, Mount Kenya.
Professional guide: Glen Cottar.
Horn lengths & circumferences at base: 21 7/8" & 13 6/8", 21" & 15"
Trophy score: 71 5/8.

White Rhino
Date: 9/70.
Location: RSA Zululand.
Professional hunter: Norman Deane.
Horn lengths & circumferences at base: 29 2/8" & 8 5/8", 20 6/8" & 17 6/8
Trophy score: 76 3/8.

Scimitar horned oryxes

Date: 1/67.
Location: Chad, Oum Chalouba.
Professional guide: Claude Vasselet.
Lengths & circumferences of horns at base: 45 2/8",
45 2/8". 6 3/8", 6 4/8"
Trophy score: 103 3/8.

Date: 1/67.
Location: Chad, Oum Chalouba.
Professional guide: Claude Vasselet.
Lengths & circumferences of horns at base: 41 6/8",
41 6/8". 6 3/8", 6 3/8"
Trophy score: 96 2/8.

Date: 1/67.
Location: Chad, Oum Chalouba.
Professional guide: Claude Vasselet.
Lengths & circumferences of horns at base: 41 2/8",
41 5/8". 6 3/8", 6 3/8".
Trophy score: 95 5/8.

Addaxes

Date: 1/67.
Location: Chad, Oum Chalouba.
Professional guide: Claude Vasselet.
Lengths & circumferences of horns at base: 37", 35".
6 3/8", 6 4/8".
Trophy score: 84 7/8

Date: 1/67.
Location: Chad, Oum Chalouba.
Professional guide: Claude Vasselet.
Lengths & circumferences of horns at base: 33 5/8",
33 2/8". 6 5/8", 6 4/8".
Trophy score: 80.

Dama Gazelles

Date: 1/67.
Location: Chad, Oum Chalouba.
Professional guide: Claude Vasselet.
Lengths & circumferences of horns at base: 14 2/8",
14 1/8". 5 4/8", 5 4/8".
Trophy score: 39 3/8

Date: 1/67.
Location: Chad, Oum Chalouba.
Professional guide: Claude Vasselet.
Lengths & circumferences of horns at base: 13 2/8",
13". 5 3/8", 5 3/8".
Trophy score: 37.

Spotted hyena
Date: 1984.
Location: Zimbabwe.
Professional Guide: Eric Wagner.
Skull length: 11 12/16".
Skull Length: 7 6/16".
Trophy score: 19 2/16.

John J Jackson III's record trophies

African elephants

Date: 8/85.
Location: Tanzania, Selous.
Hunting guide: Larry Ward.
Tusk weights: 74 ½ lb, 82 ½ lb.
Trophy score: 157.

Date: 6/87.
Location: Ethiopia, Gambella.
Hunting guide: Col Neguissie Esshete.
Tusk weights: 72 lb, 53 lb.
Trophy score: 125

Date: 12/87.
Location: Ethiopia, Teppi.
Hunting guide: Nassos Roussos.
Tusk weights: 63 lb, 60 lb.
Trophy score: 123.

Lion

Date: 8/85
Location: Tanzania, Selous.
Hunting guide: Larry Ward.
Skull length & width: 14 4/16", 9 9/16"
Trophy score: 23 13/16.

Leopard
   Date: 11/88.
   Location: Tanzania, Selous.
   Hunting company/guide: Jean-Louis Masson/;Gerard
Pasanisi.
   Skull length & width: 8 8/16", 5 8/16"
   Trophy score: 14.

Spotted hyena
   Date: 6/87.
   Location: Ethiopia, Danakil.
   Hunting guide: Col. Negussie Eshete.
   Skull length/width: 10 9/16", 6 6/16".
   Trophy score: 16 15/16.

Japto Soerjosoemarno's record trophies and SCI awards

SCI Awards

Grand Slam Africa Big Five Award (2000)
Grand Slam Dangerous Game of Africa Award (2015)
Global Hunting Award - Copper (2015)
Hunting Achievement Award - Bronze (2015)
Introduced Animals of North America Award - Silver (2015)
TopTen Award - Silver (2011)
Animals of South Pacific - Bronze (1994)
Wild Goats of the World Award - Copper (1994)

SCI Record Book Trophies

White Rhino
Date: 8/95.
Location: RSA Natal.
Hunting company/guide: G Jones, Hunters & Guides.
Horn lengths & circumferences at base: 29 2/8" & 10 6/8", 27 4/8" & 24 2/8"
Trophy Score: 91 6/8.

Lion

Date: 8/95.
Location: Tanzania, Selous.
Hunting company/guide: Pano Calavrias, Kiboko
Safaris.
Skull length/width: 14 8/16", 10 14/16"
Trophy score: 25 6/16.

Leopard

Date: 9/95.
Location: Tanzania, Selous.
Hunting company/guide: Pano Calavrias, Kiboko
Safaris.
Skull length & width: 9 4/16", 6 4/16"
Trophy score: 15 8/16.

Hossein 'Soudi' Golabchi's record trophies & SCI awards

World Conservation & Hunting Award (2013)
World Hunting Award (2000)
SCI Major Awards Honor – ASIA: 1st
Pinnacle of Achievement - Fourth Pinnacle (1994)
Crowning Achievement (1997)
Africa 15 Award (2013)
North American 12 Award (2013)
Grand Slam Cats of the World Award (1993)
Grand Slam White-tailed Deer Award (1993)
Grand Slam European Deer Award (2013)
Grand Slam Elk of North America Award (2000)
Grand Slam Bears of the World Award (1992)
Grand Slam North American Wild Sheep Award (1991)
Grand Slam Africa Big Five Award (1994)
Grand Slam Moose of the World Award (1991)
Grand Slam North American Caribou Award (1997)
Grand Slam North American Deer Award (1994)
Grand Slam Africa 29 Award (1996)
Grand Slam Dangerous Game of Africa (1998)
Inner Circle Award Antlered Game of the Americas Award - Silver (1997)
Spiral-horned Antelopes of Africa Award - Diamond (1995)
Chamois of the World Award - Diamond (1995)
Desert Game of the World Award - Diamond (2013)
Global Hunting Award Recipients - Diamond (1999)
Gazelles of the World Award - Diamond (1998)

Hunting Achievement Award - Diamond (2000)
Introduced Animals of North America Award -
Bronze (1995)
Ibex of the World Award - Diamond (1995)
Mountain Game of the World Award - Diamond
(2009)
Red Deer/Wapiti of the World Award - Diamond
(1997)
Wild Pigs and Peccaries of the World Award -
Diamond (1998)
Predators of the World Award - Diamond (2013)
Pygmy Antelope of Africa Award - Diamond (2013)
Ringed-horn Antelope of Africa Award - Diamond
(2013)
Animals of Asia Award - Diamond (1994)
Animals of Europe Award - Diamond (1999)
Animals of South America Award - Diamond (1998)
Animals of Africa Award – Gold (1997)
Wild Oxen of the World Award - Diamond (2000)
Wild Sheep of the World Award - Diamond (1993)
Antlered Game of the World Award - Diamond
(1998)
TopTen Award - Diamond (1994)
Animals of North America Award - Diamond (2013)
Animals of South Pacific Award - Diamond (1999)
Wild Goats of the World Award - Diamond (1993)

Record trophies

White Rhino
Date: 4/93.
Location: RSA, NW Transvaal.
Hunting company/guide: D van Staden/Kwalata Safaris.
Length & circumference of horns at base: 27 1/8" & 12 2/8", 26 7/8" & 24 2/8".
Trophy score: 90 4/8.

Lions

Date: 11/91.
Location: Tanzania, Rungwa.
Hunting guide: Gerard Miller.
Length & width of skull: 15 1/16", 9 4/16"
Trophy score: 24 5/16.

Date: 11/91.
Location: Tanzania, Masailand.
Hunting company/guide: Gerard Miller, Tanzania Hunting Safaris.
Length & width of skull: 14 8/16", 9 2/16"
Trophy score: 23 10/16.

Printed in Great Britain
by Amazon

41970642R00177